2018년 런던 삽화화시 《생산지-조선》 선전화

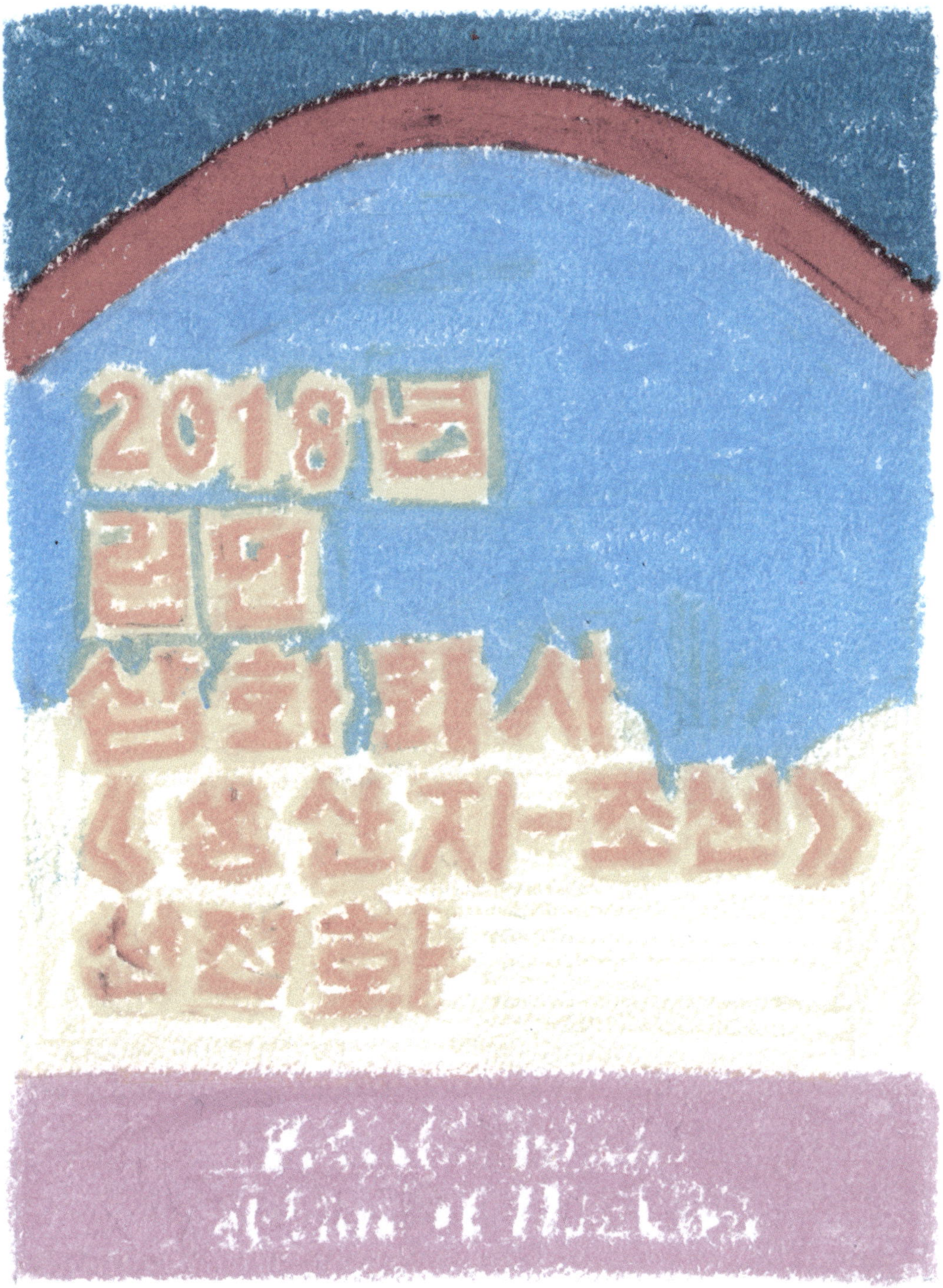

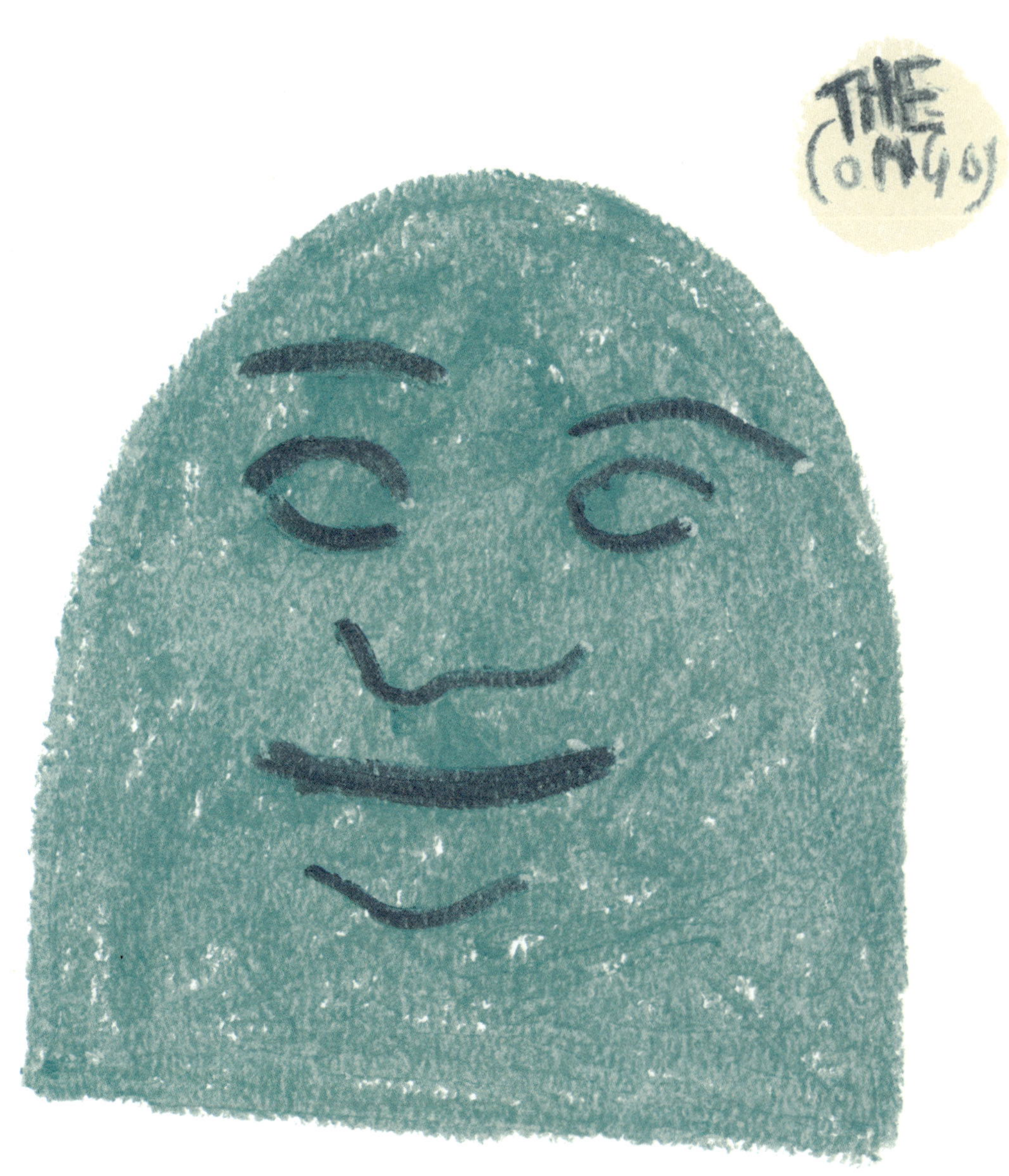
THE
CONGO

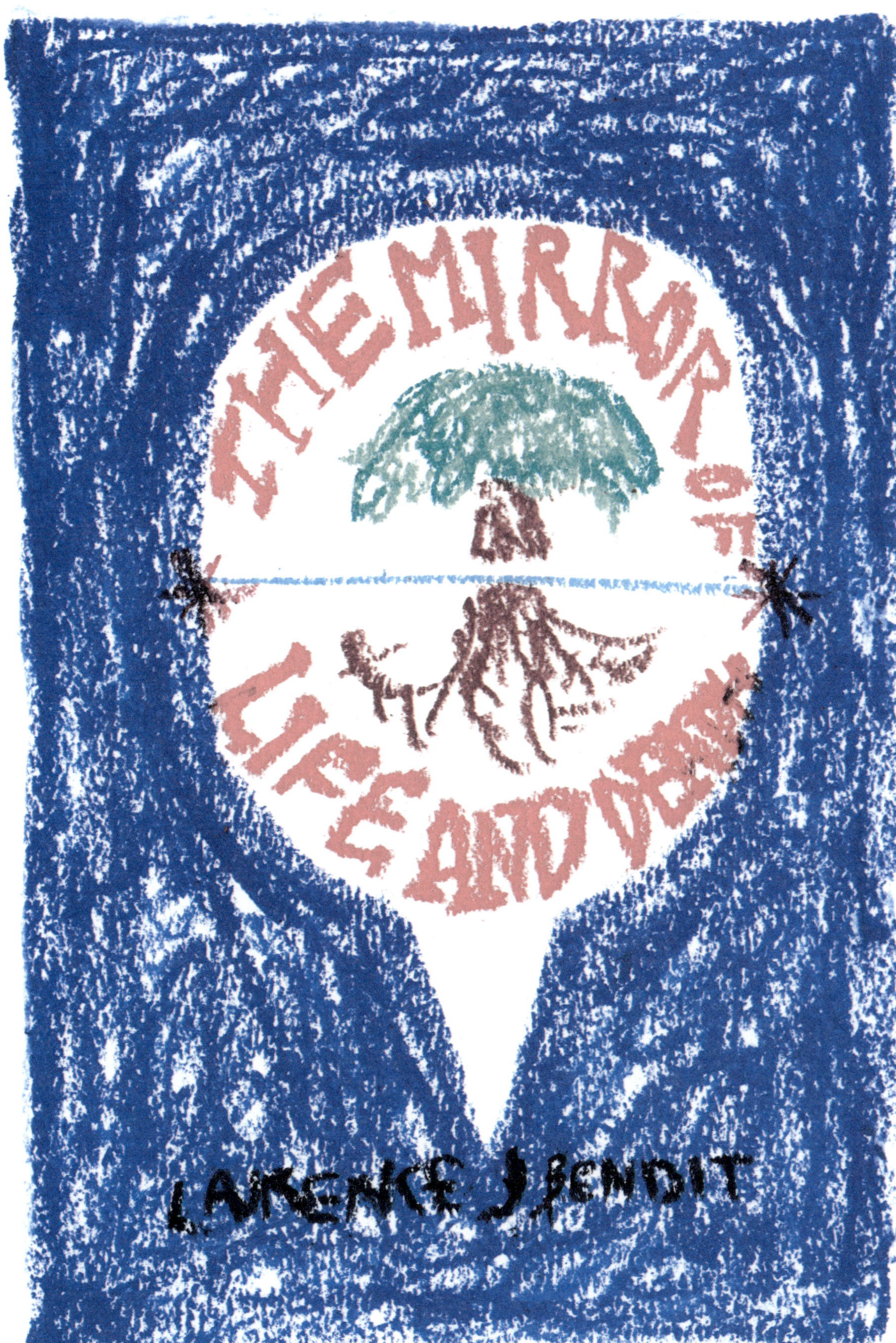
THE MIRROR OF
LIFE AND DEATH
LAURENCE J BENDIT

Sat. 1, 8 &
15 July '17

in
ter
de
pen
den

we need
to talk,

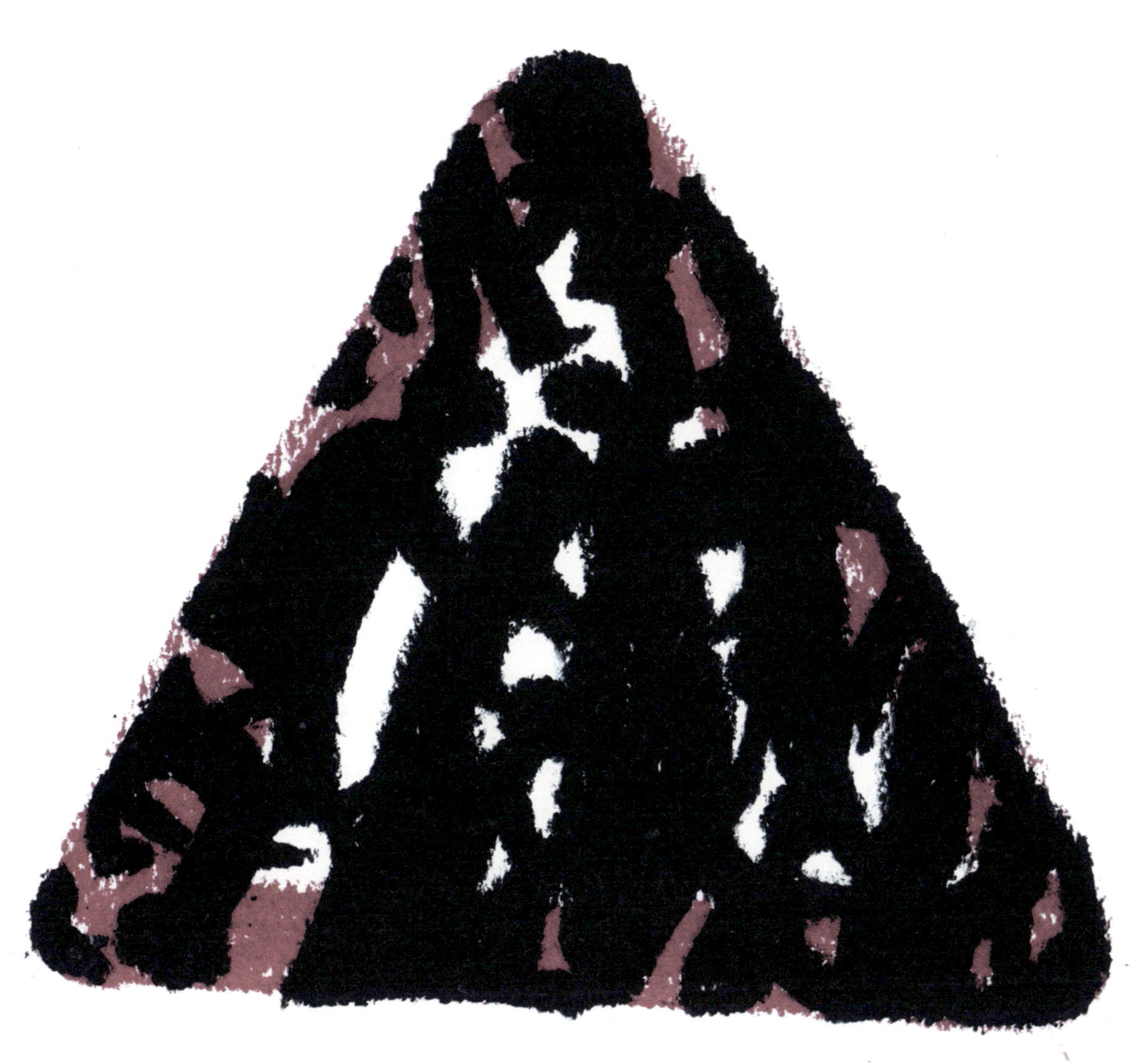

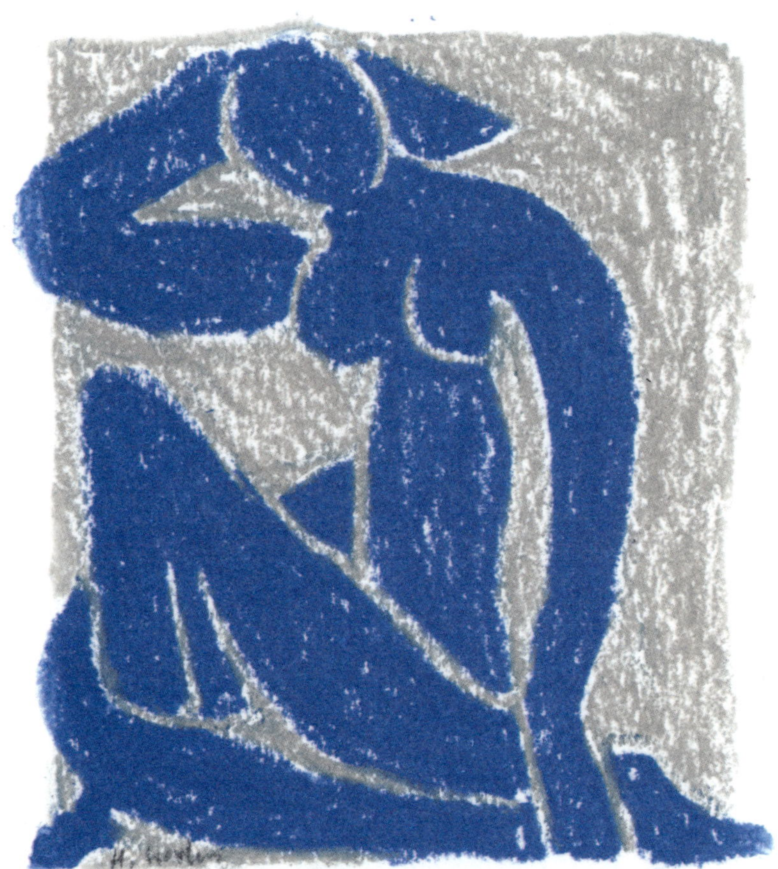

Henri Matisse The Cut-Outs

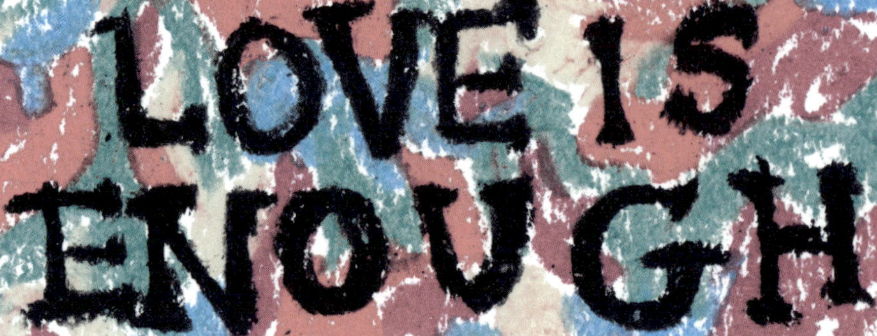

William Morris
& Andy Warhol

Curated by Jeremy Deller
6 December 2014–
8 March 2015

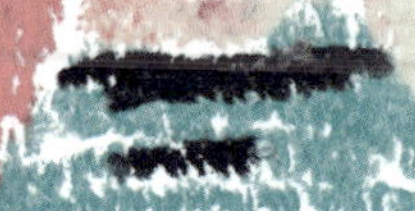
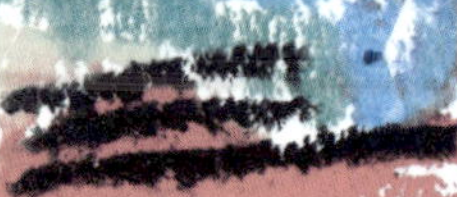
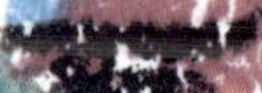

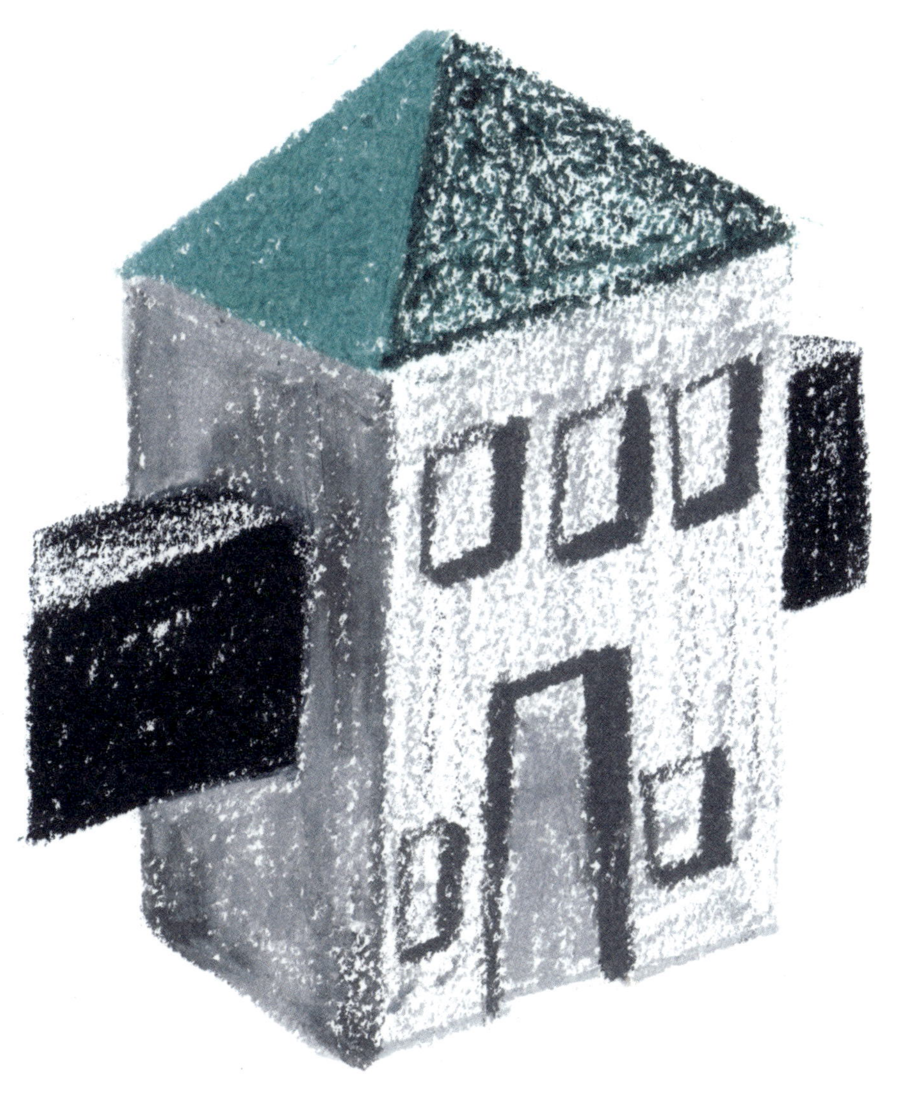

HAMMER HOUSE Simon Martin

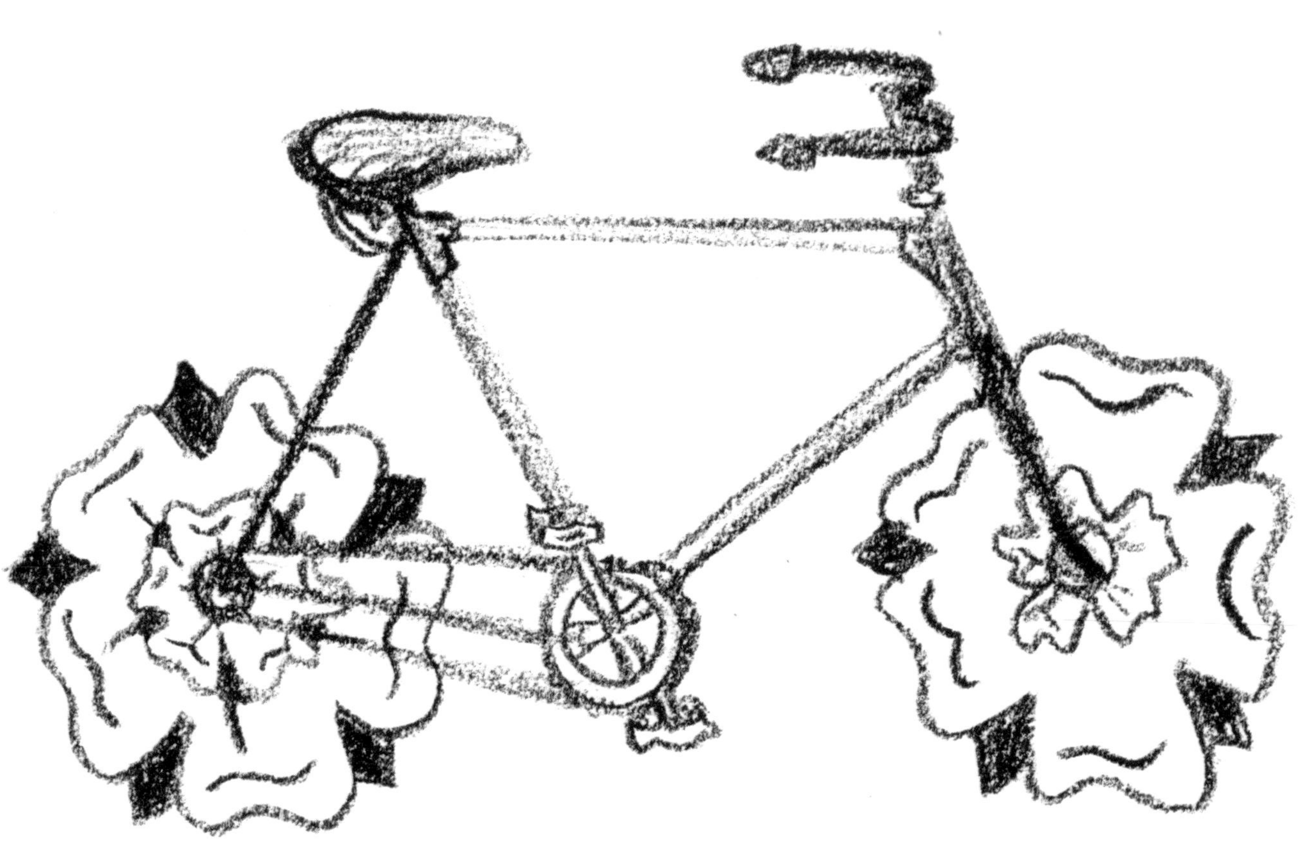

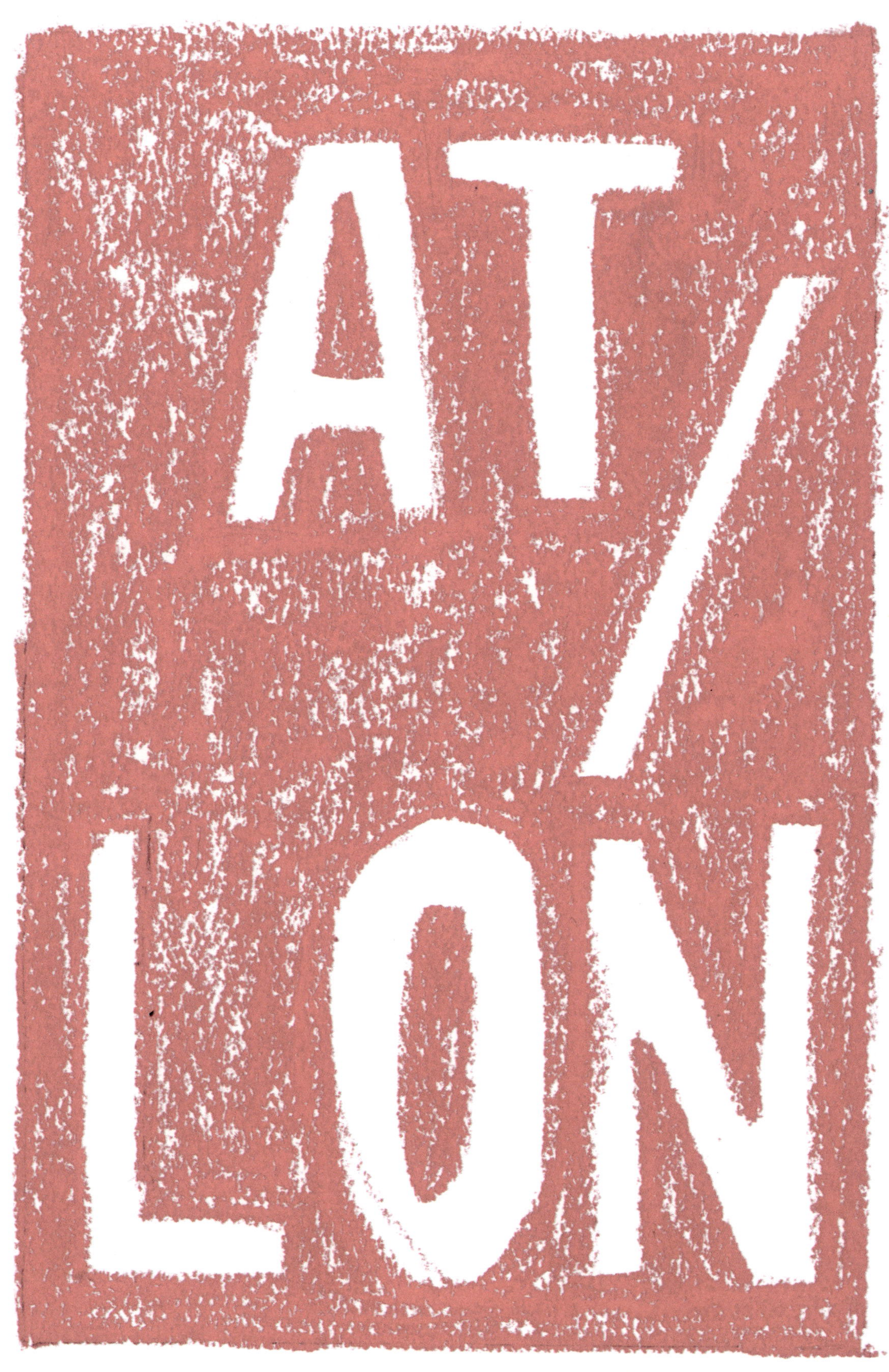
AT/
LON

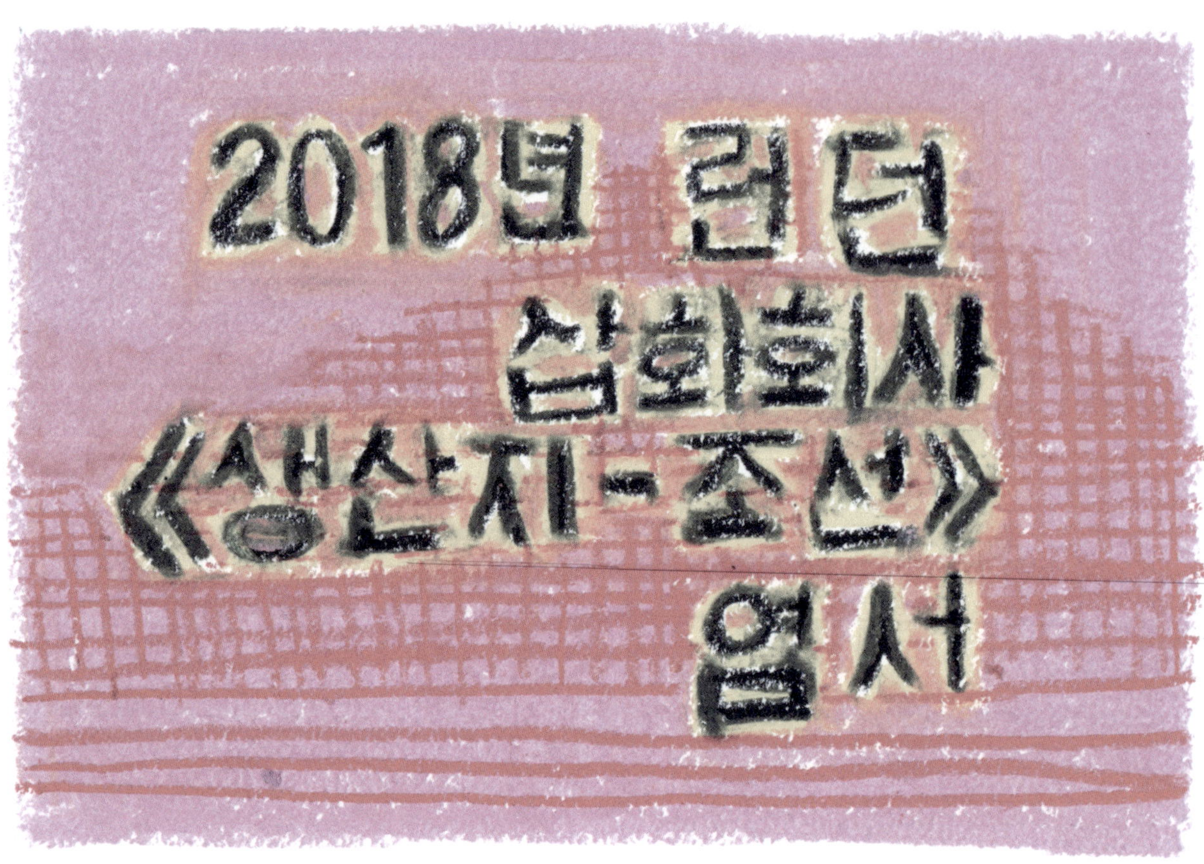
2018년 런던
삽화회사
《생산지-조선》
엽서

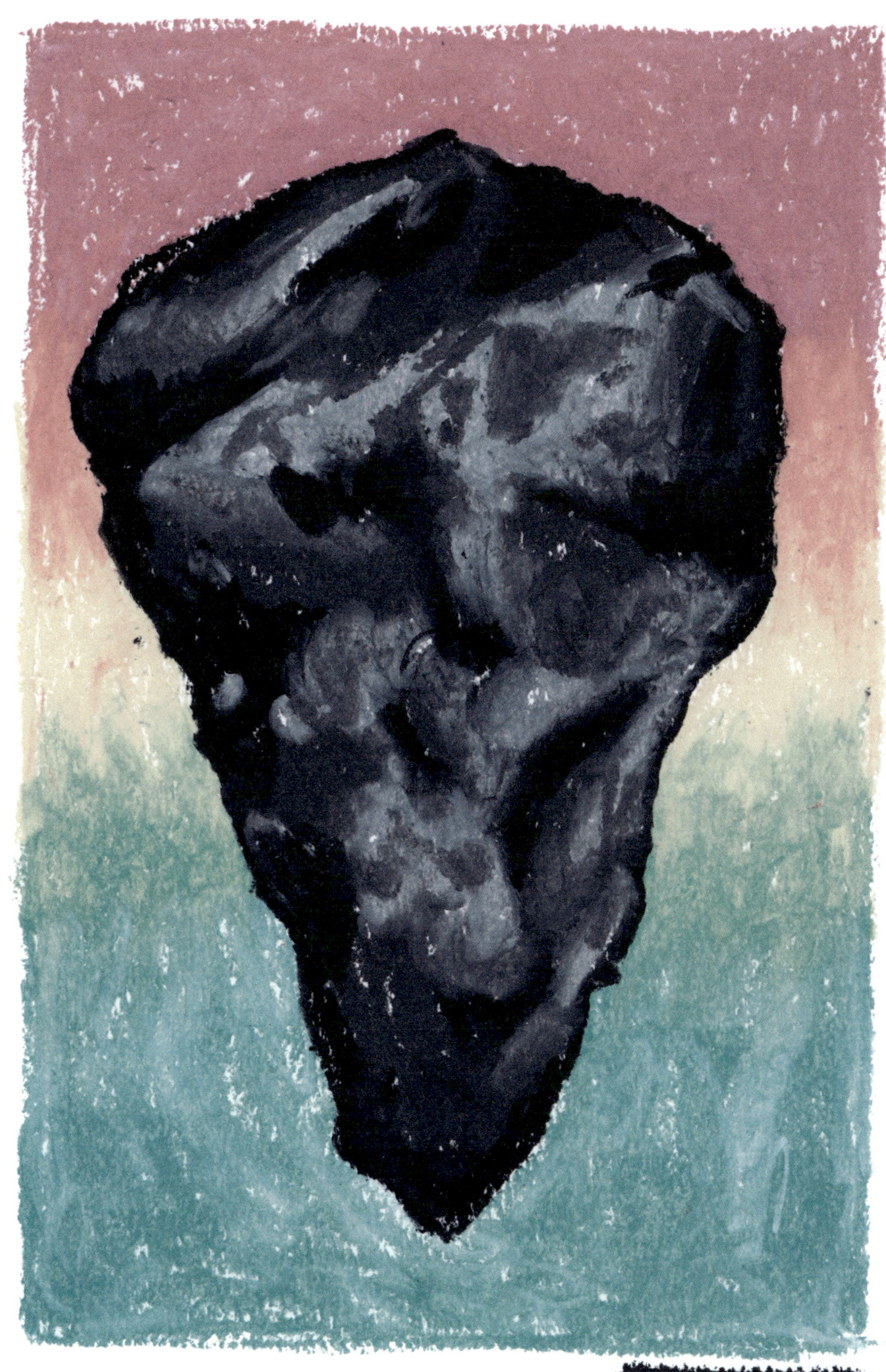

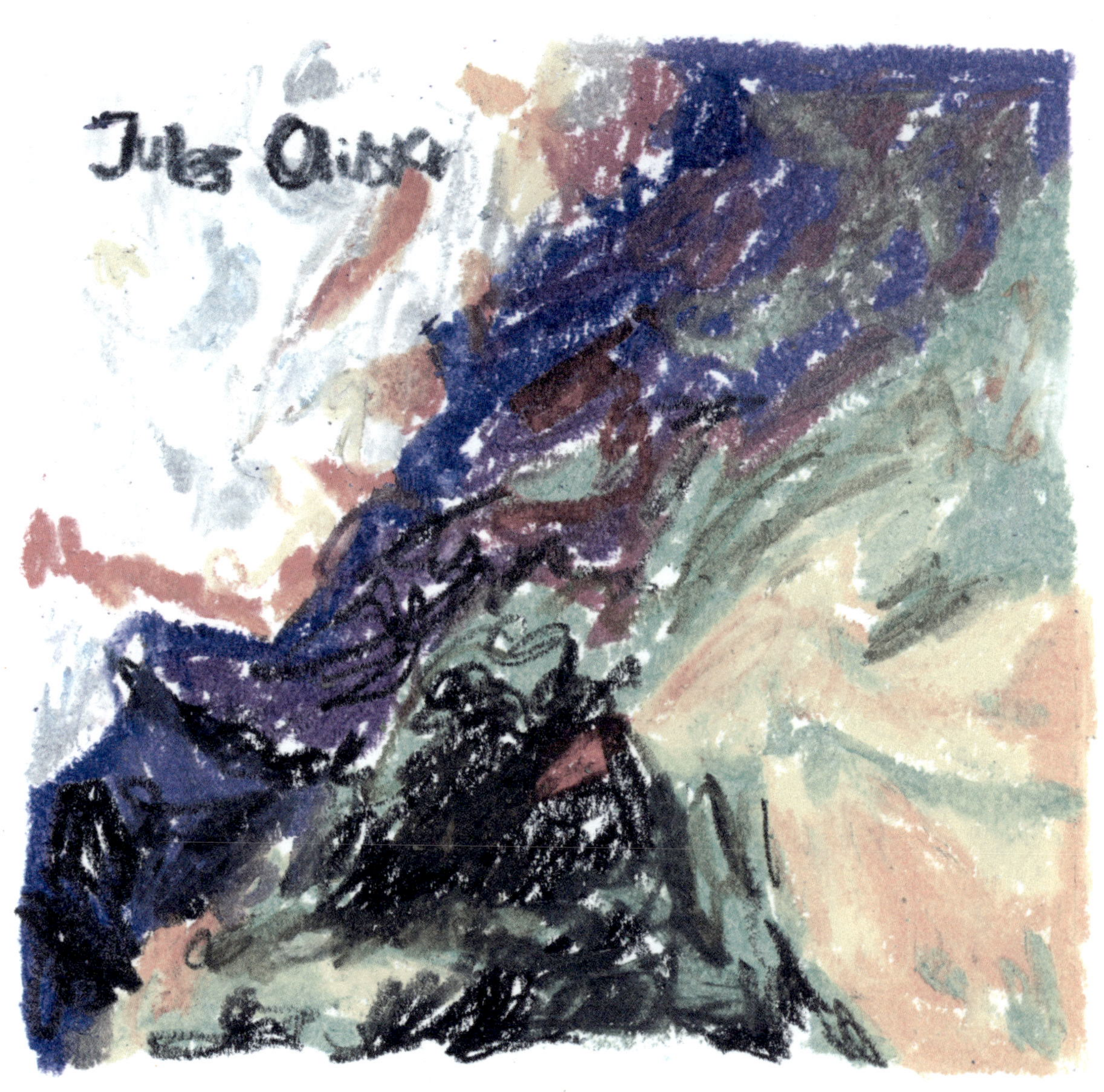
Jules Olitski

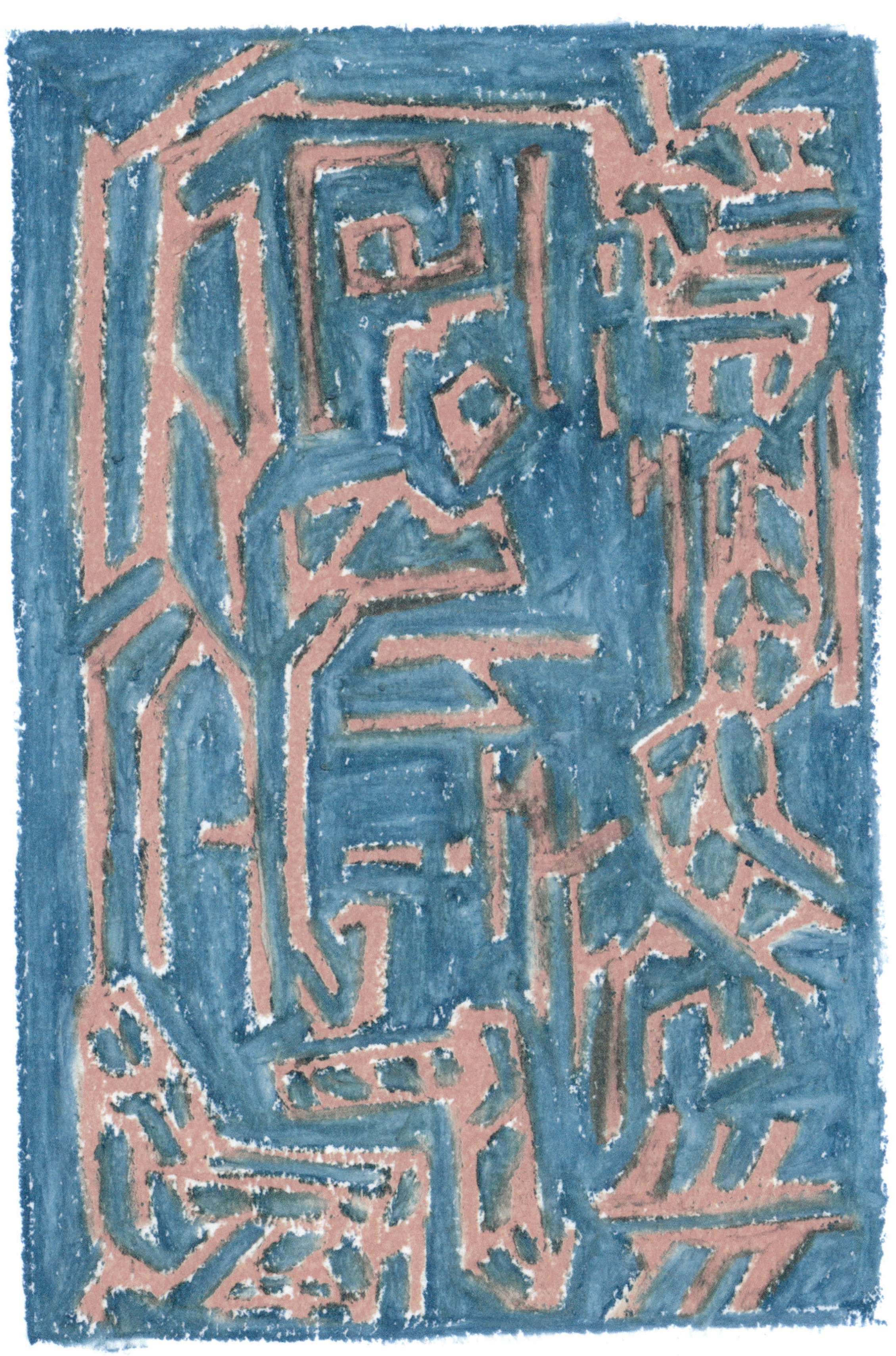

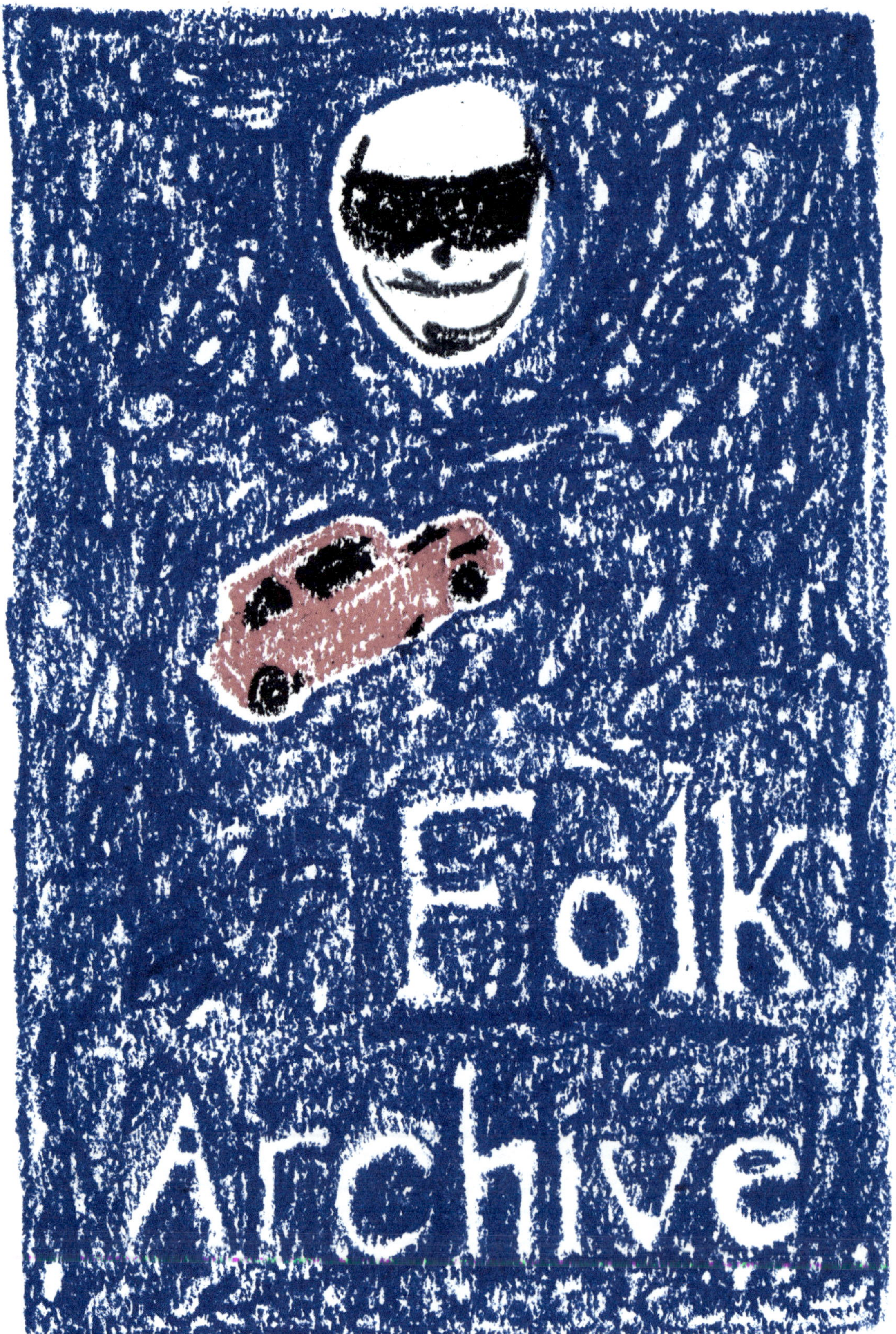
Folk
Archive

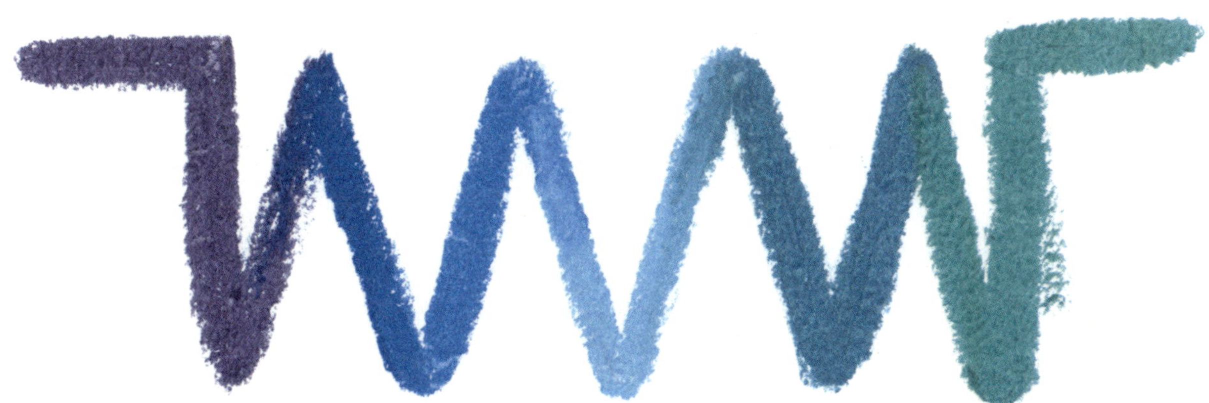

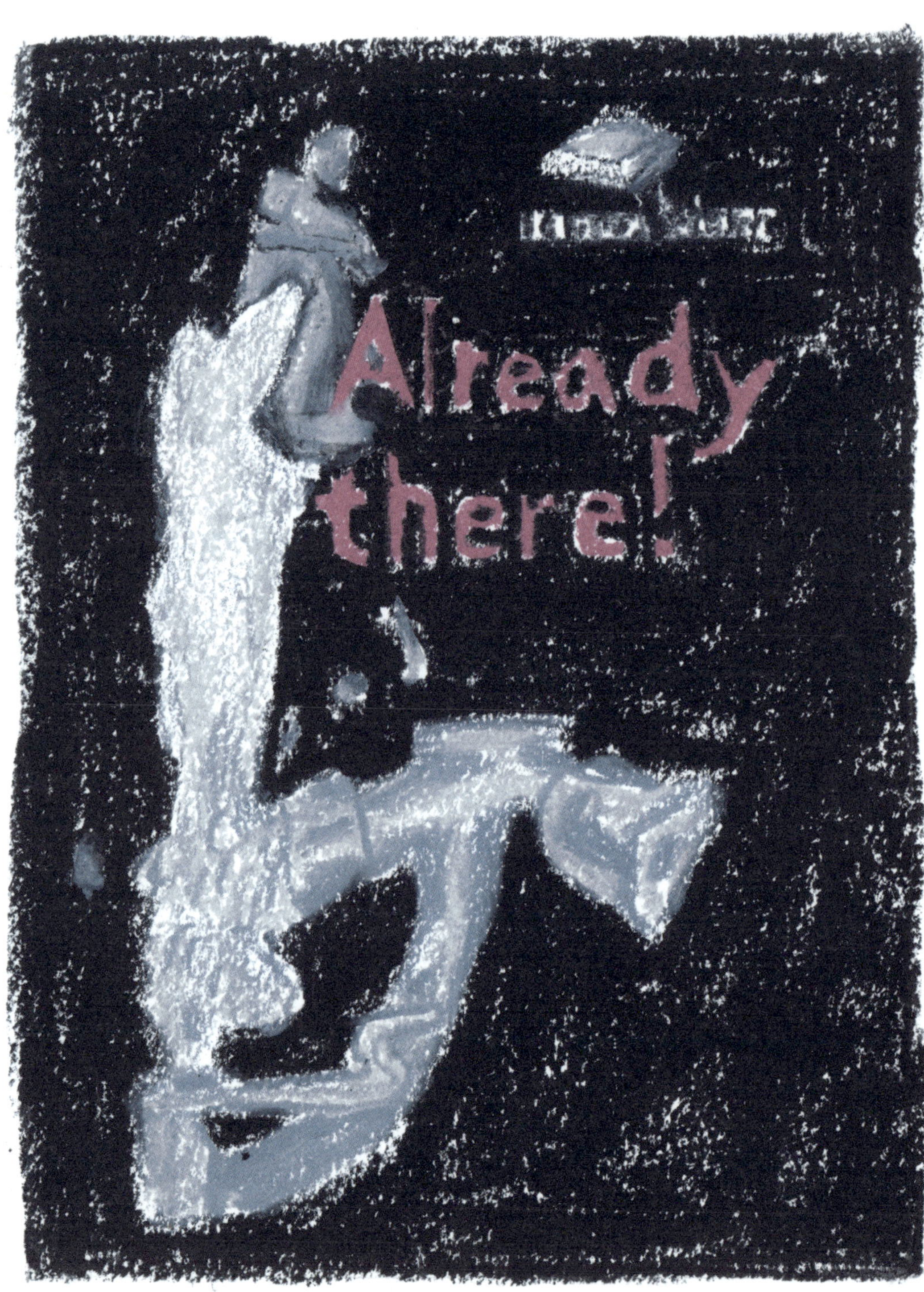
Already
there!

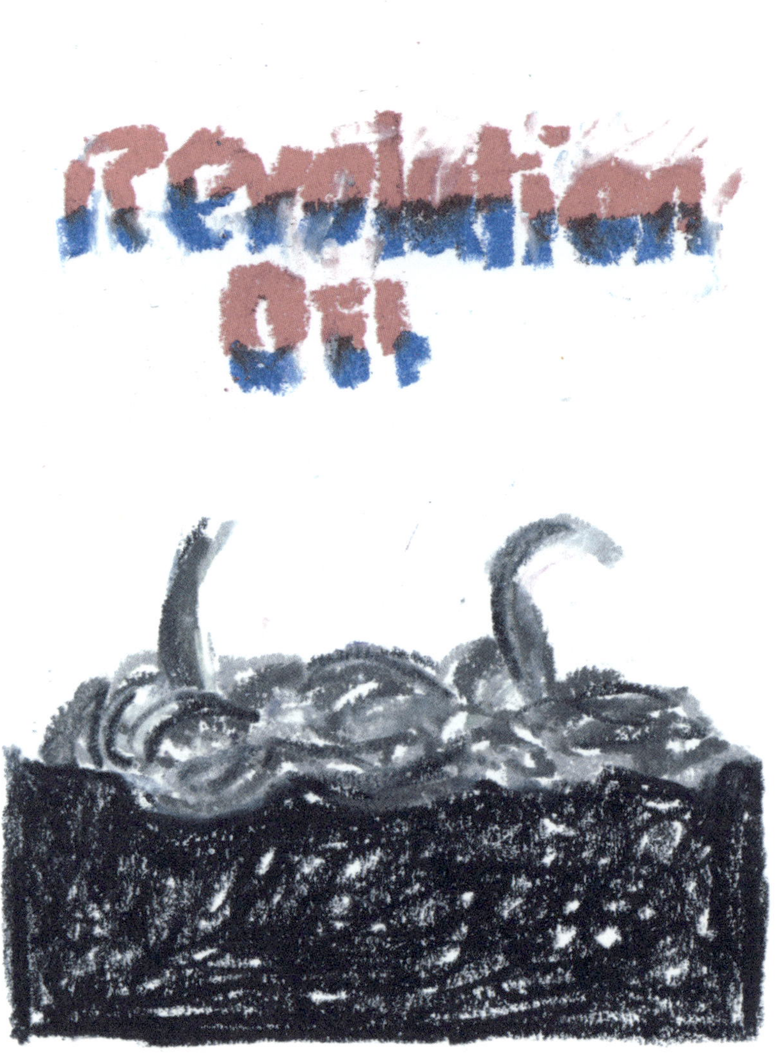
Revolution
Oil

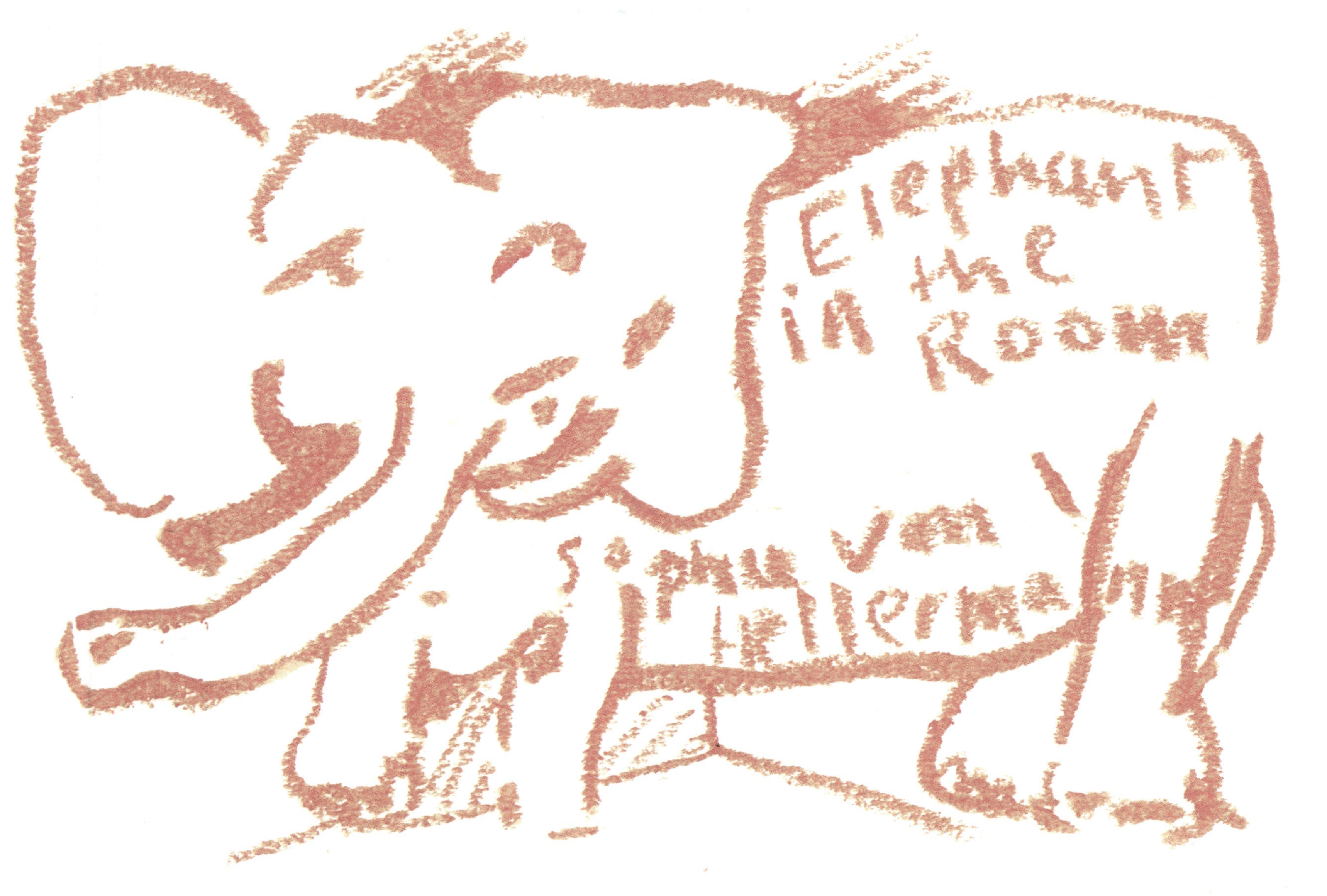
Elephant in the Room
Sophy von Hellermann

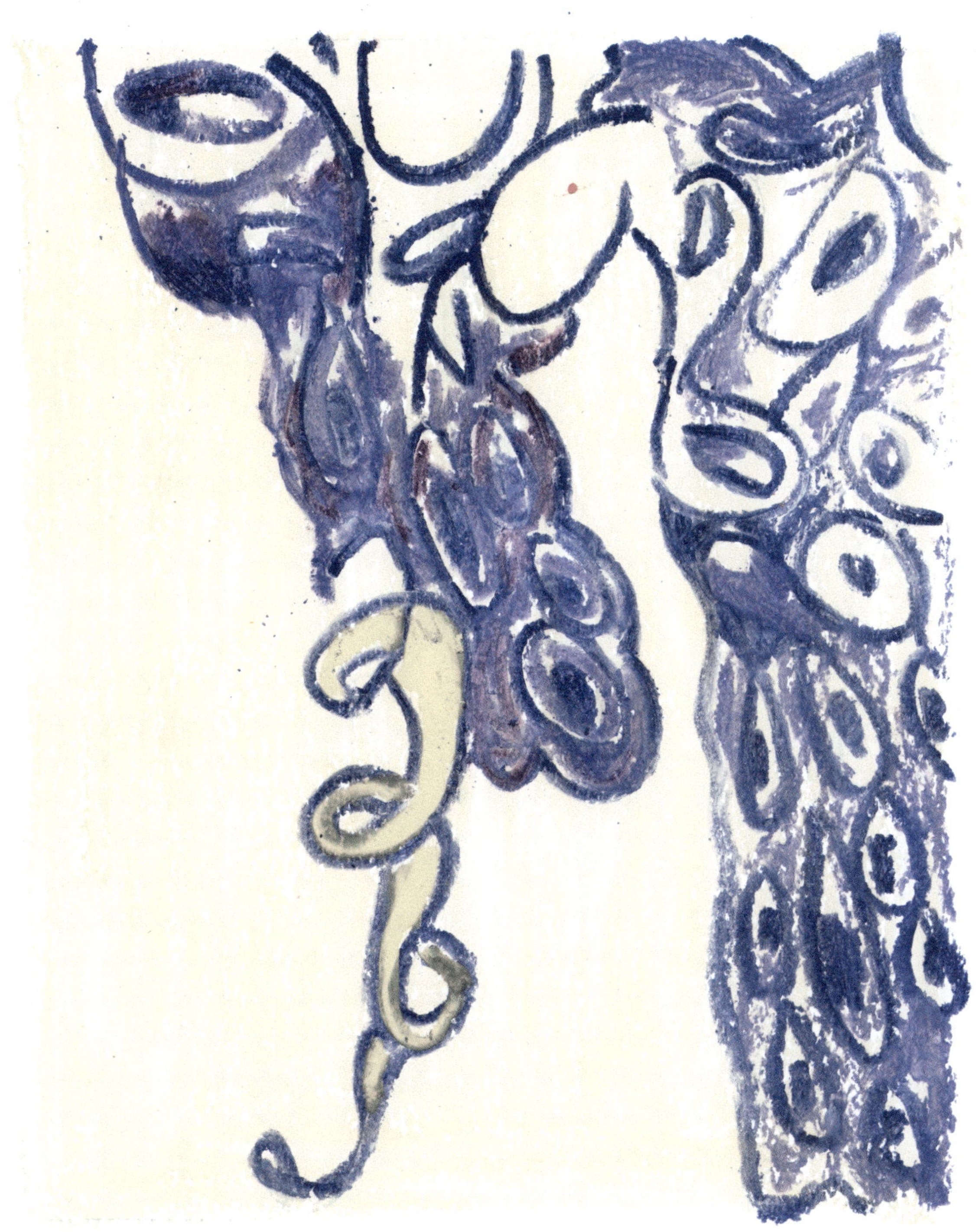

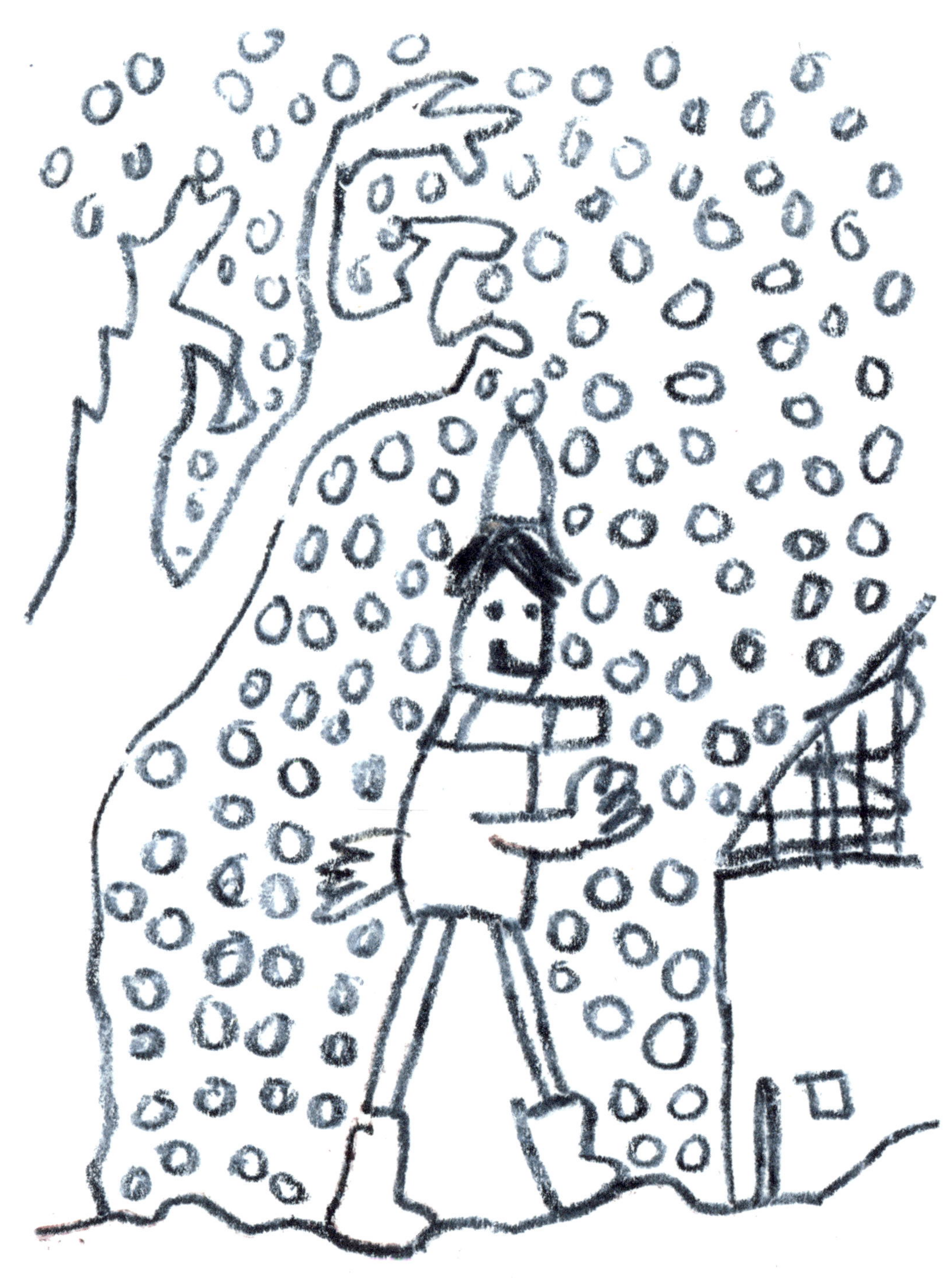

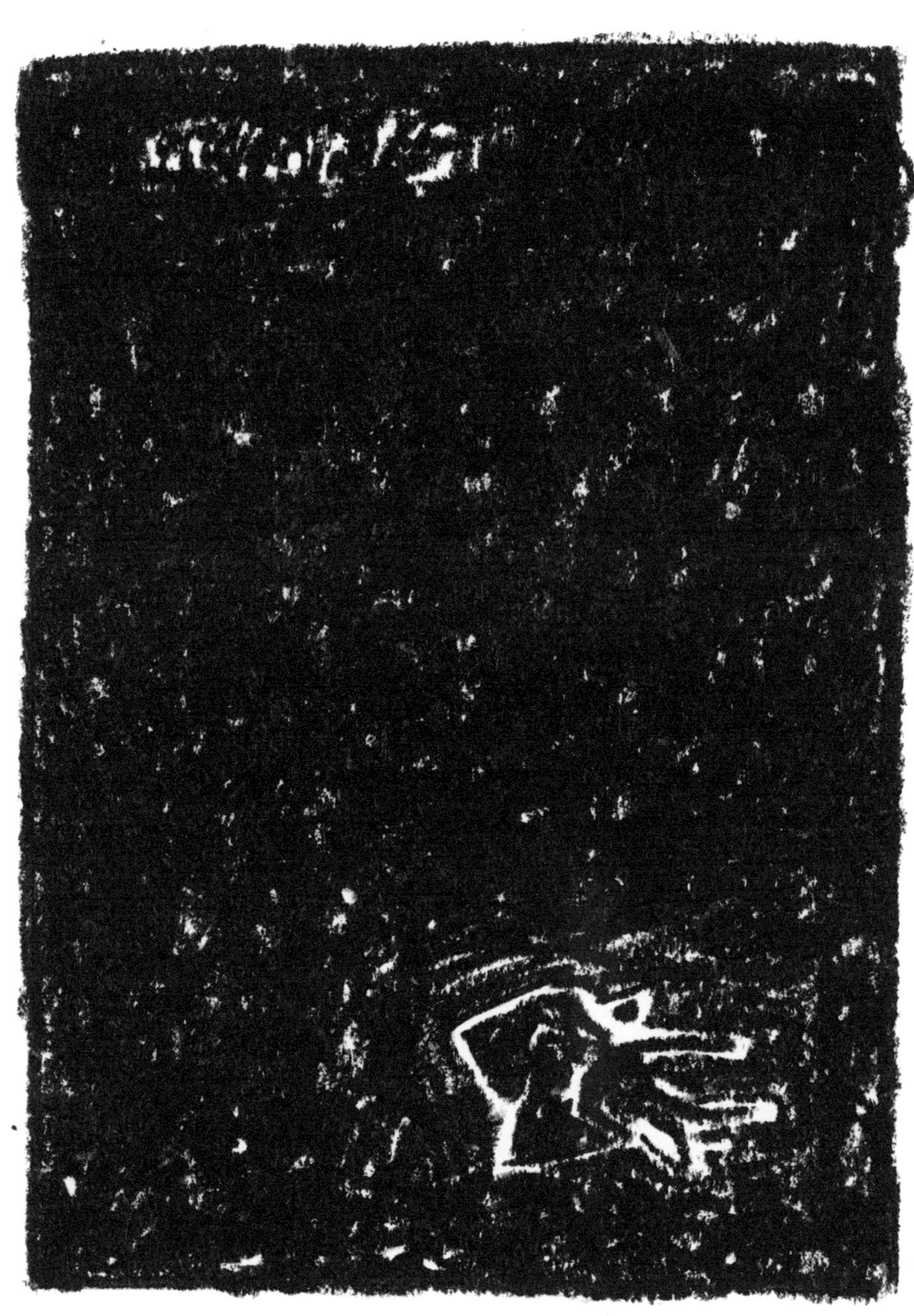

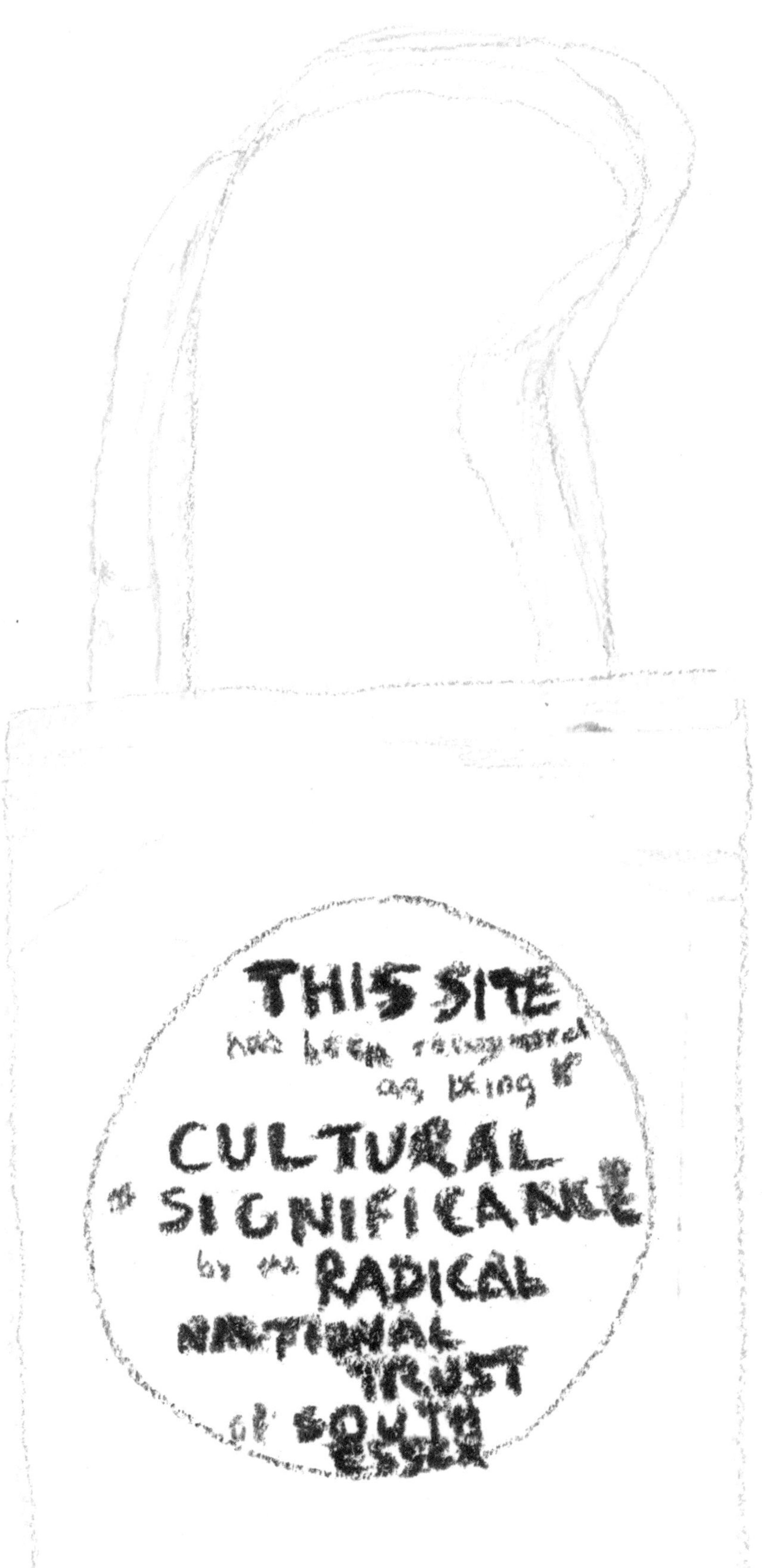
THIS SITE
CULTURAL
SIGNIFICANCE
RADICAL
NATIONAL
TRUST
SOUTH
ESSEX

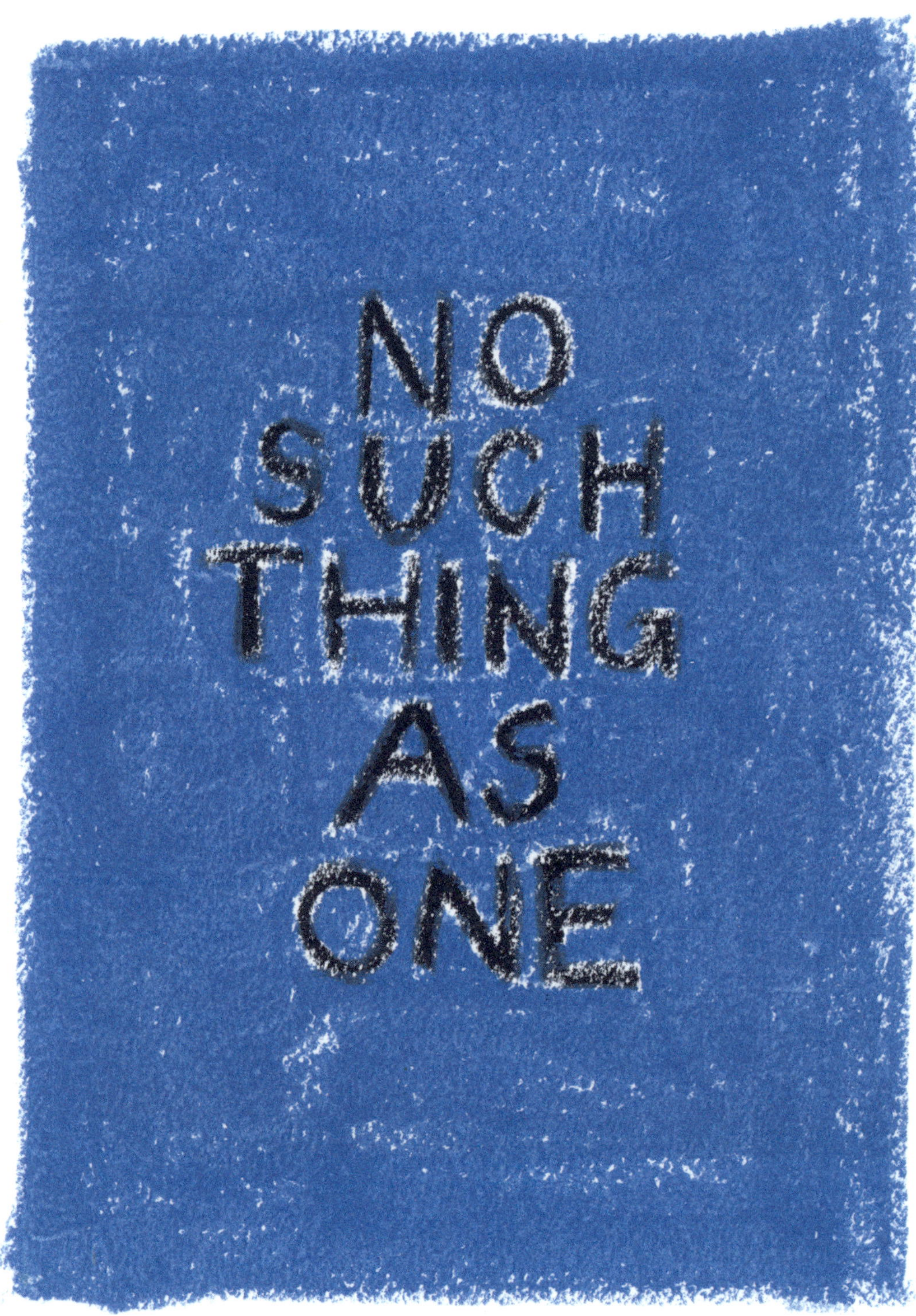
NO
SUCH
THING
AS
ONE

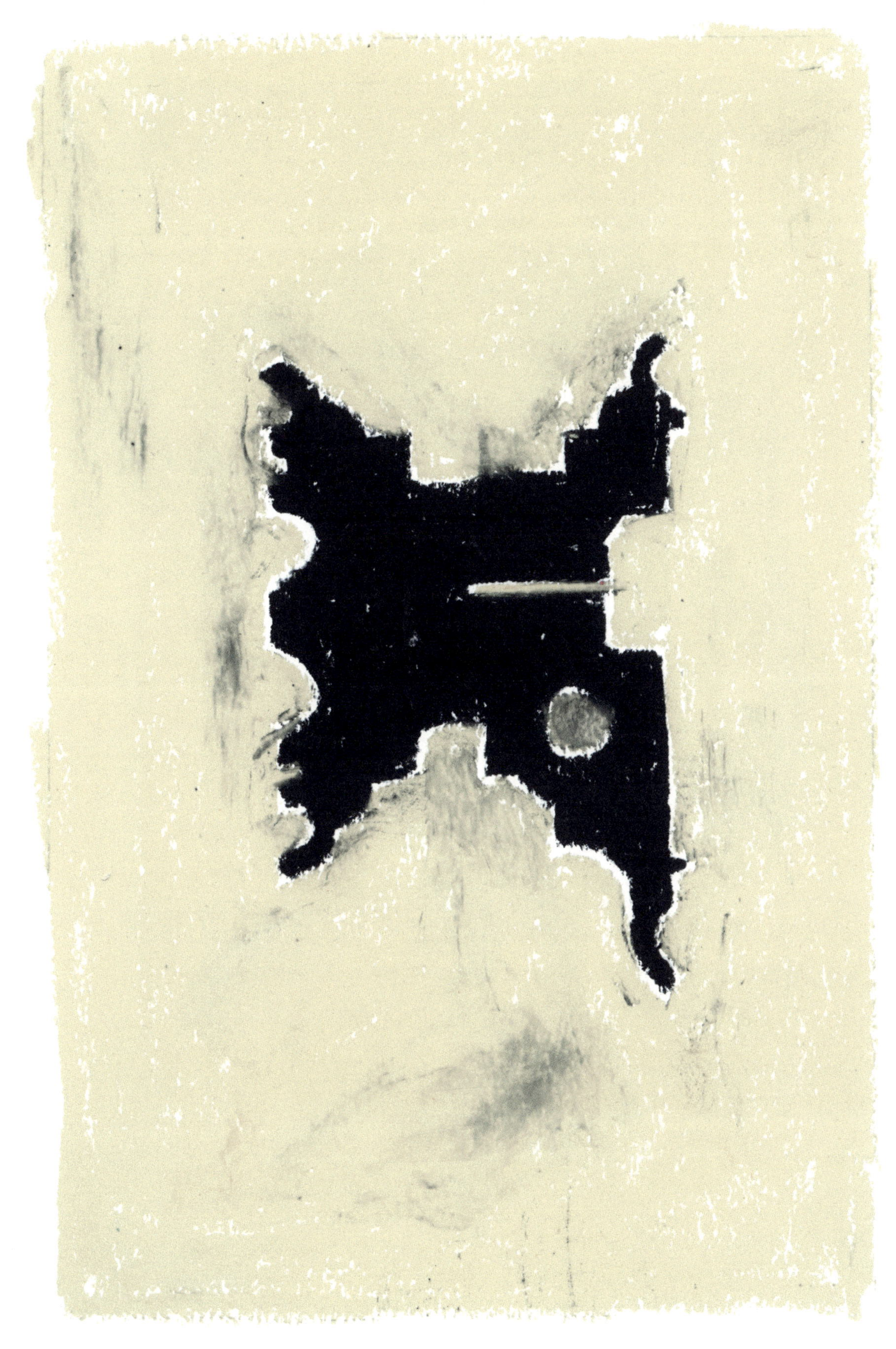

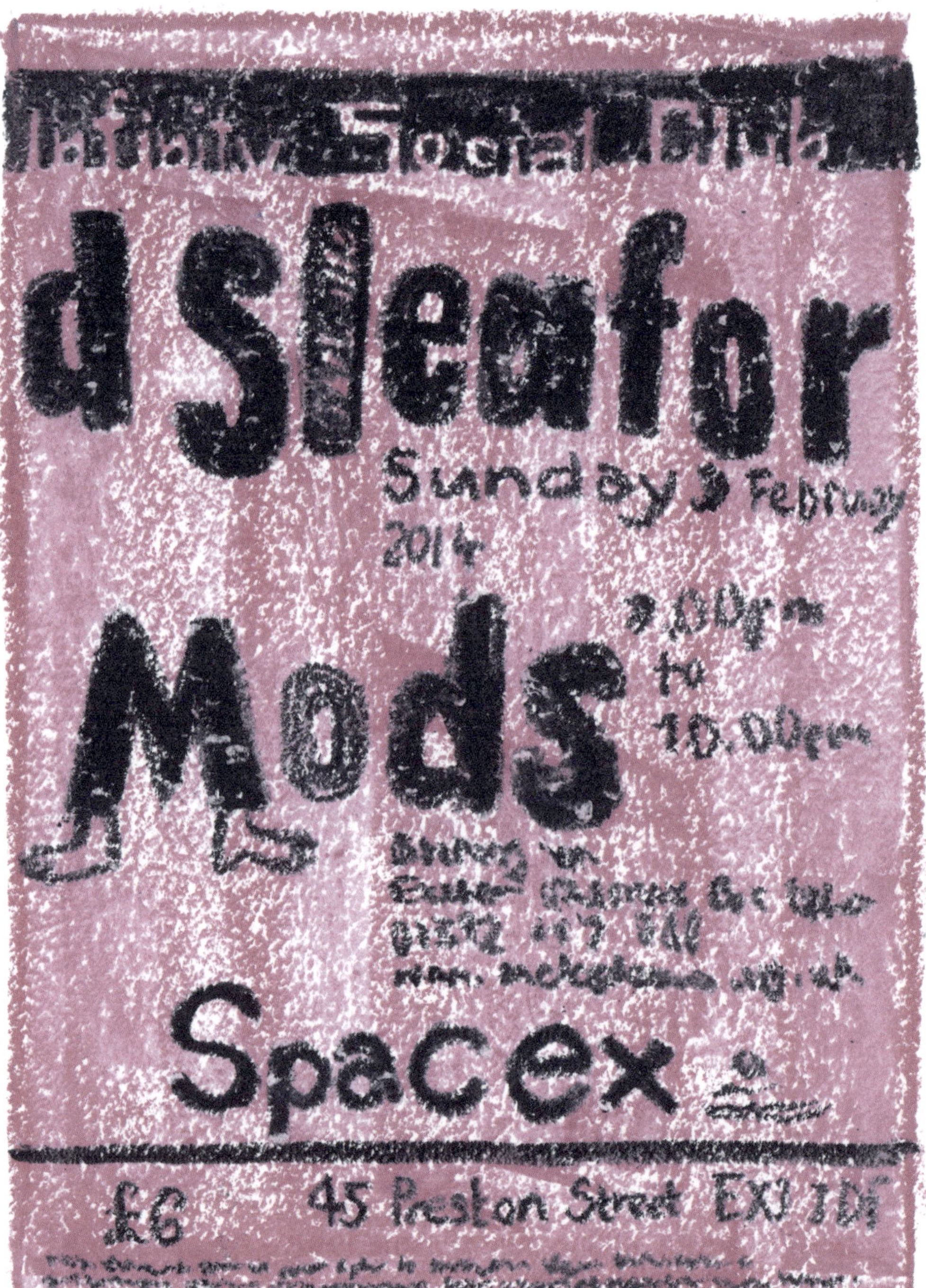
dSleafor
Sunday 3 February
2014
Mods
7.00pm
to
10.00pm
Spacex
£6
45 Preston Street EX1 1DF

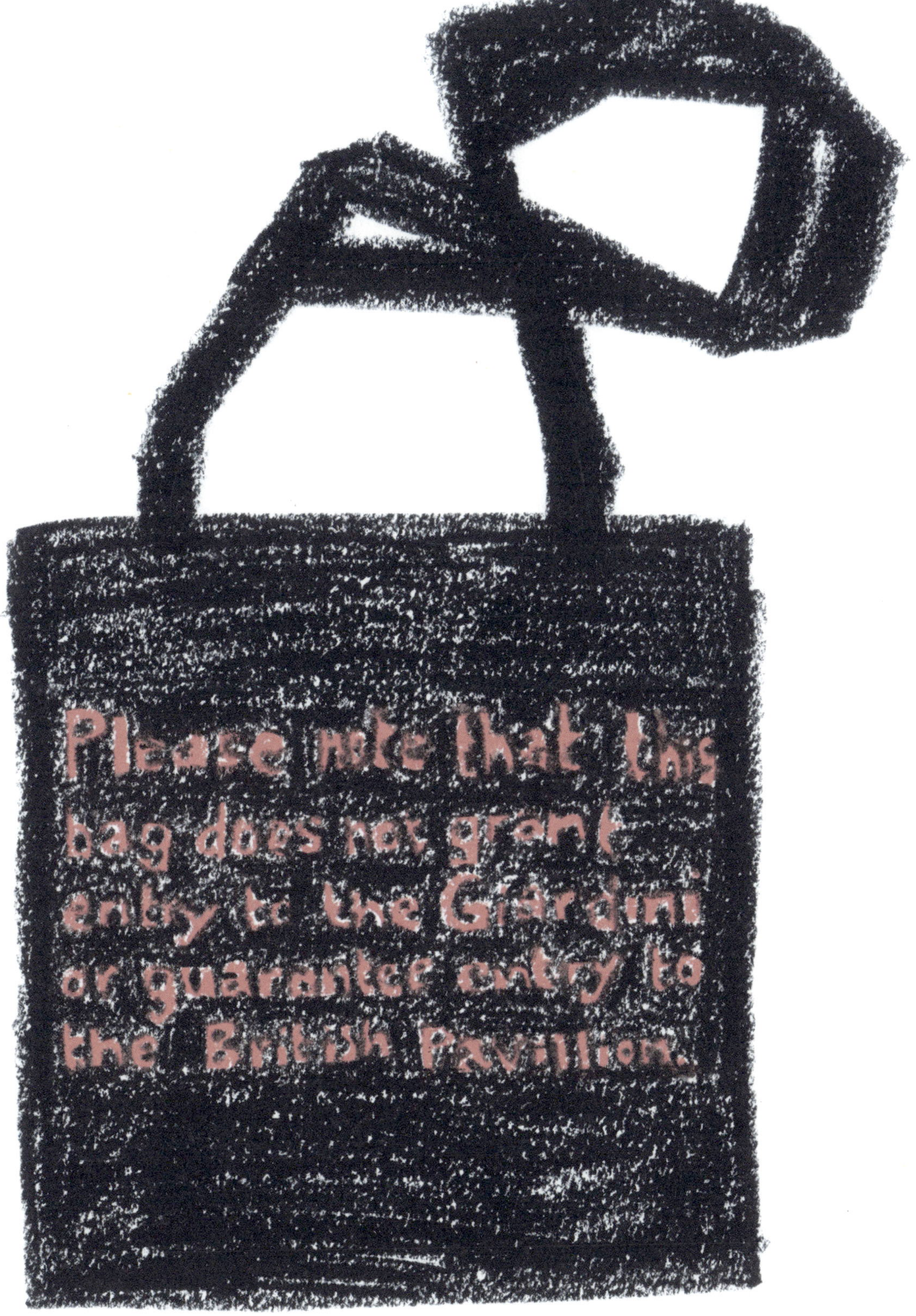

Please note that this bag does not grant entry to the Giardini or guarantee entry to the British Pavillion.

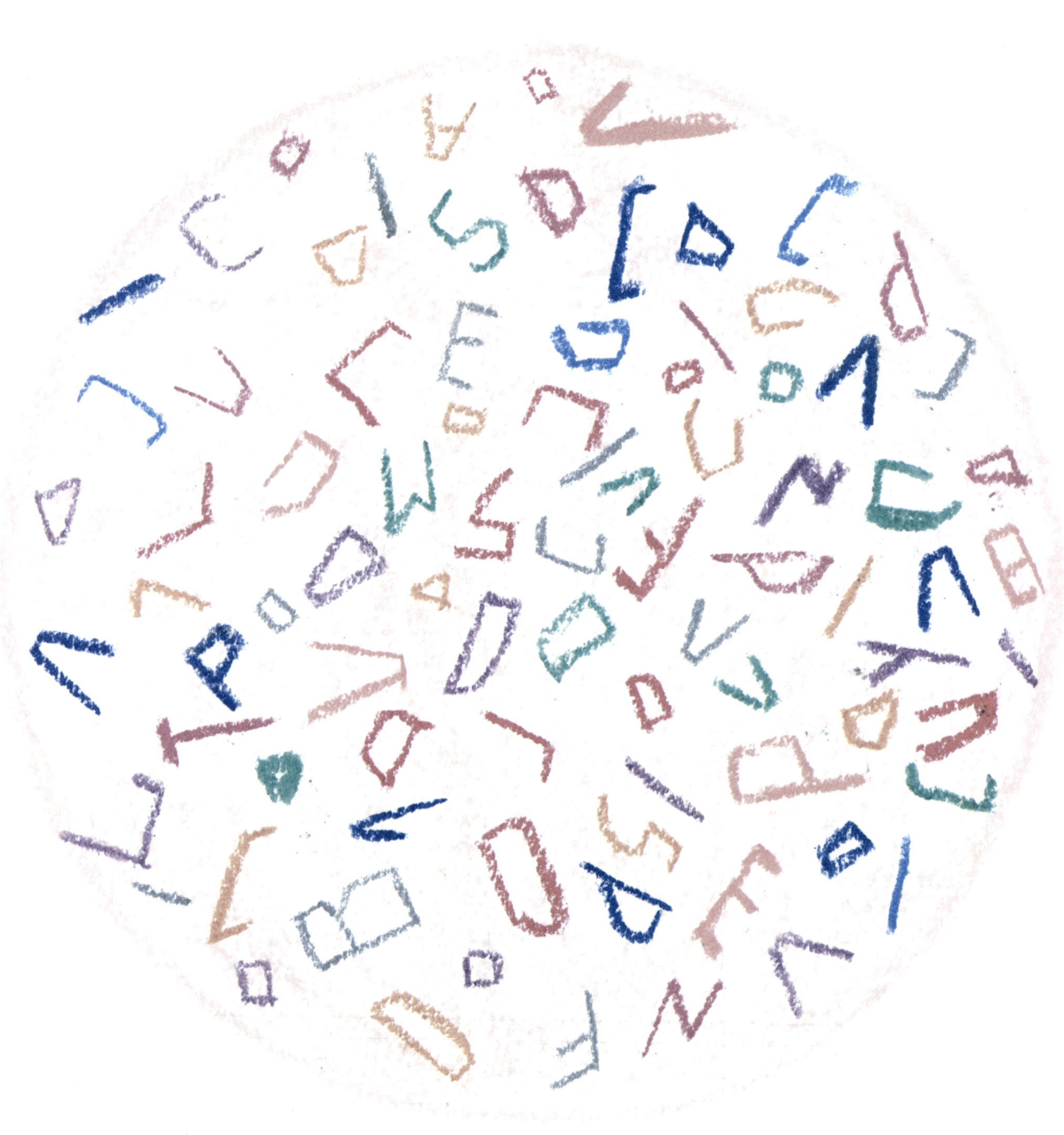

BARCELONA

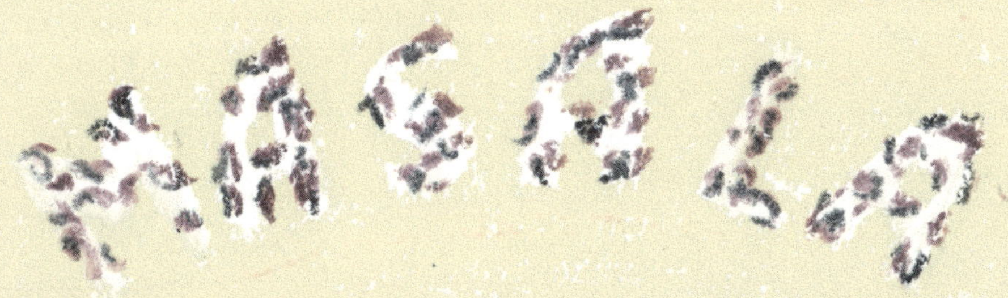

NARRATIVES & INTERACTIONS in CULTURAL SPACE

Edited by
Robert E. D'souza
Daniel Cid Morgas

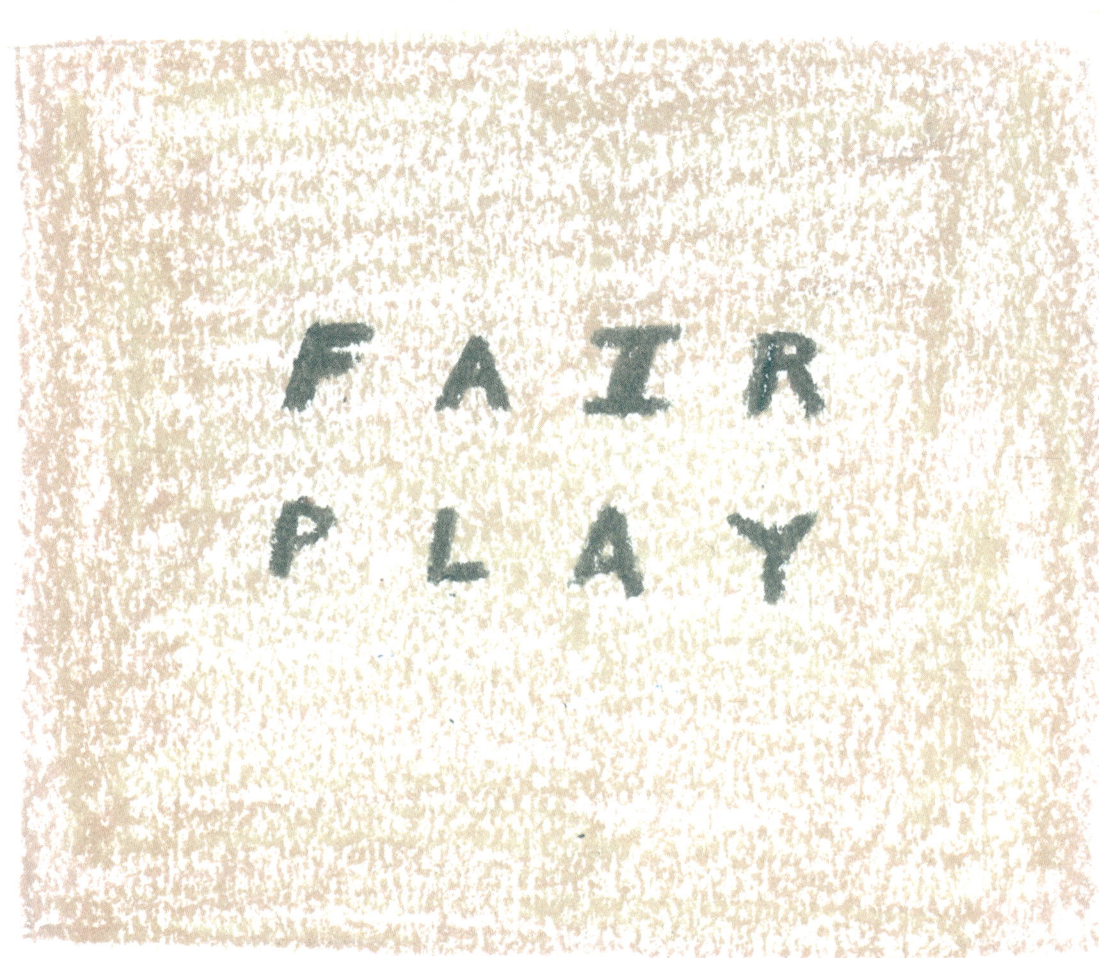
FAIR
PLAY

13 Presidents

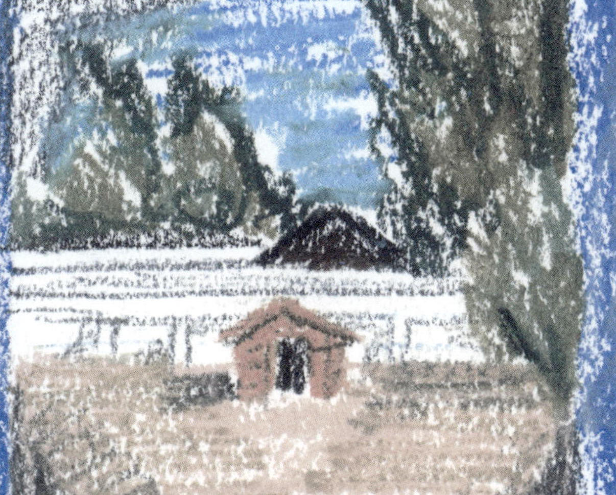

Marisa J. Futernick

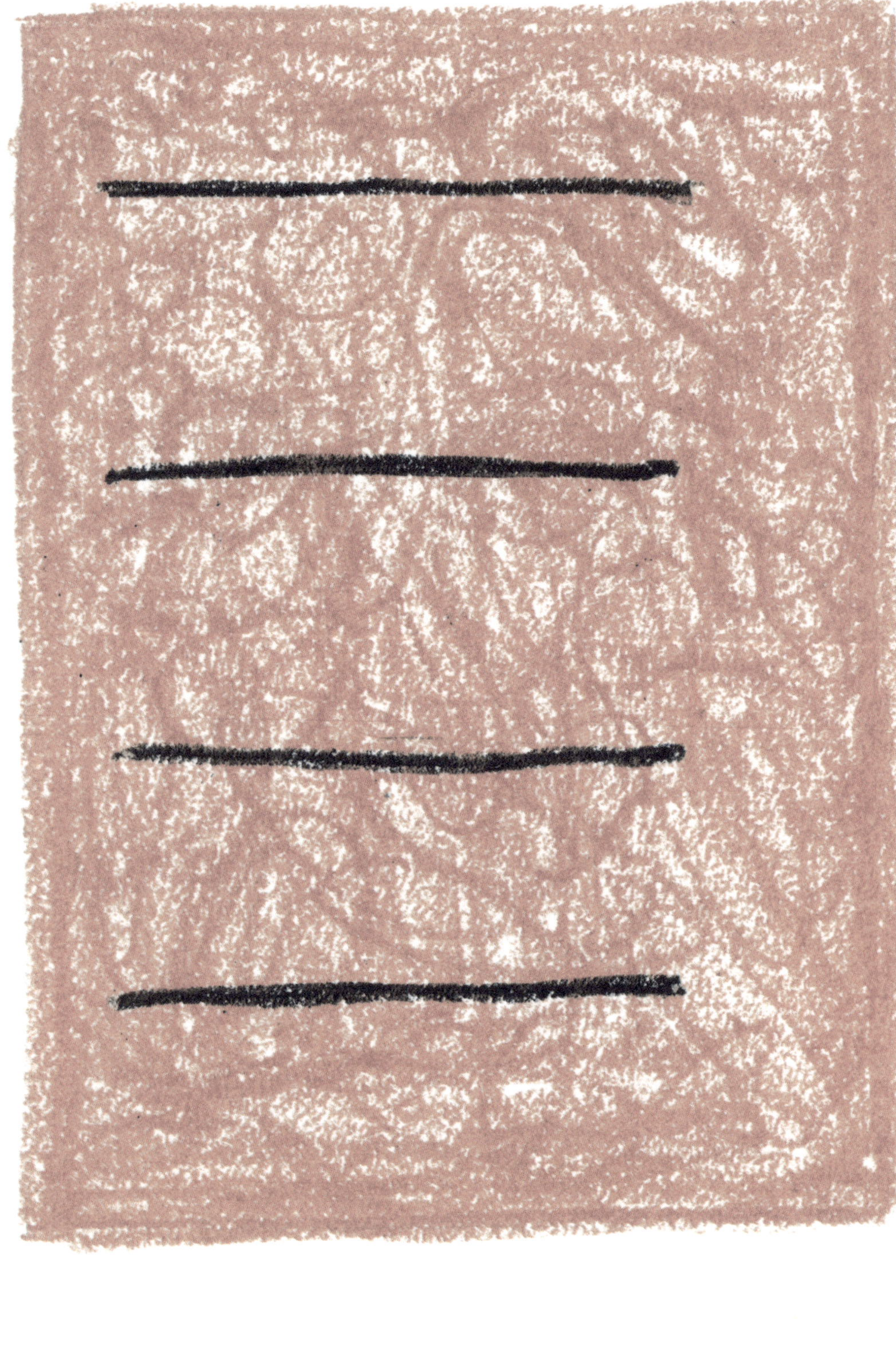

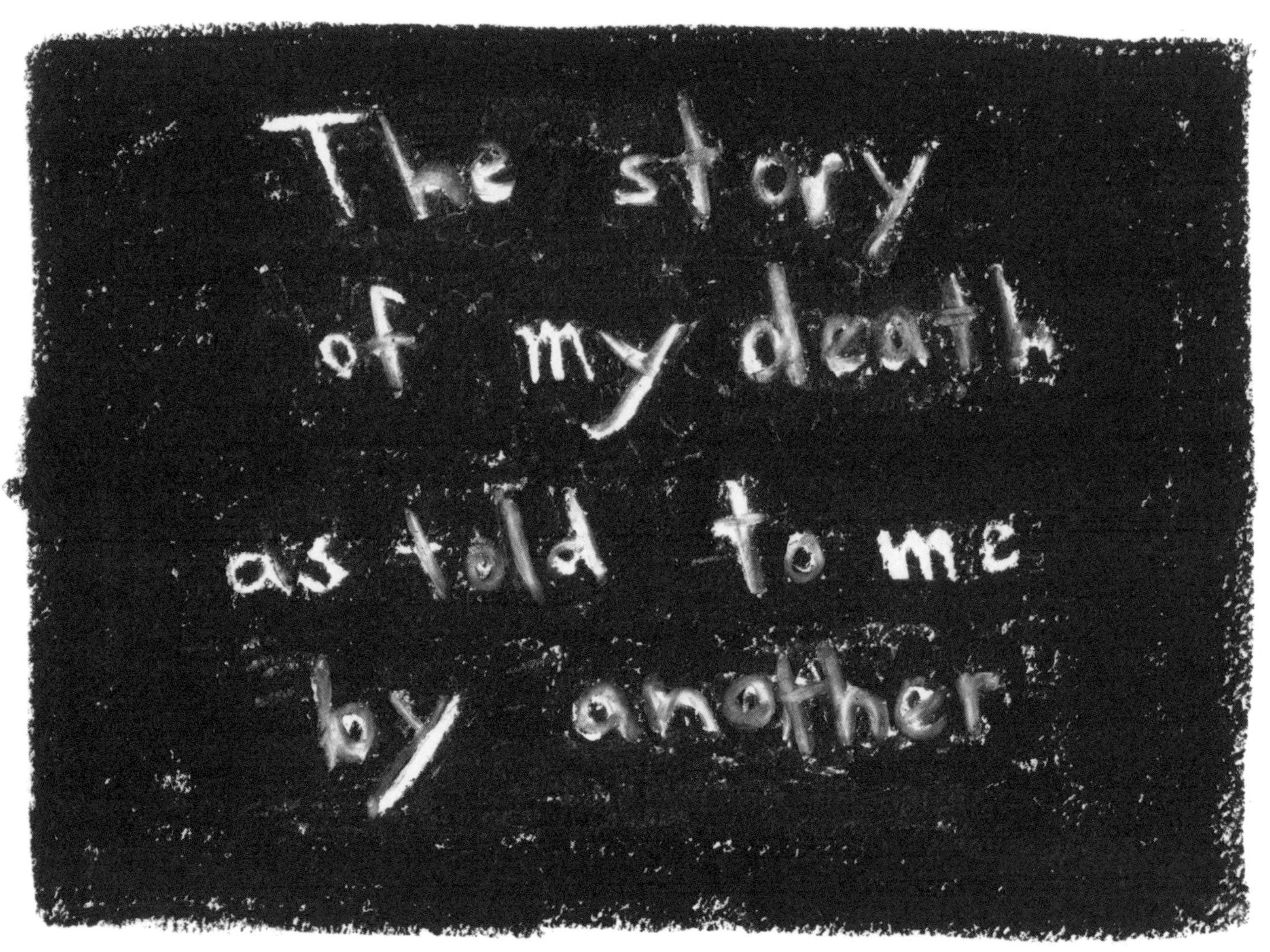
The story
of my death
as told to me
by another

Elizabeth Price

SUNLIGHT

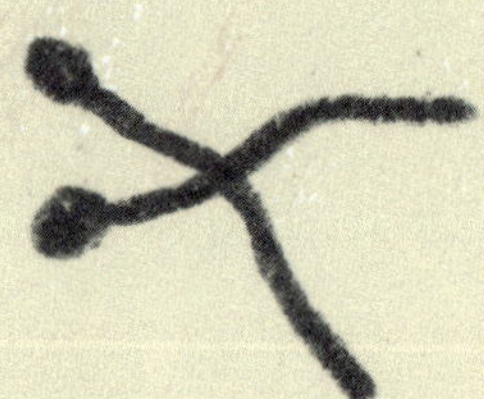

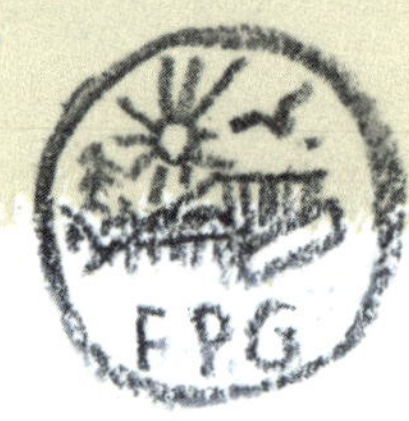

[illegible]

Marc Camille Chaimowicz
Mike Nelson
Allen Ruppersberg
Tris Vonna-Michell

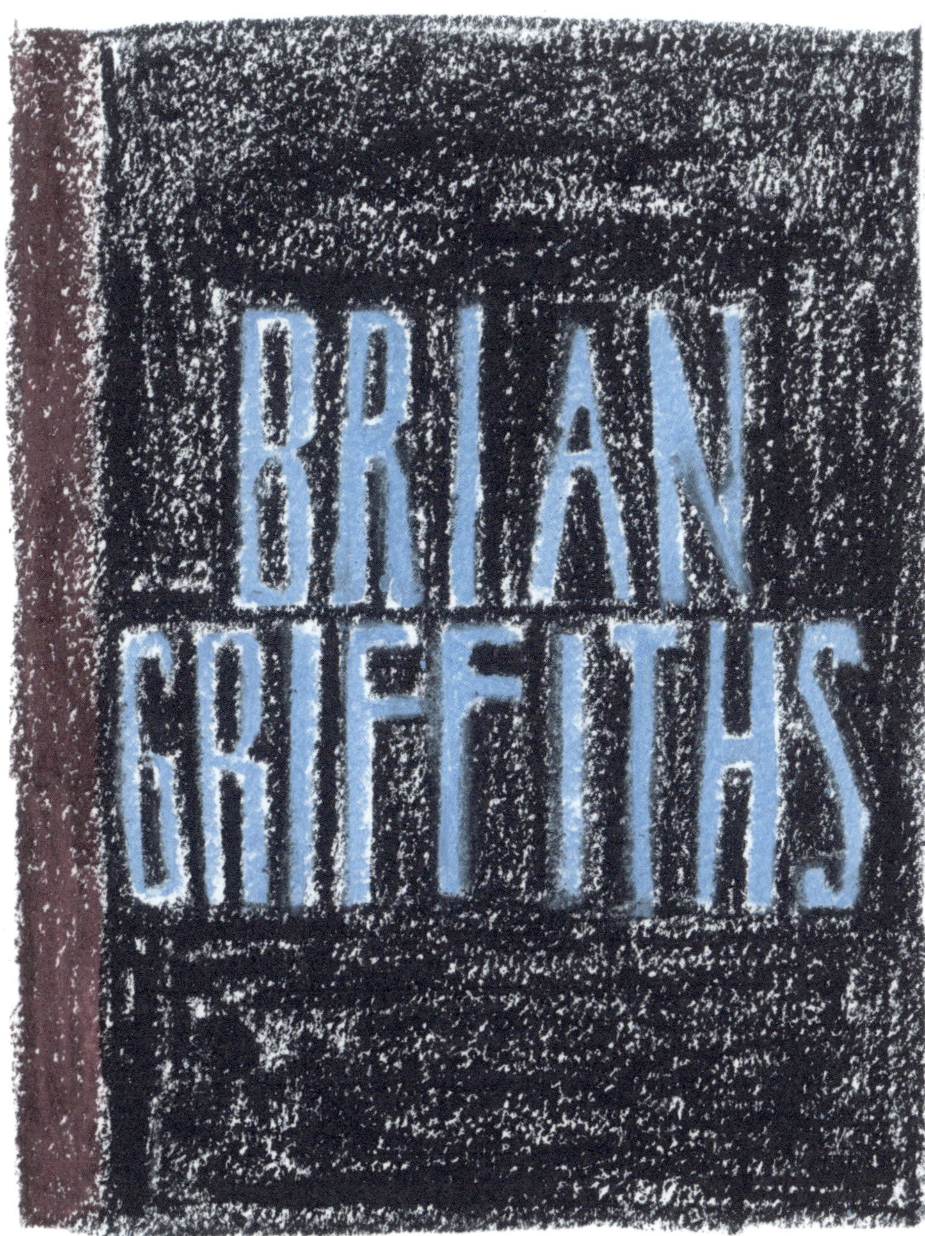
BRIAN
GRIFFITHS

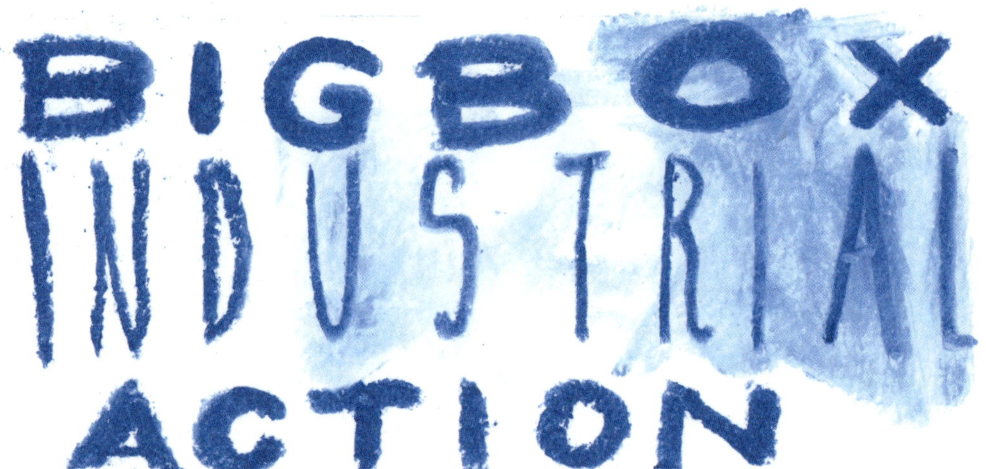

4-SET HALF HOUR PERFORMANCES

POW WOW
BORBORYGMUS
GILDED AGE
SWEET SEIZURE

SIXTEENTH of FEBRUARY
6.15pm TWENTY THIRD of FEBRUARY
FIRST of MARCH
EIGHTH of MARCH

FREE ADMISSION

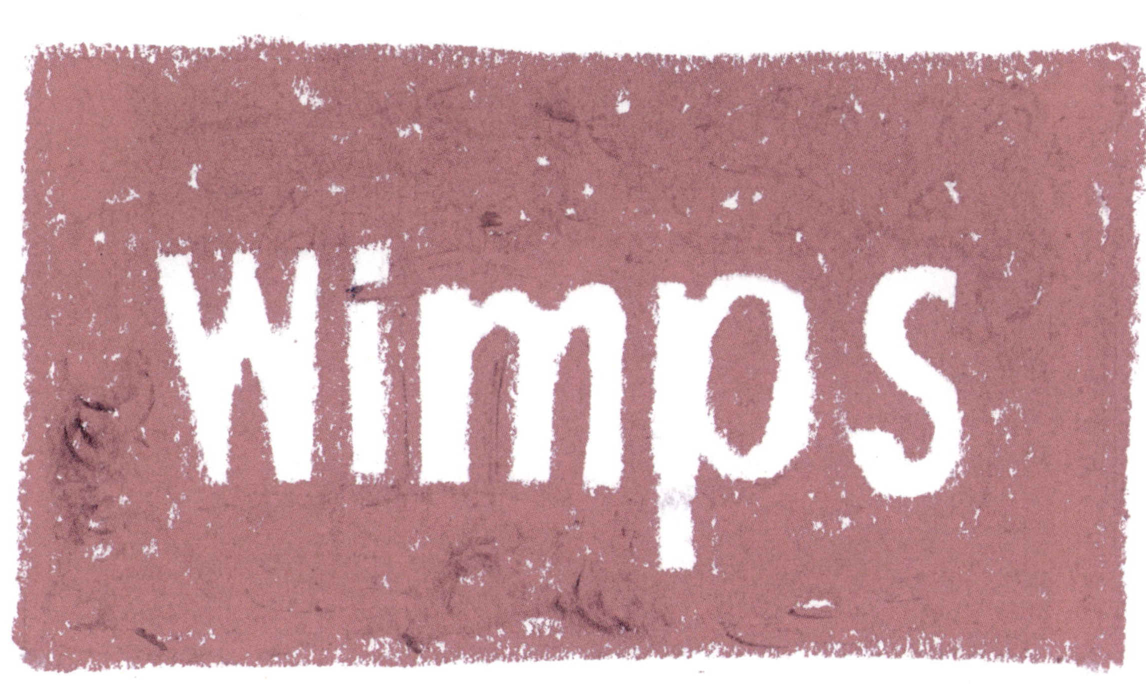
Wimps

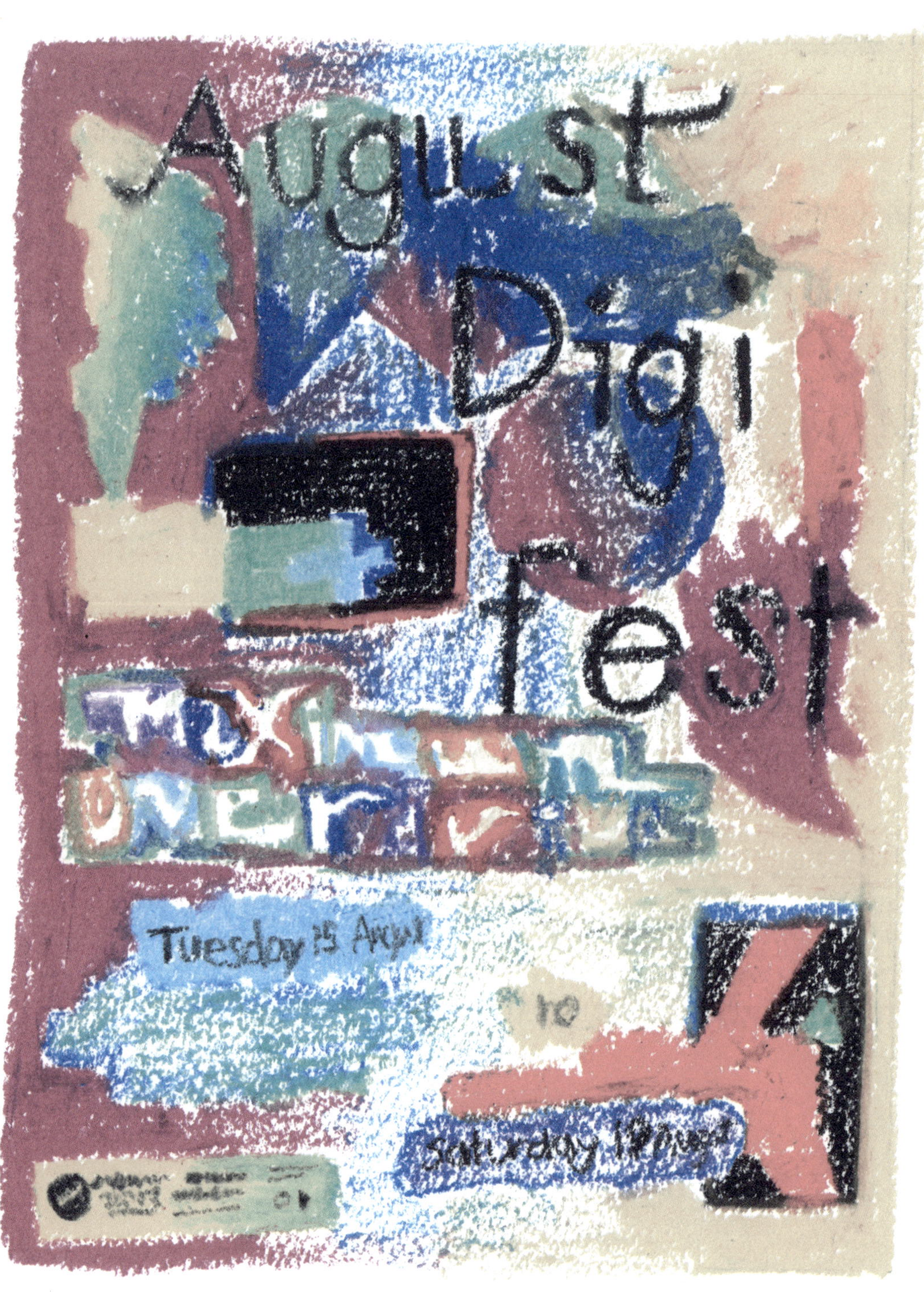
August
Digi
fest
Tuesday 15
to
Saturday

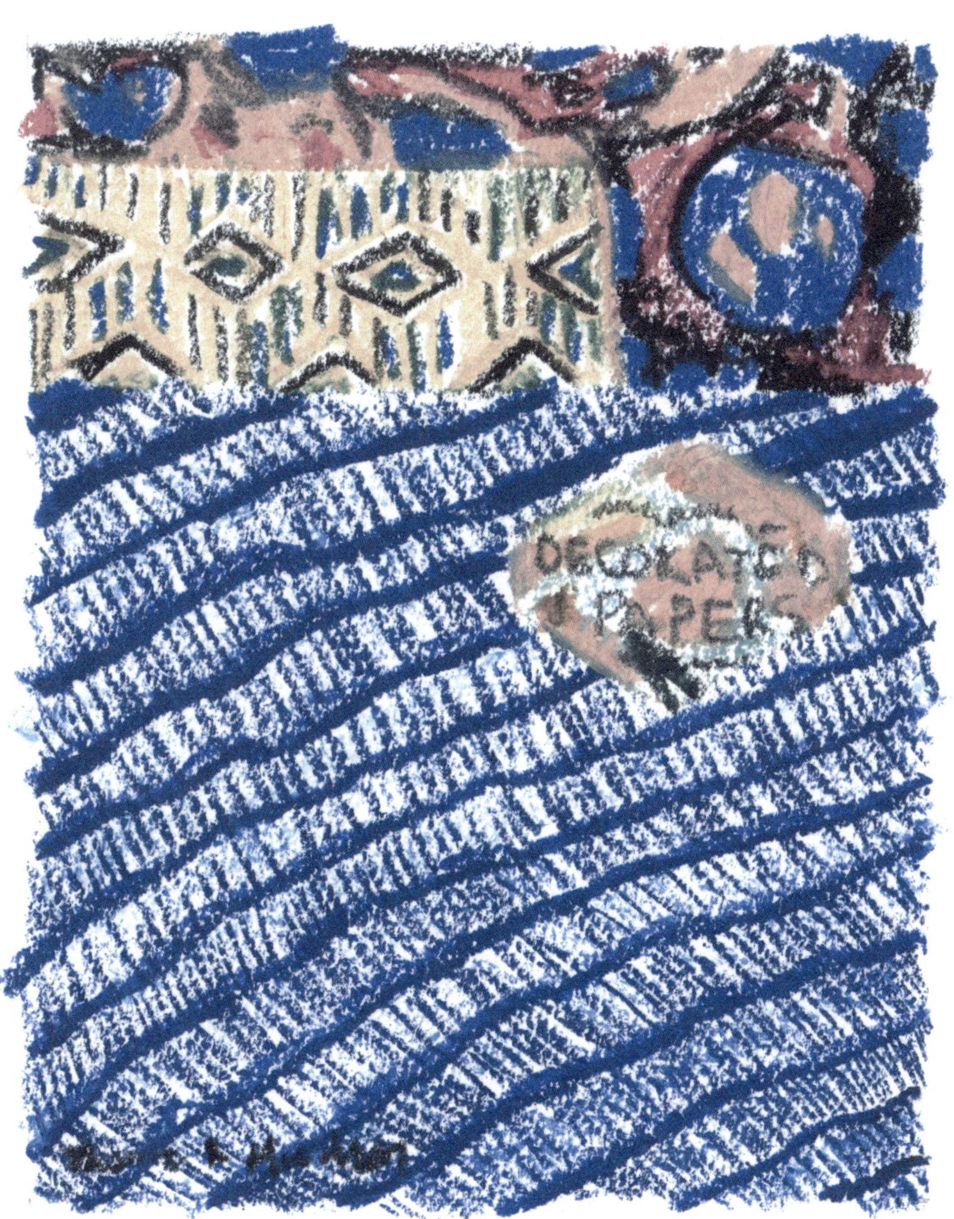
DECORATED
PAPERS

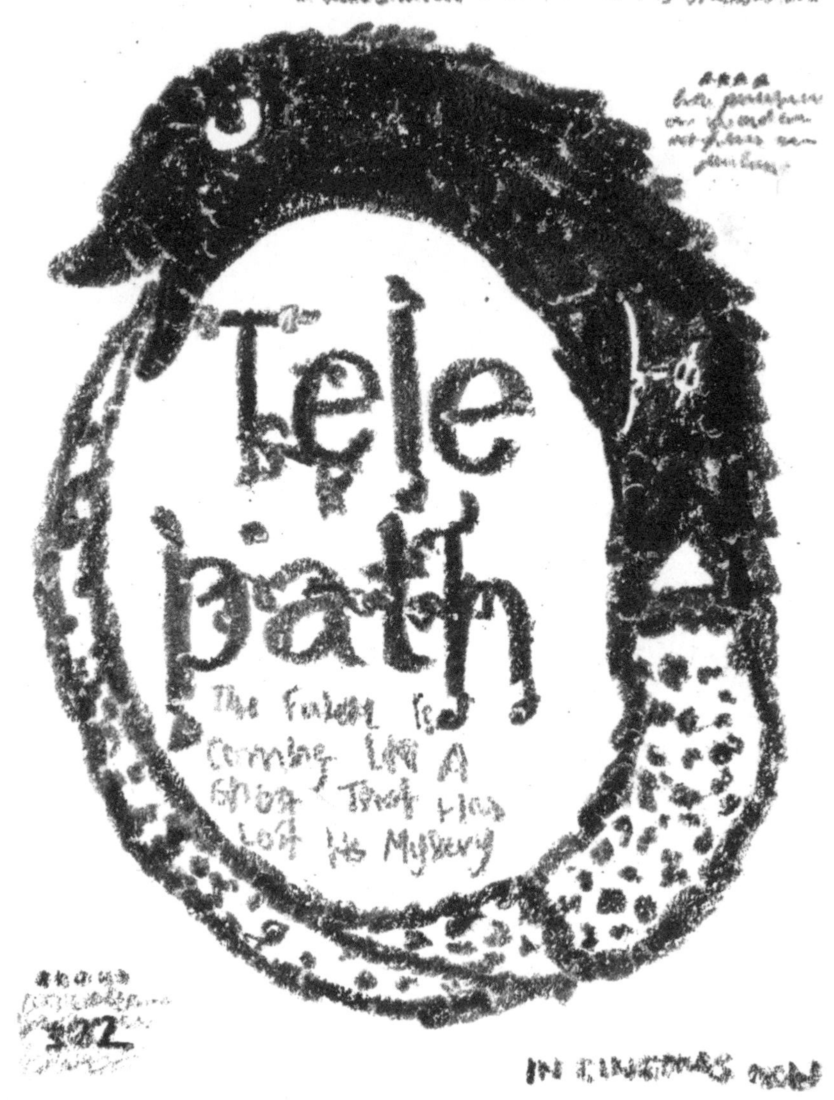
A RADICAL FILM STUDIO PRODUCTION
Tele
path
IN CINEMAS NOW

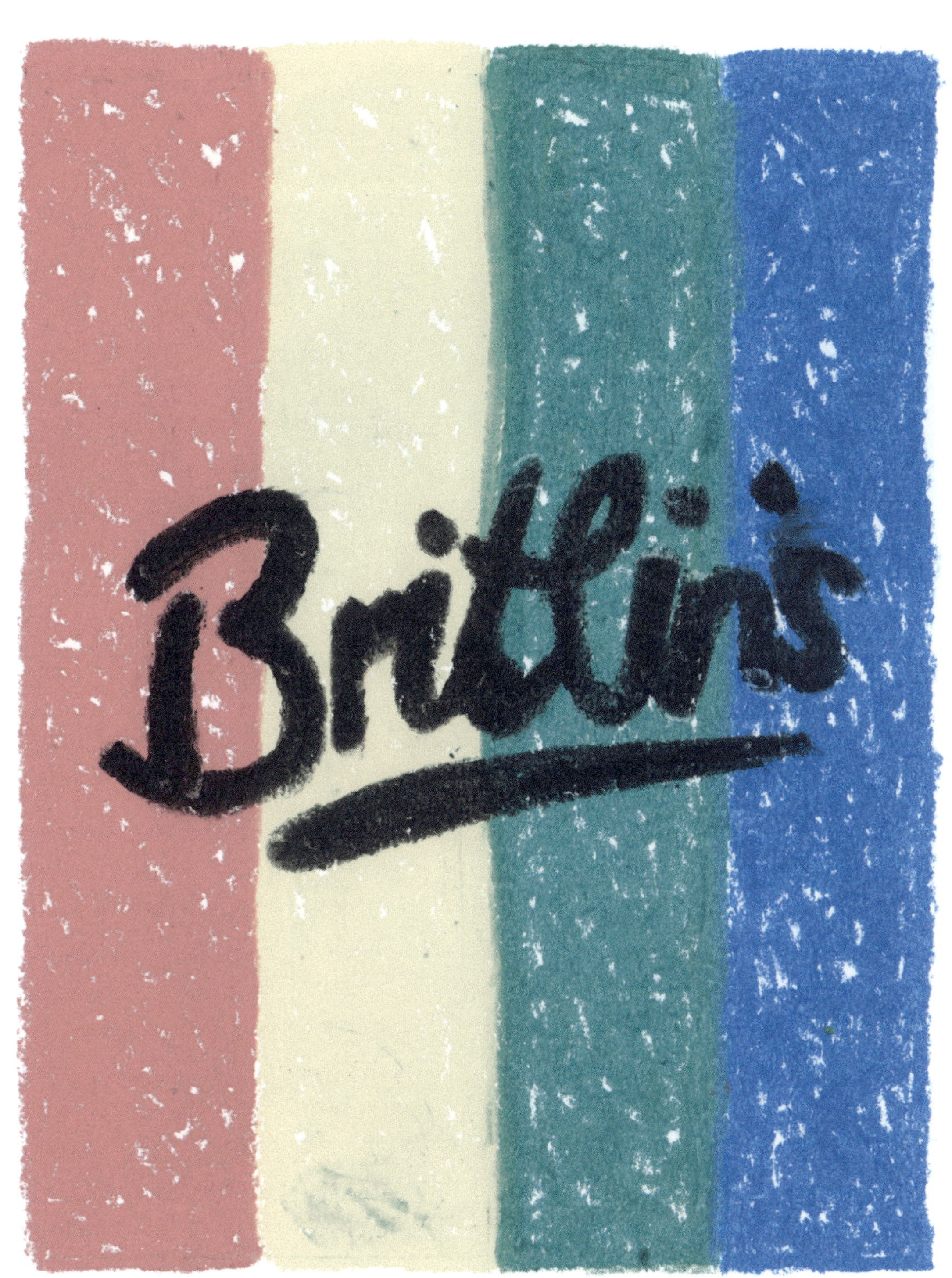
Britlin's

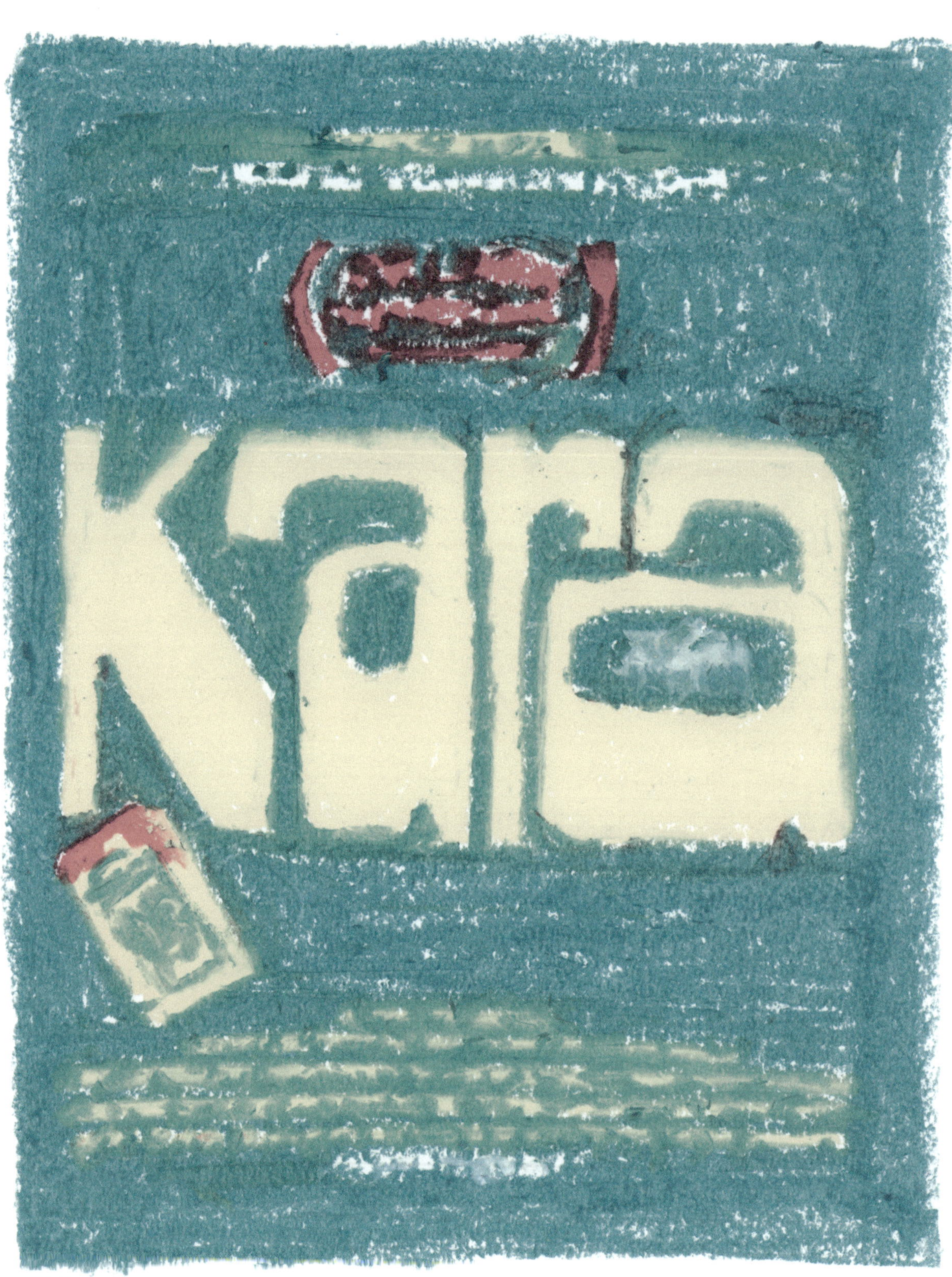
Kara

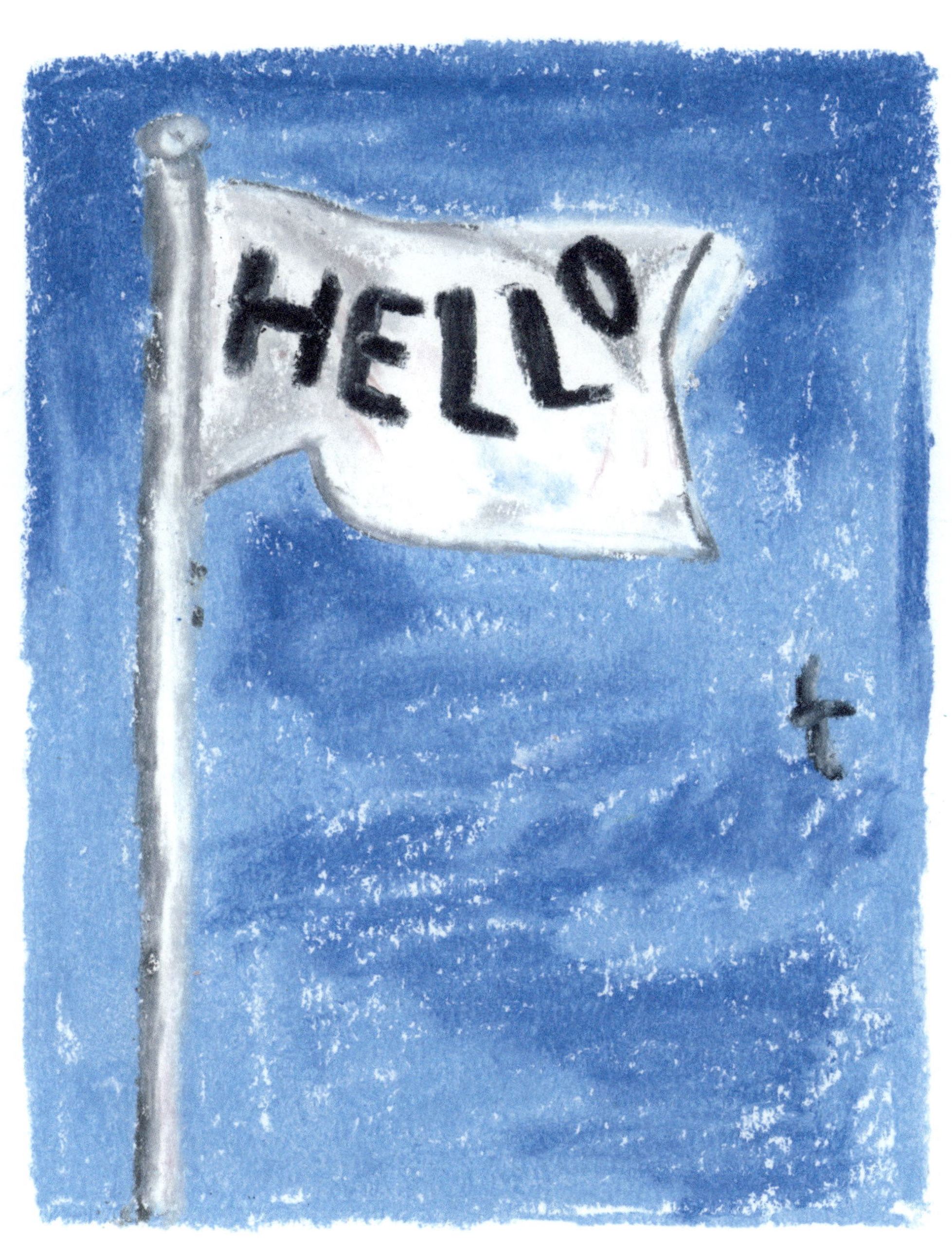
HELLO

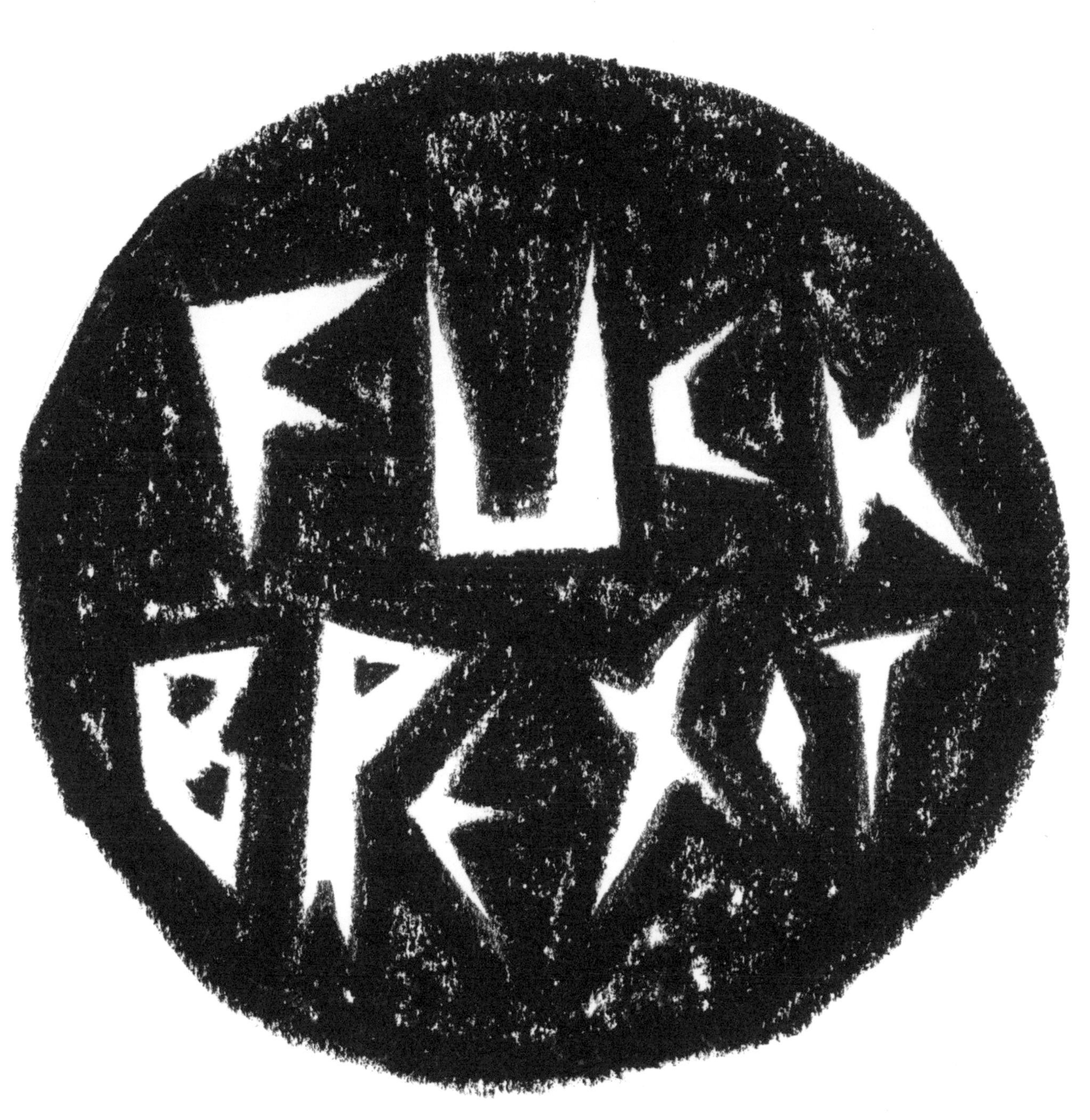
FUCK
BREXIT

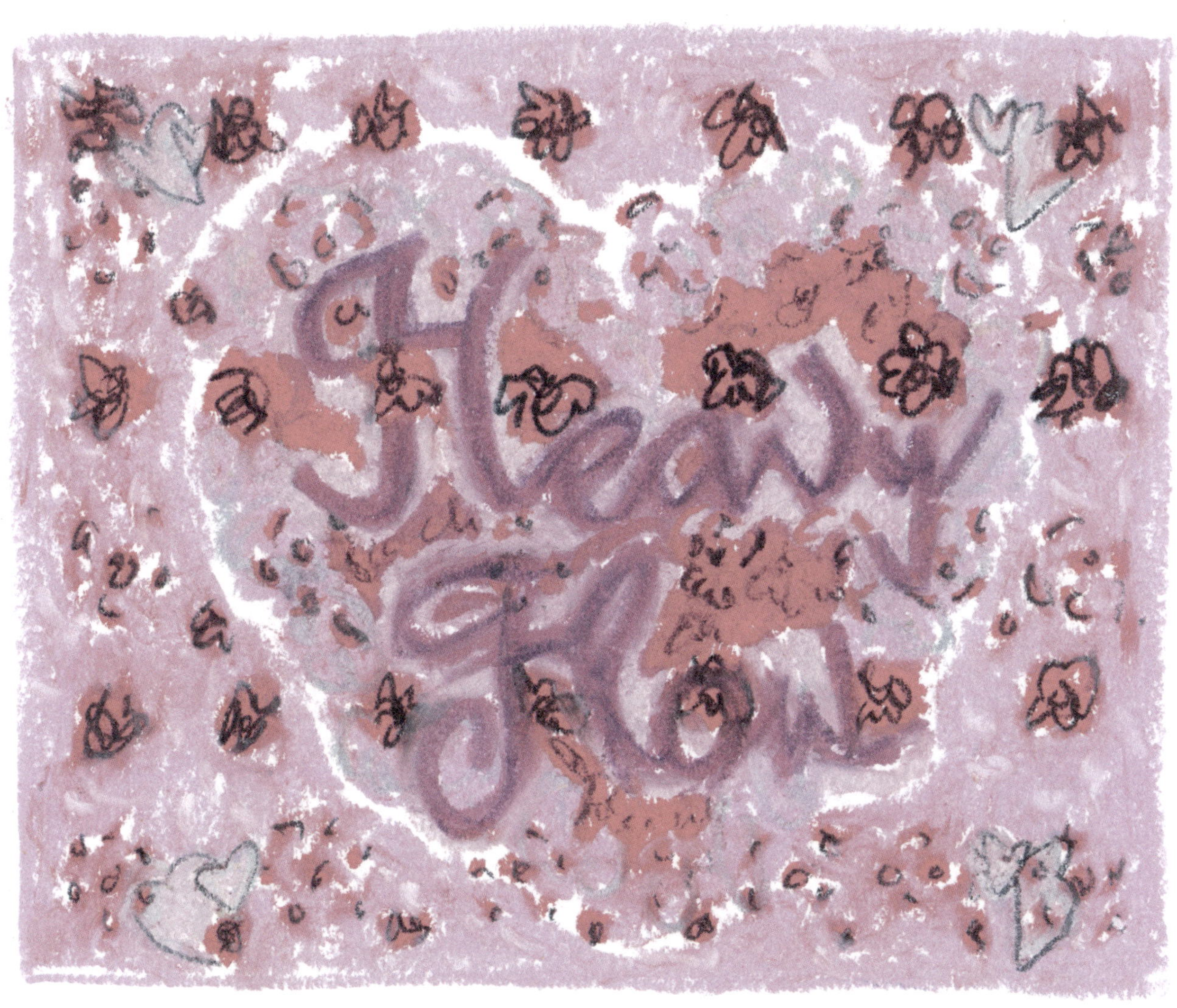
Heavy
Flow

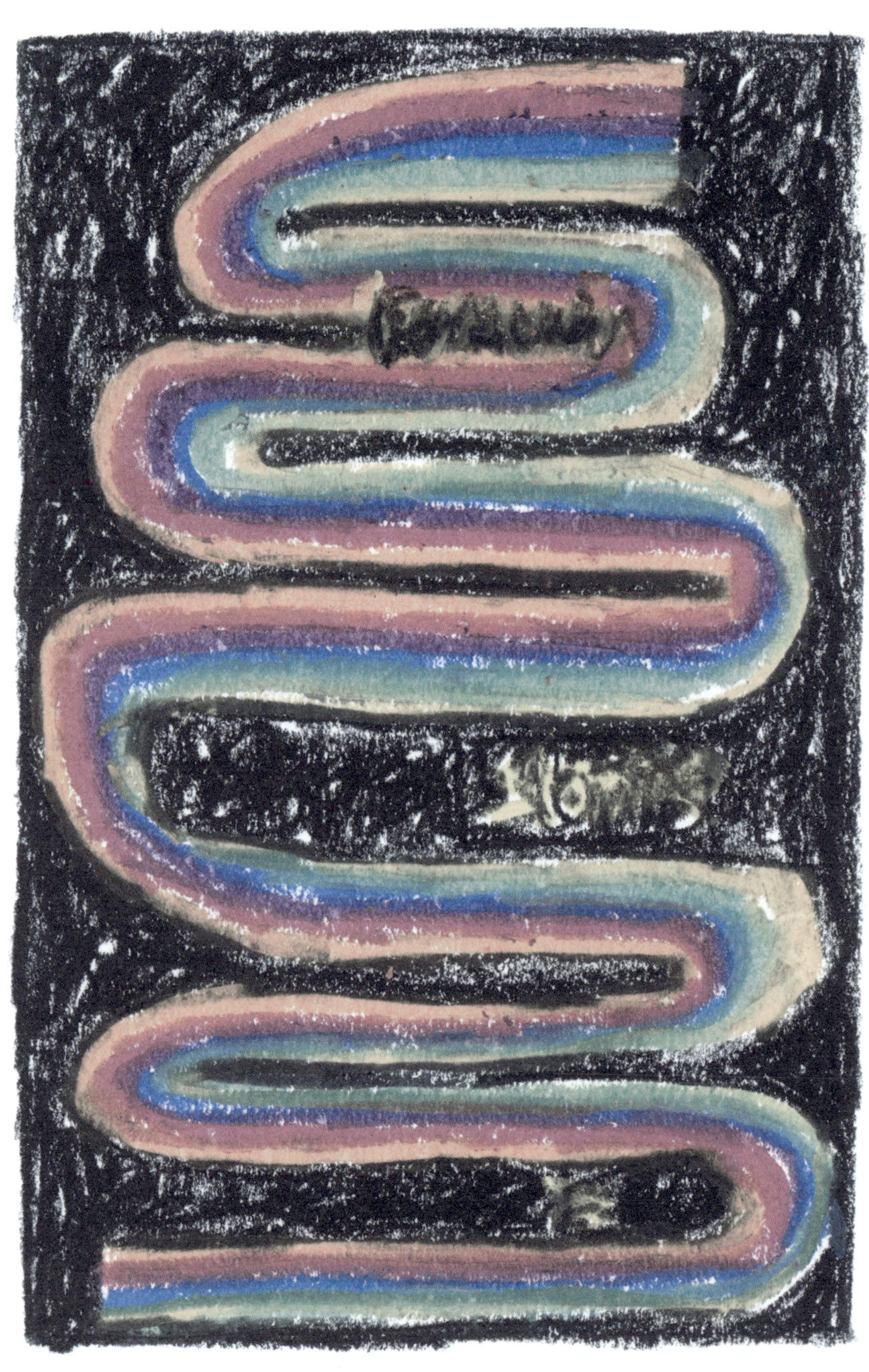

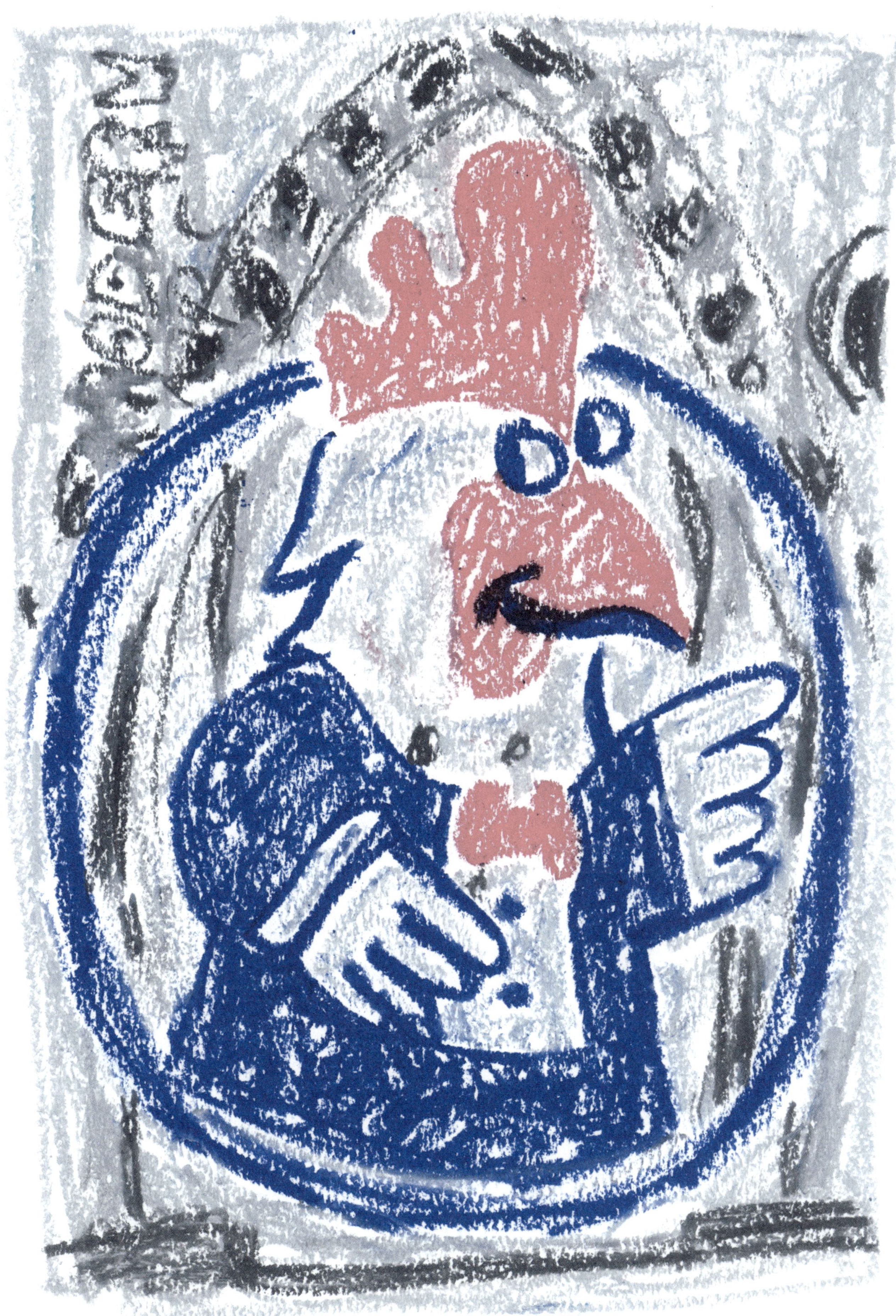

UNITED
WE FALL

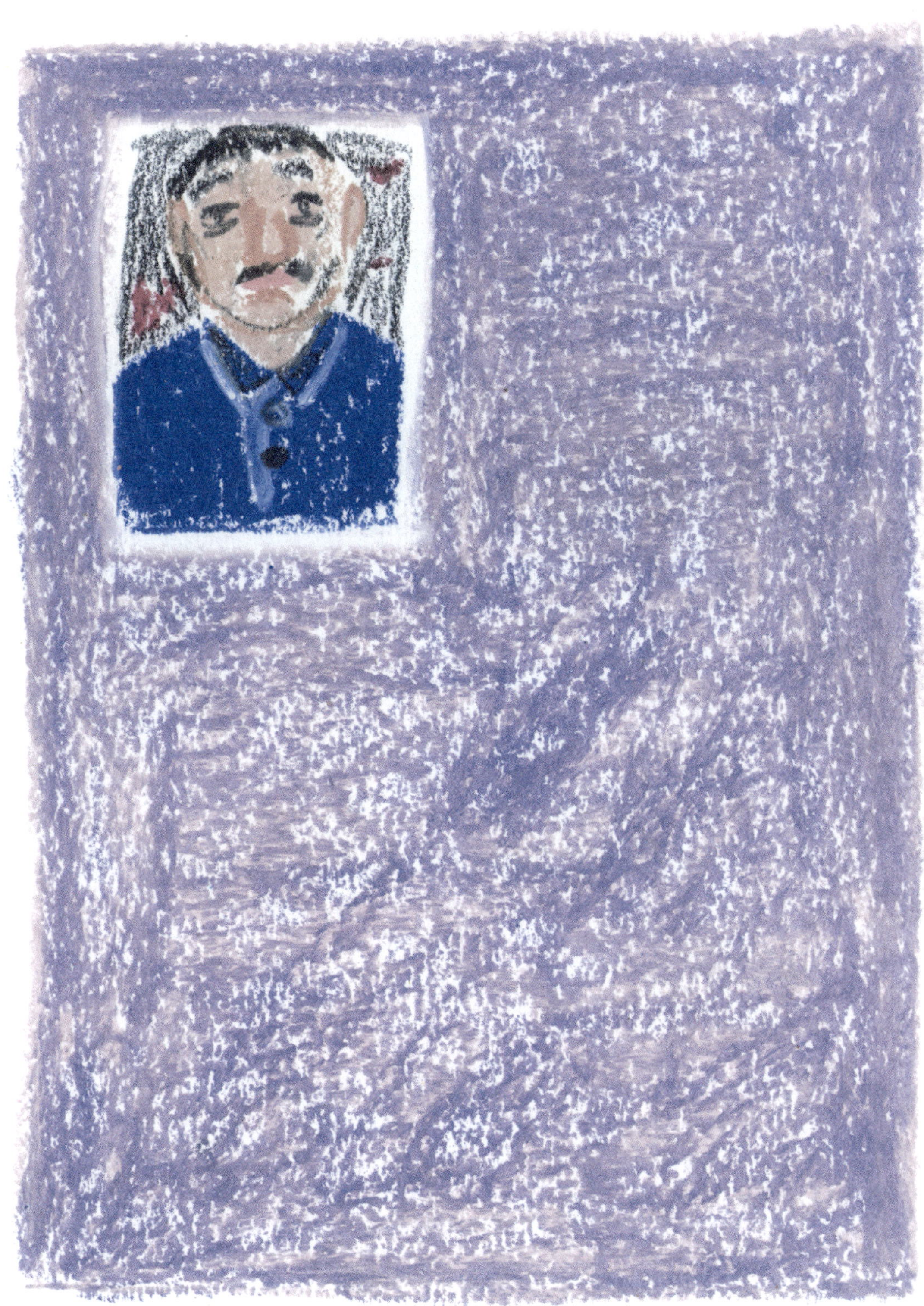

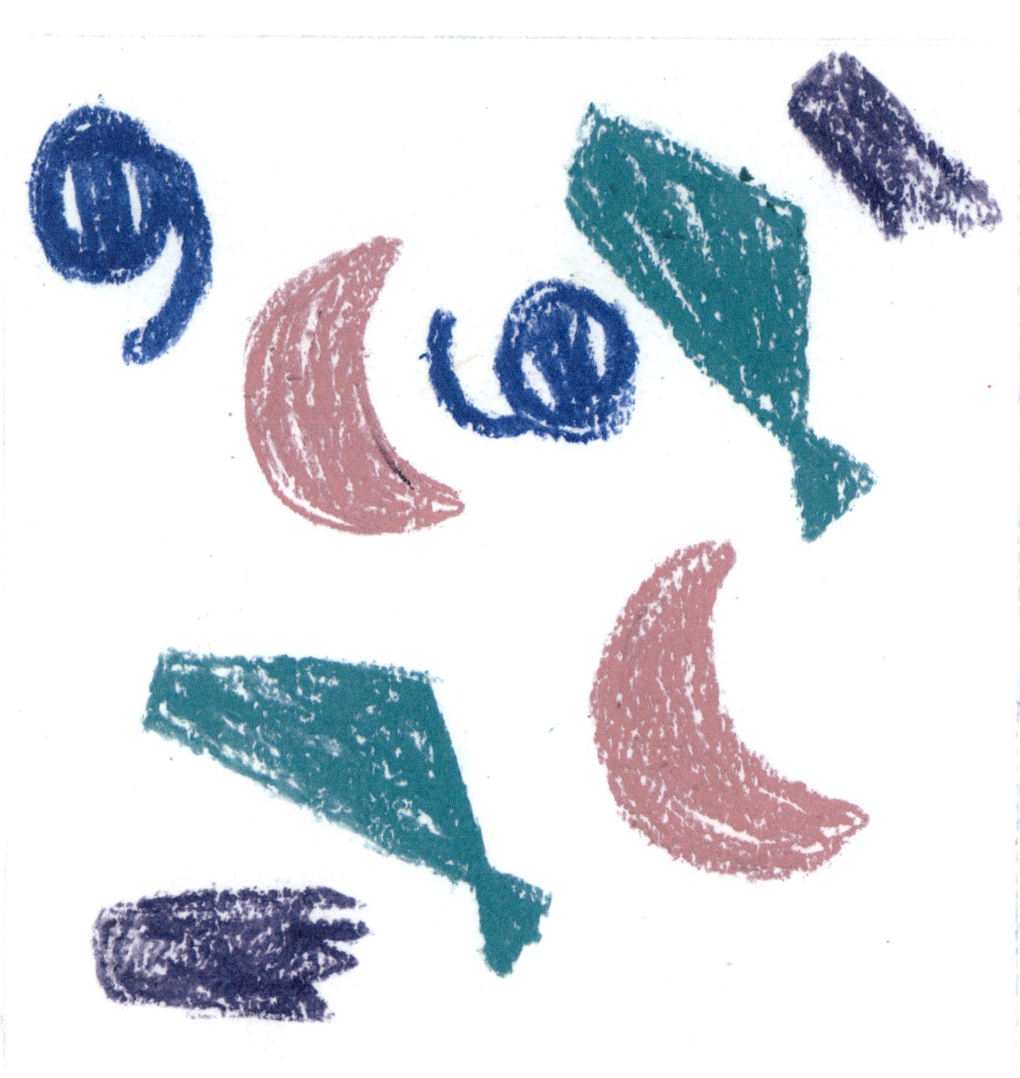

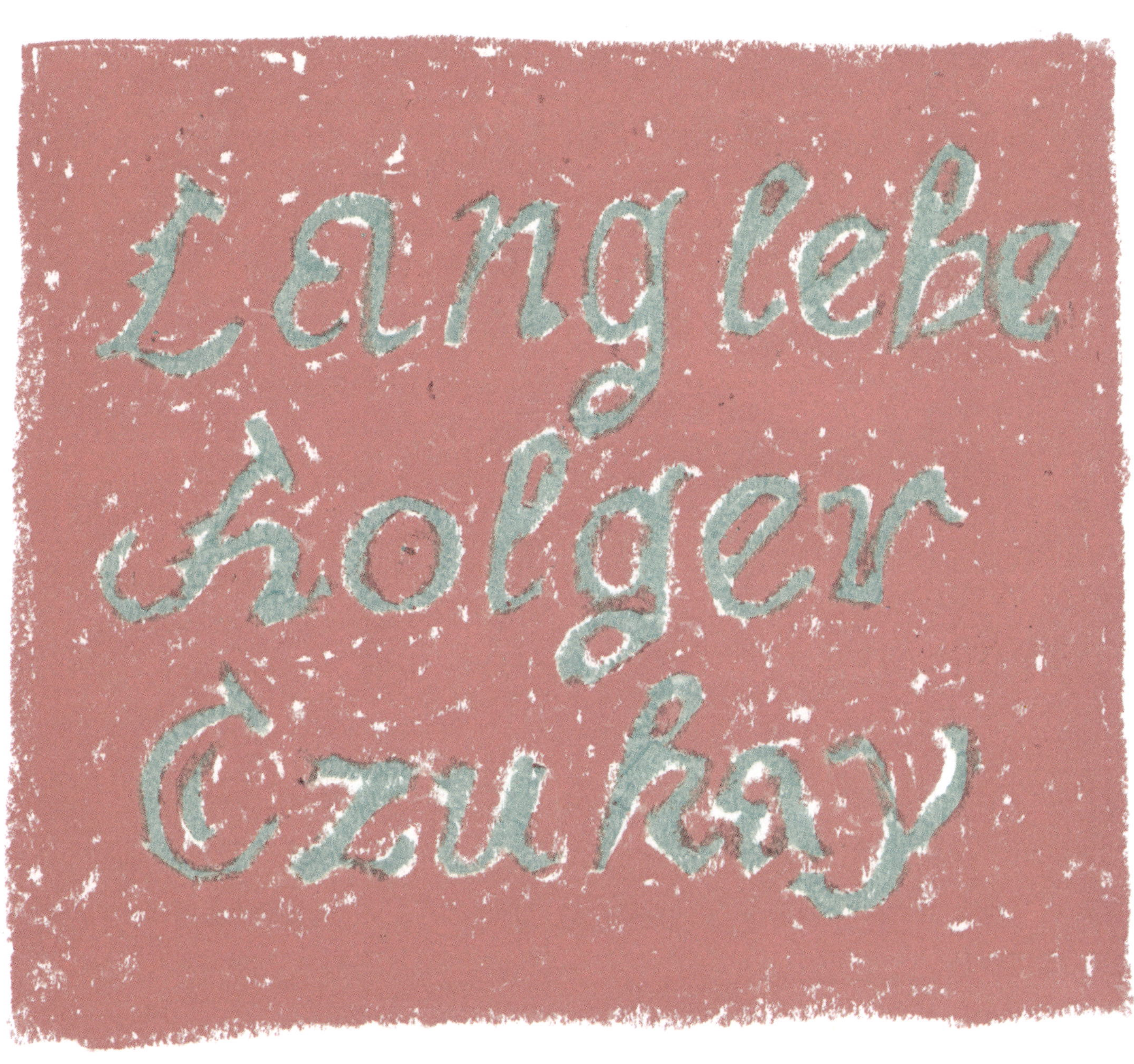
Lang lebe
Holger
Czukay

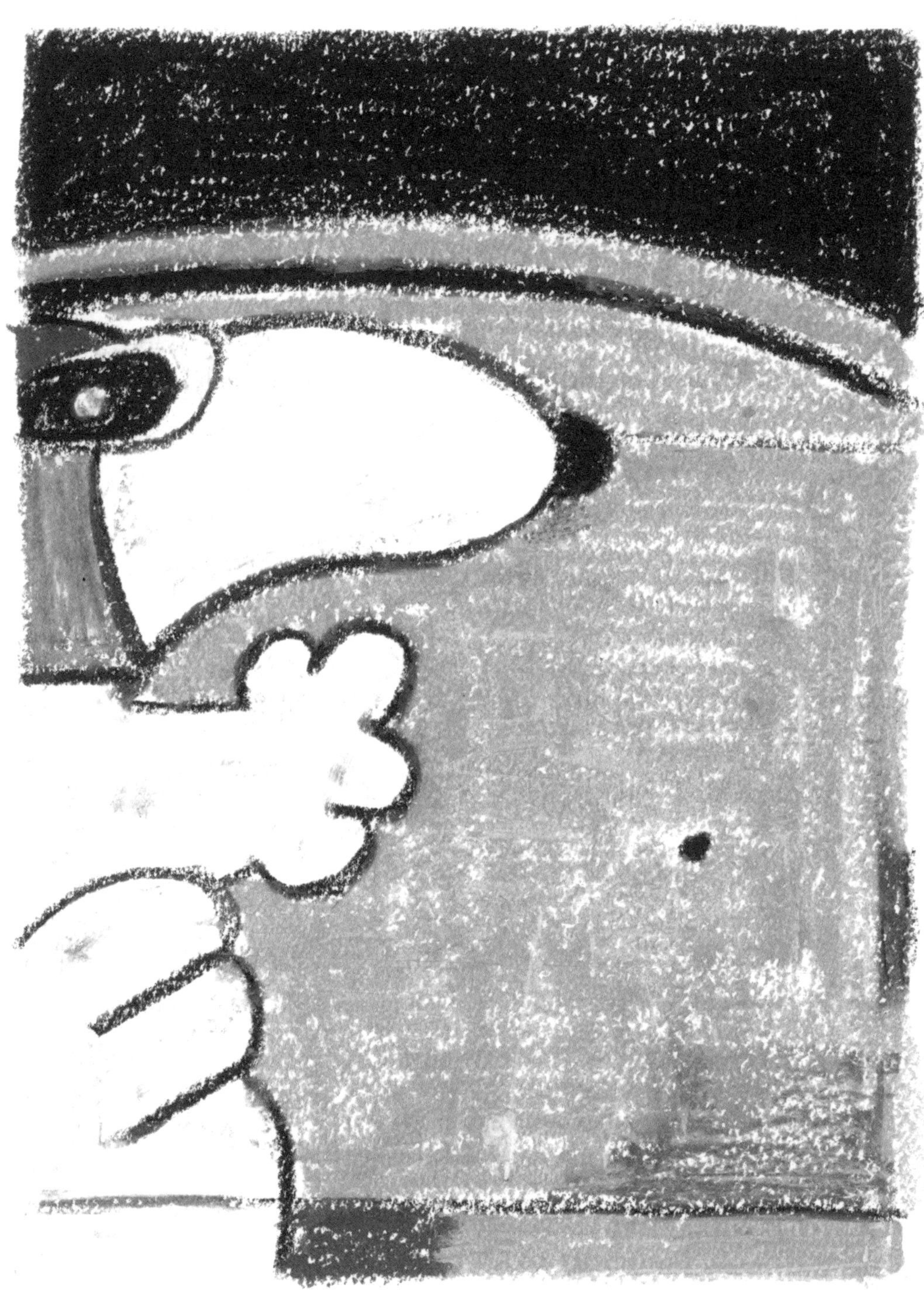

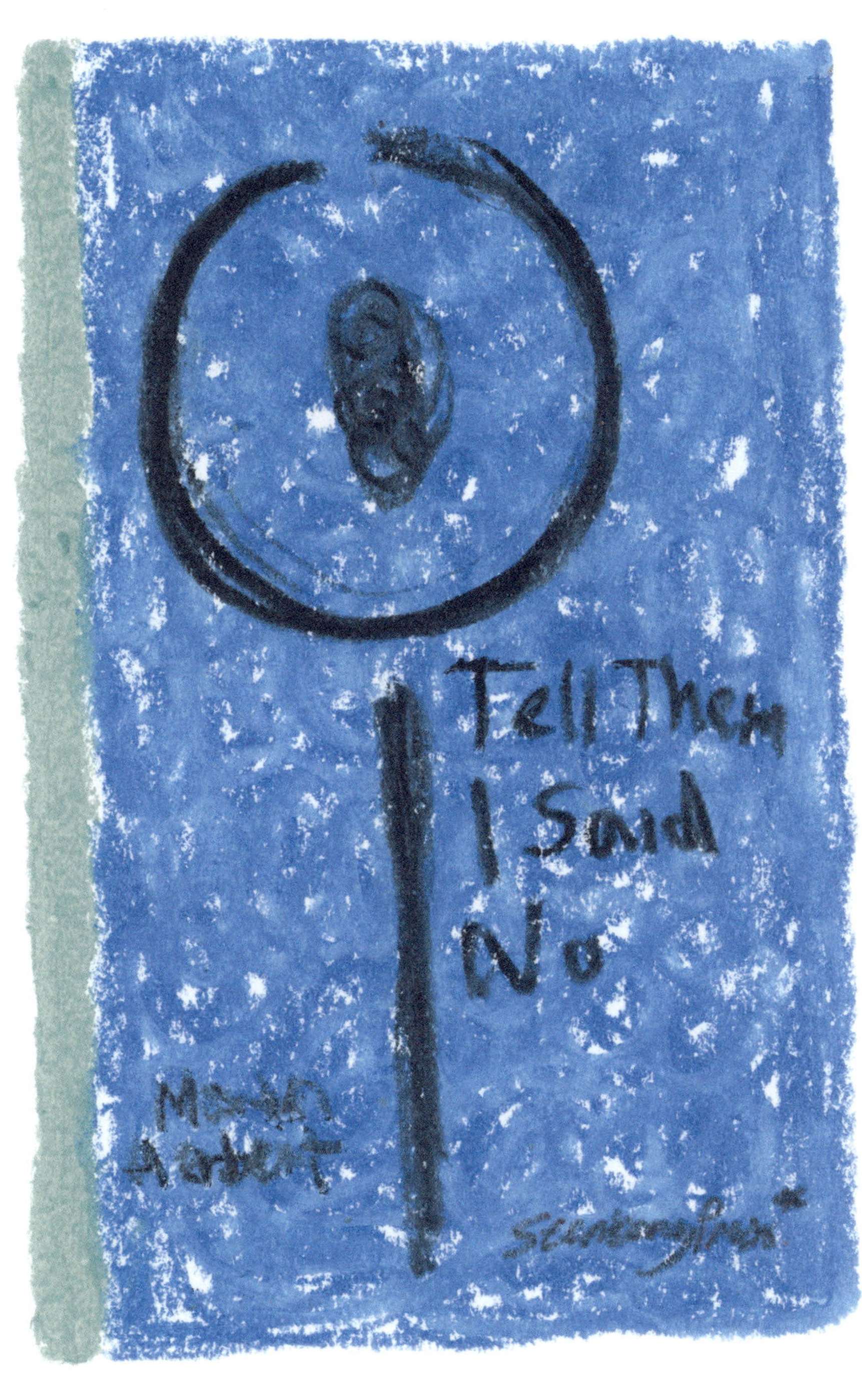

Tell Them
I Said
No

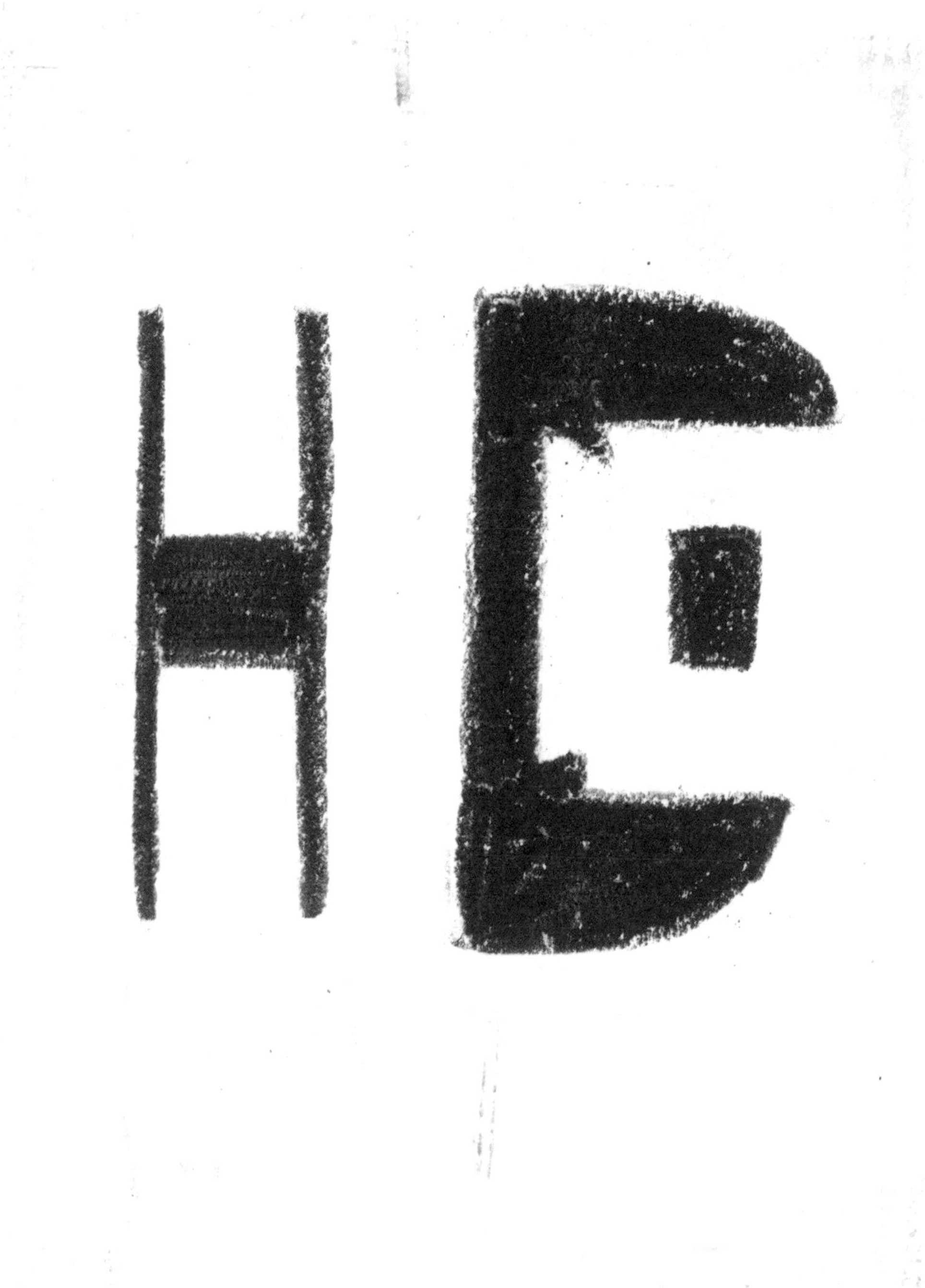

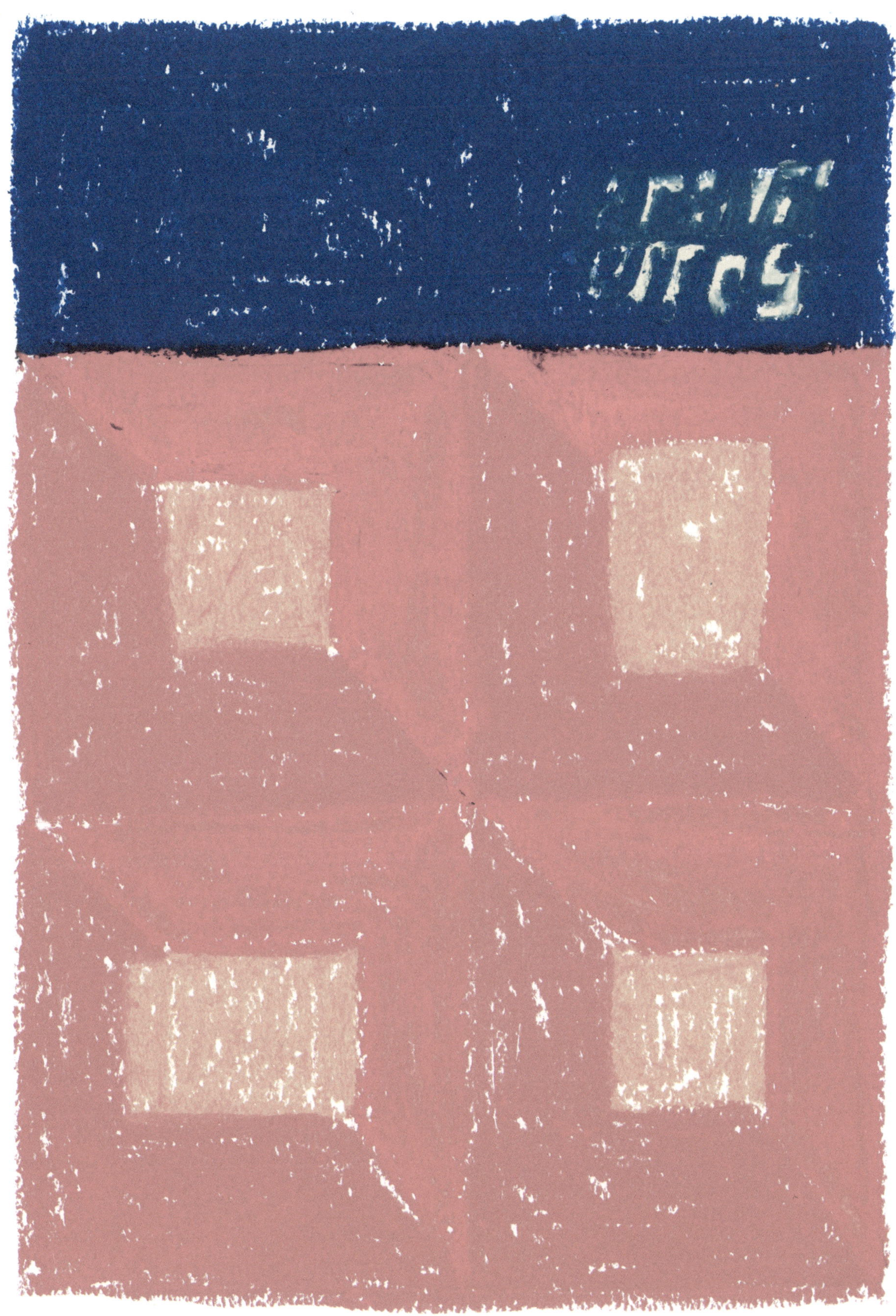

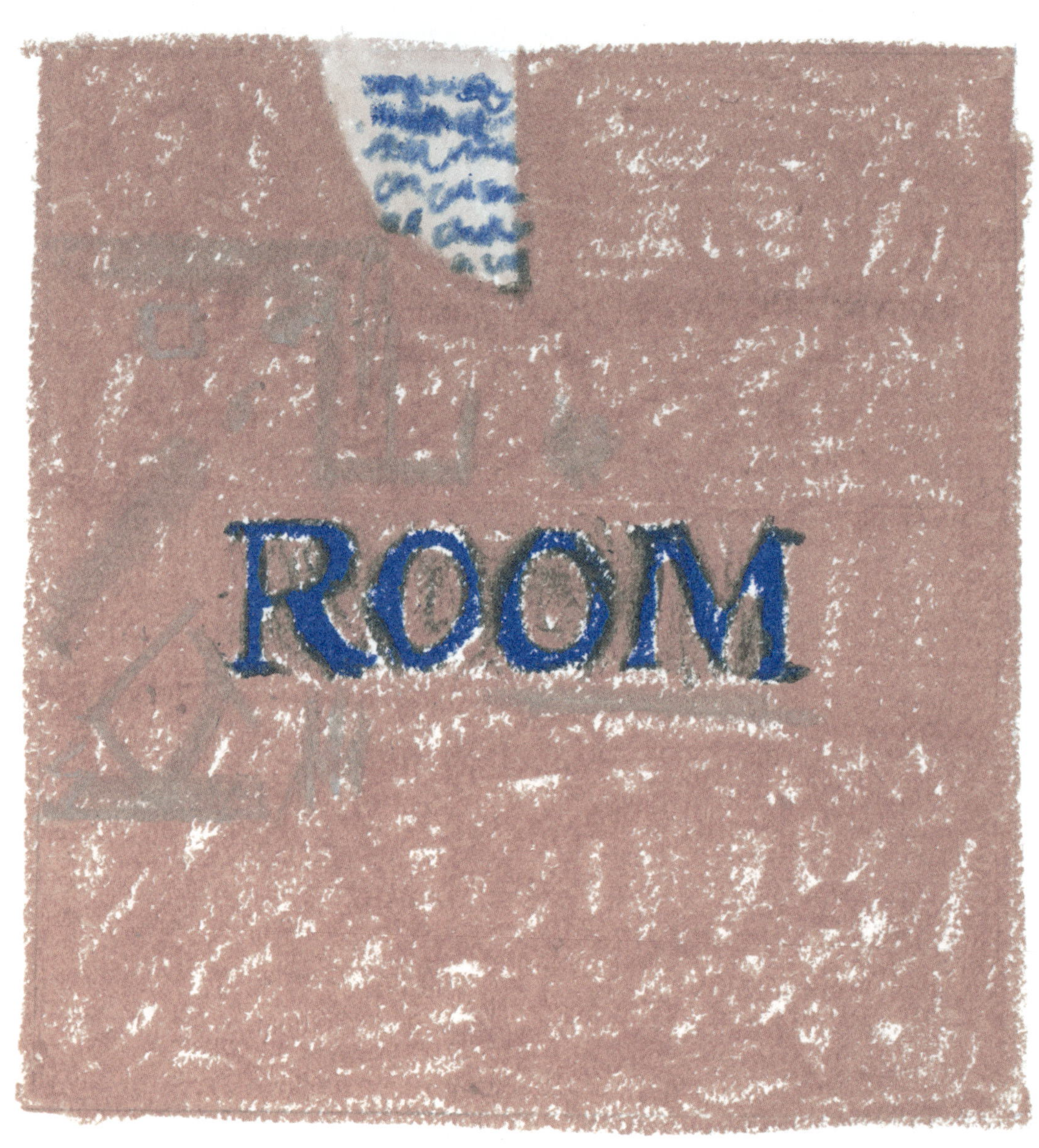
ROOM

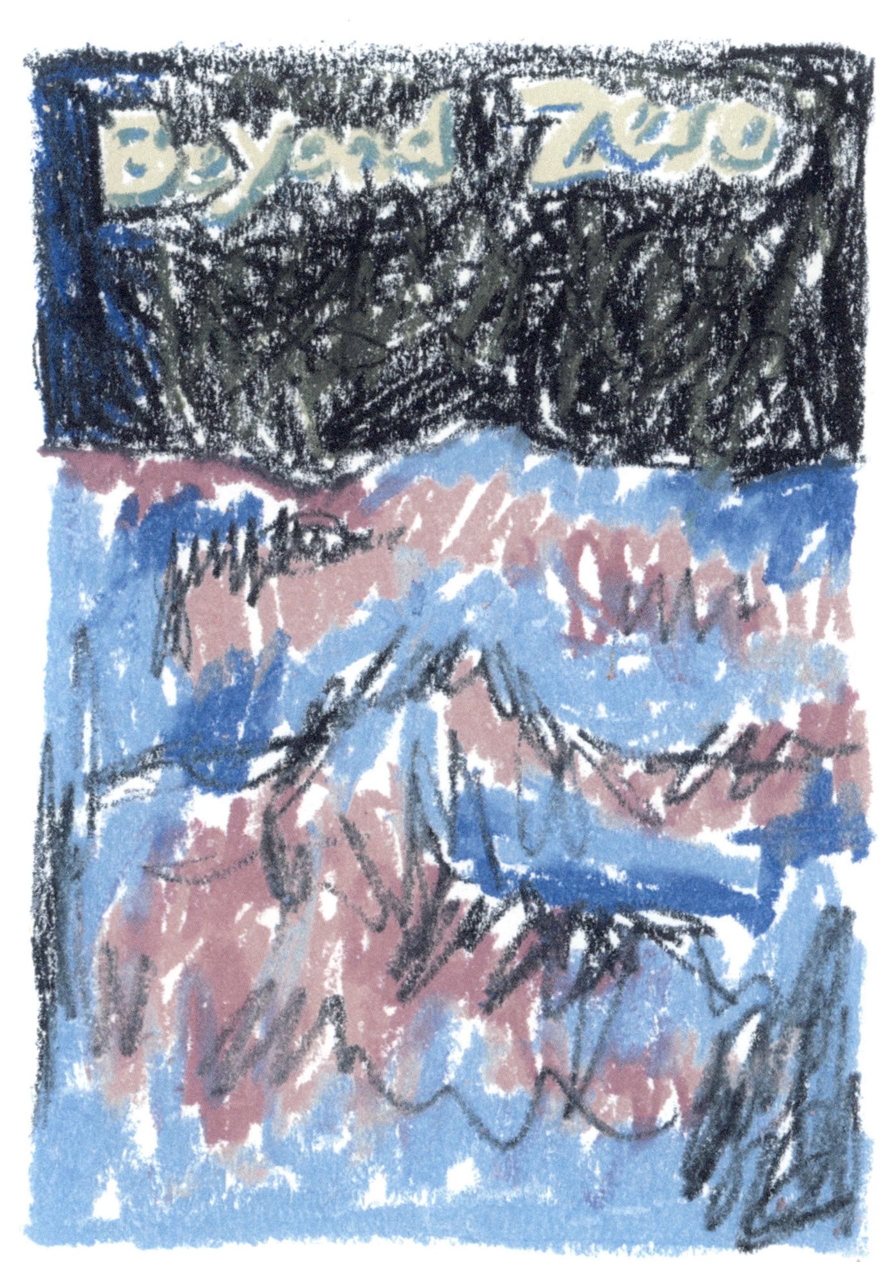
Beyond Zero

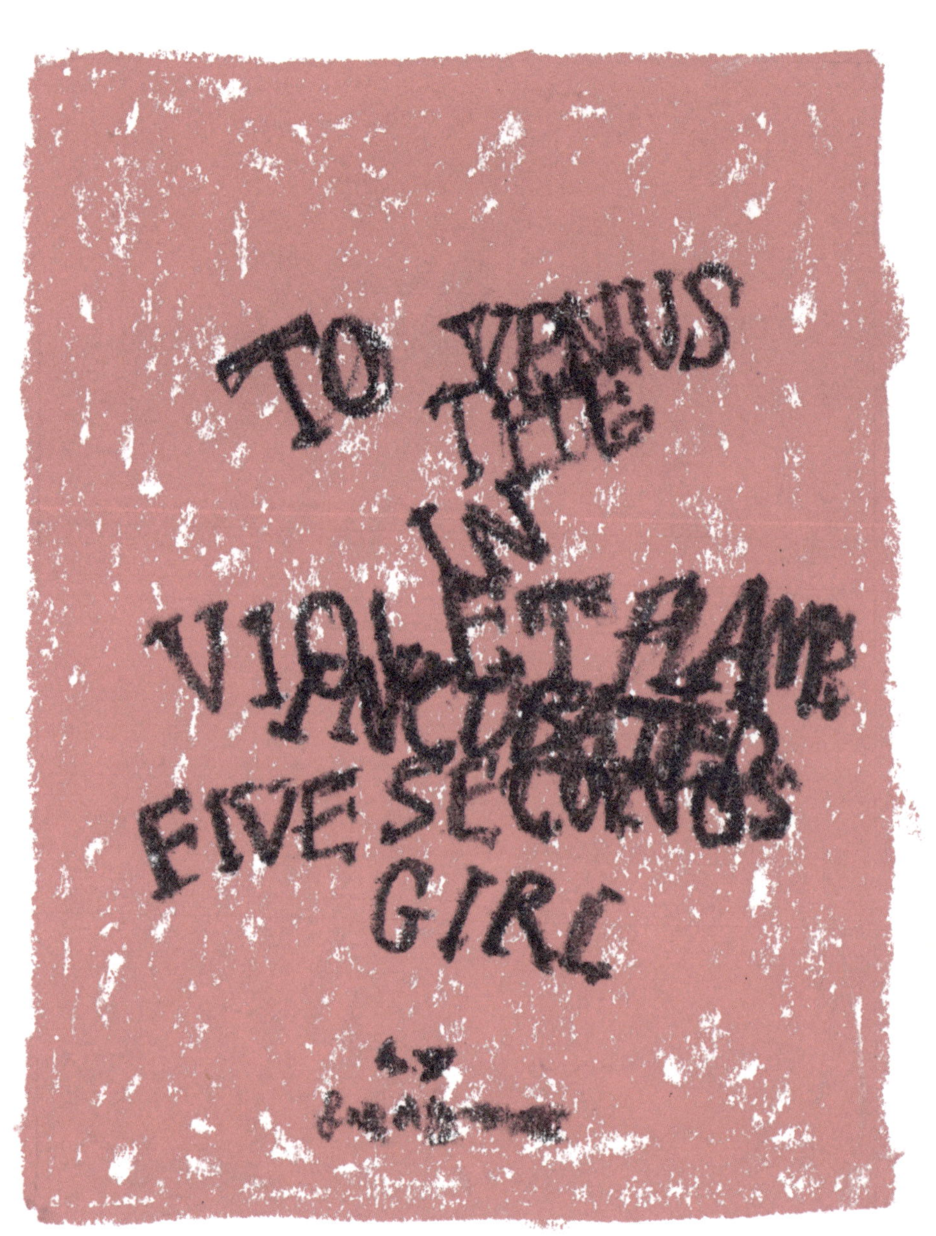
TO VENUS
THE
IN
VIOLET FLAME
FIVE SECONDS
GIRL
by

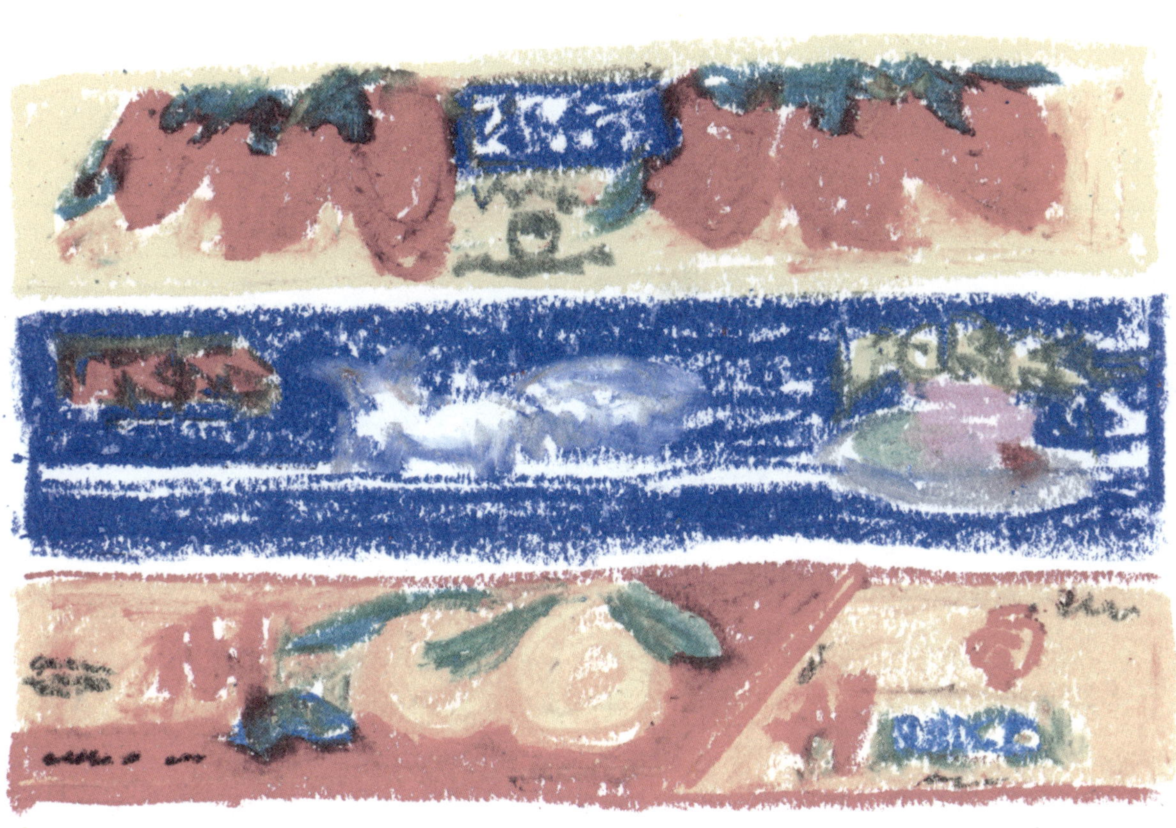

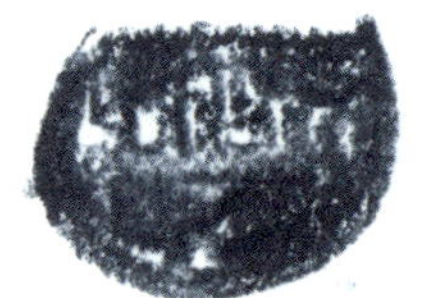

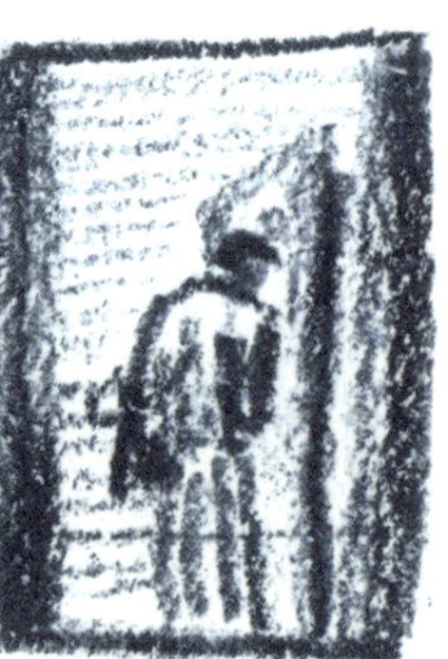

Laurie Anderson

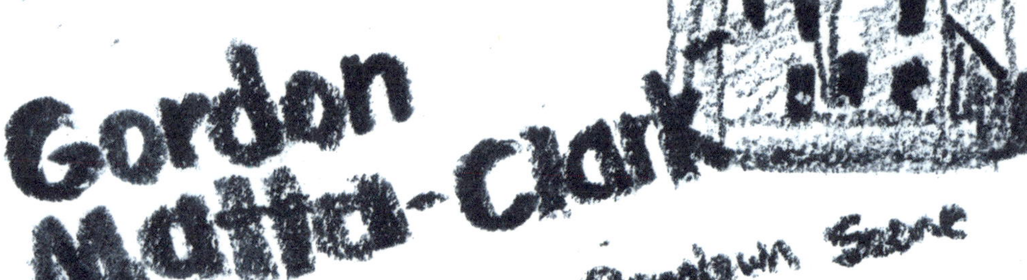

Pioneers of the Downtown Scene New York 1970s

3 Mar – 22 May/11

barbican artgallery

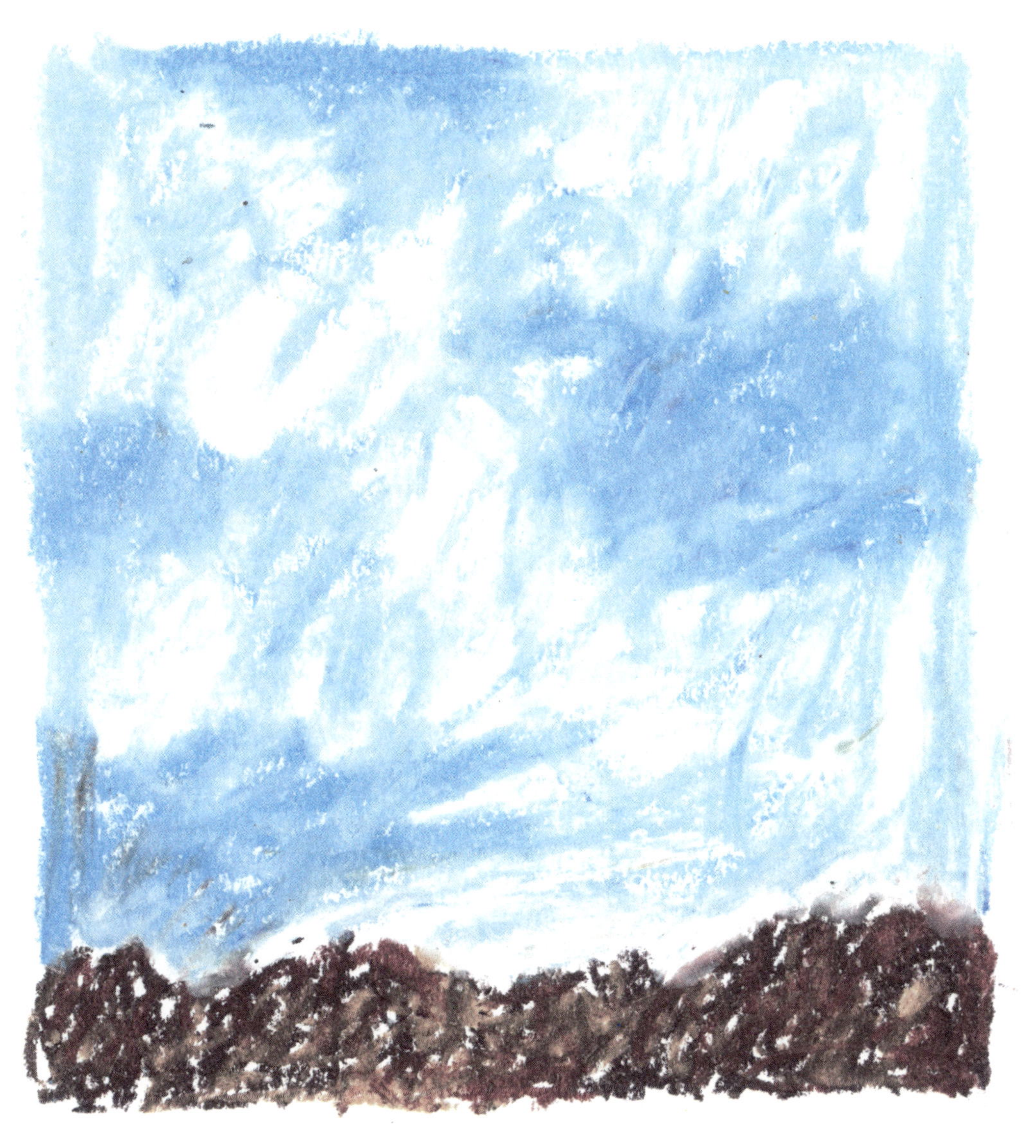

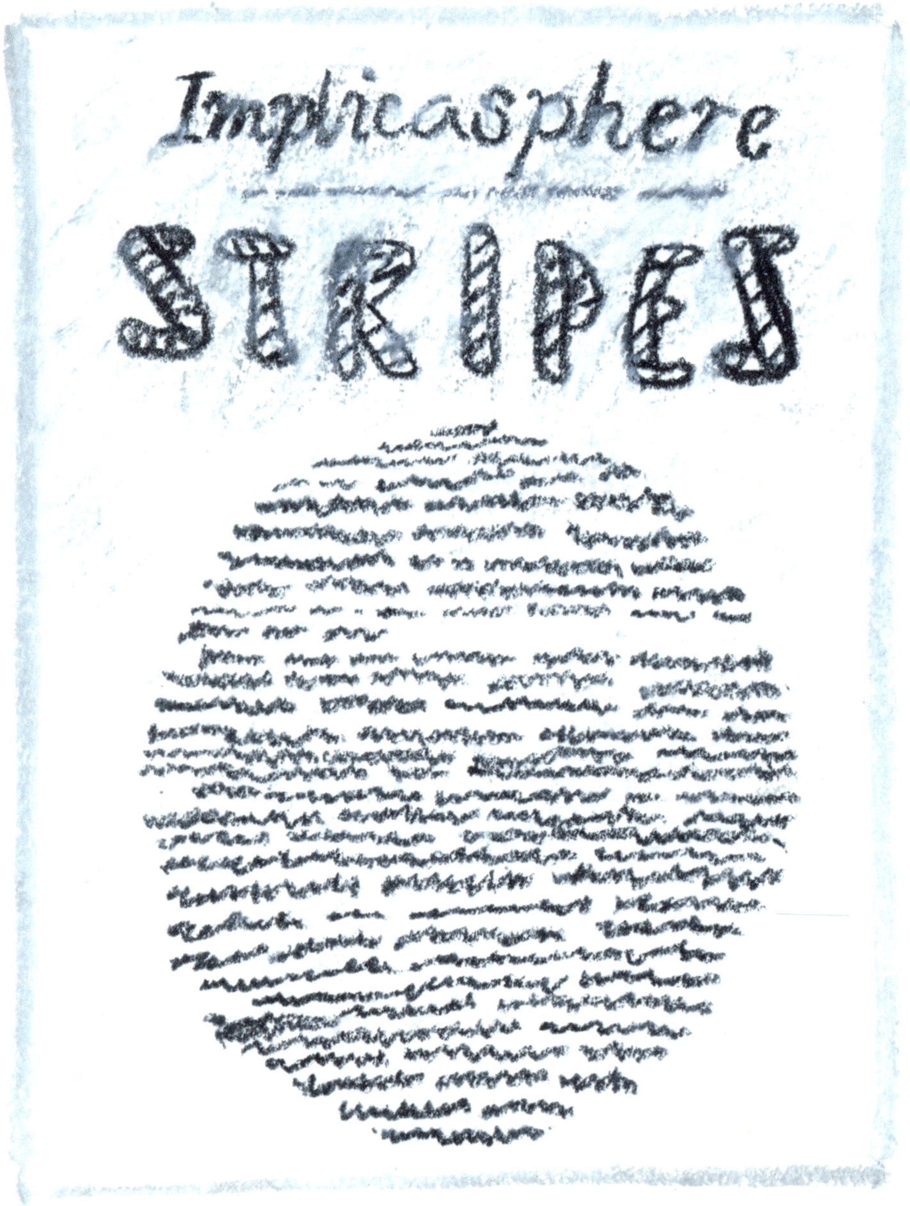
Implicasphere
STRIPES

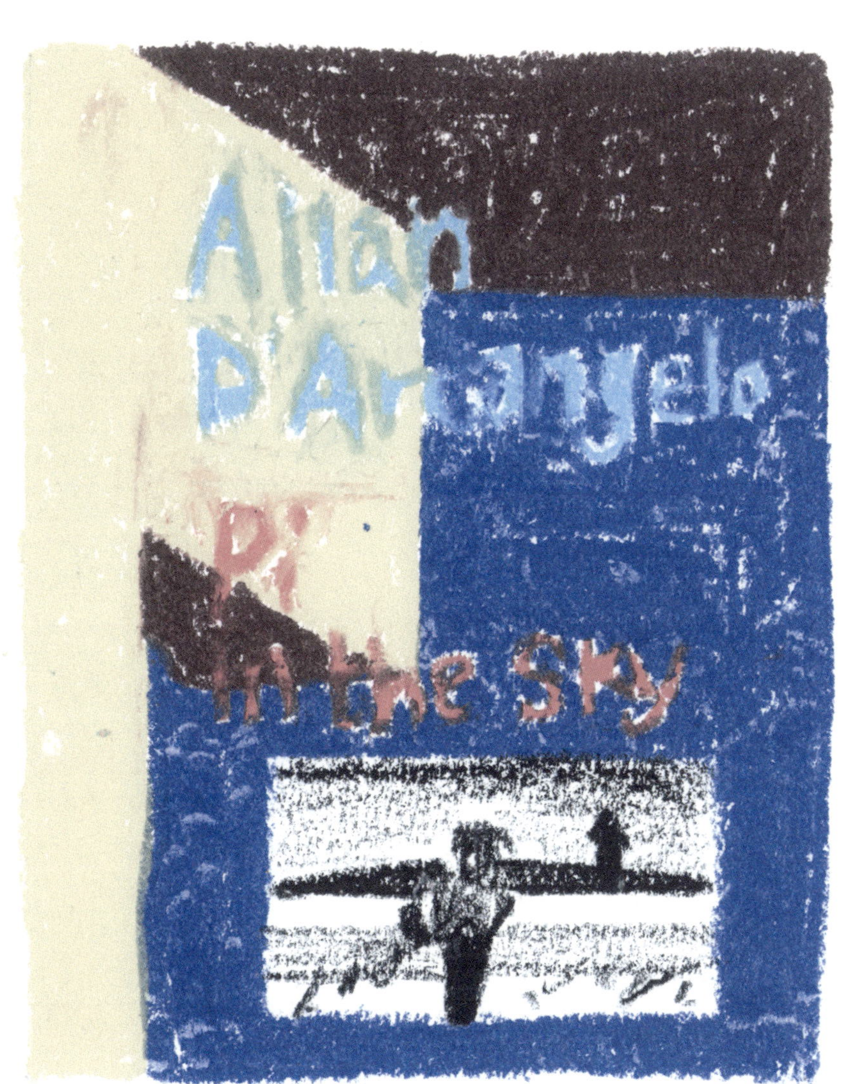
Allan
Pi
in the Sky

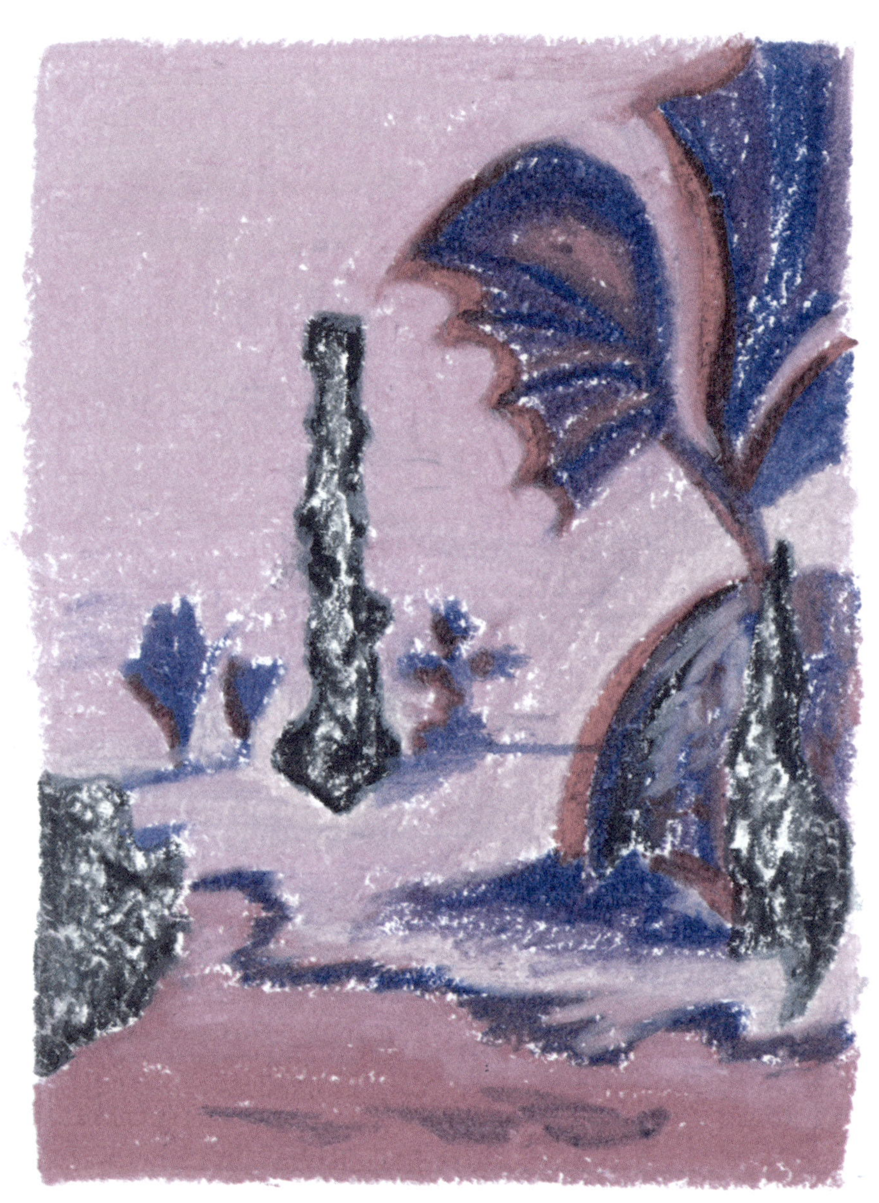

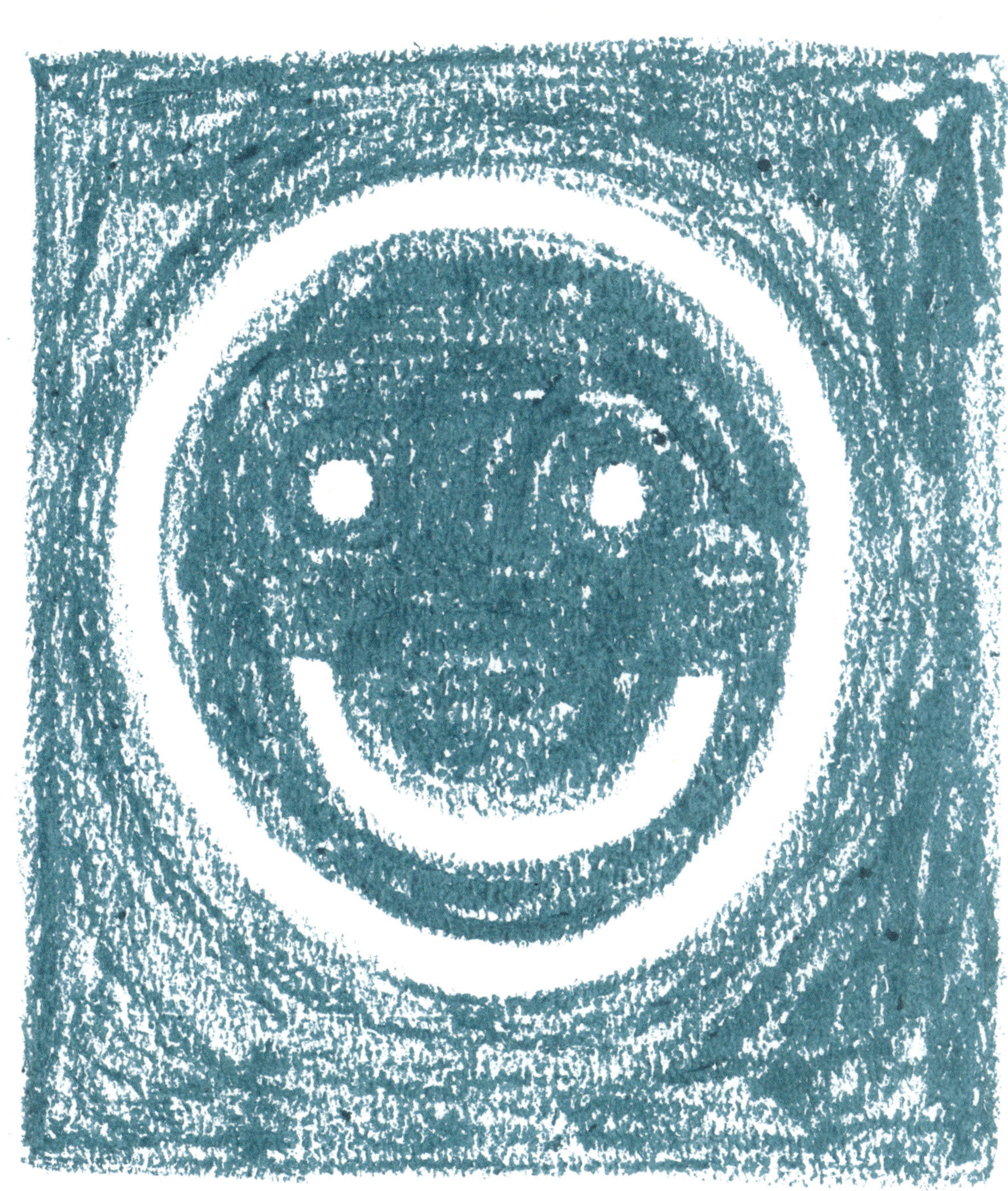

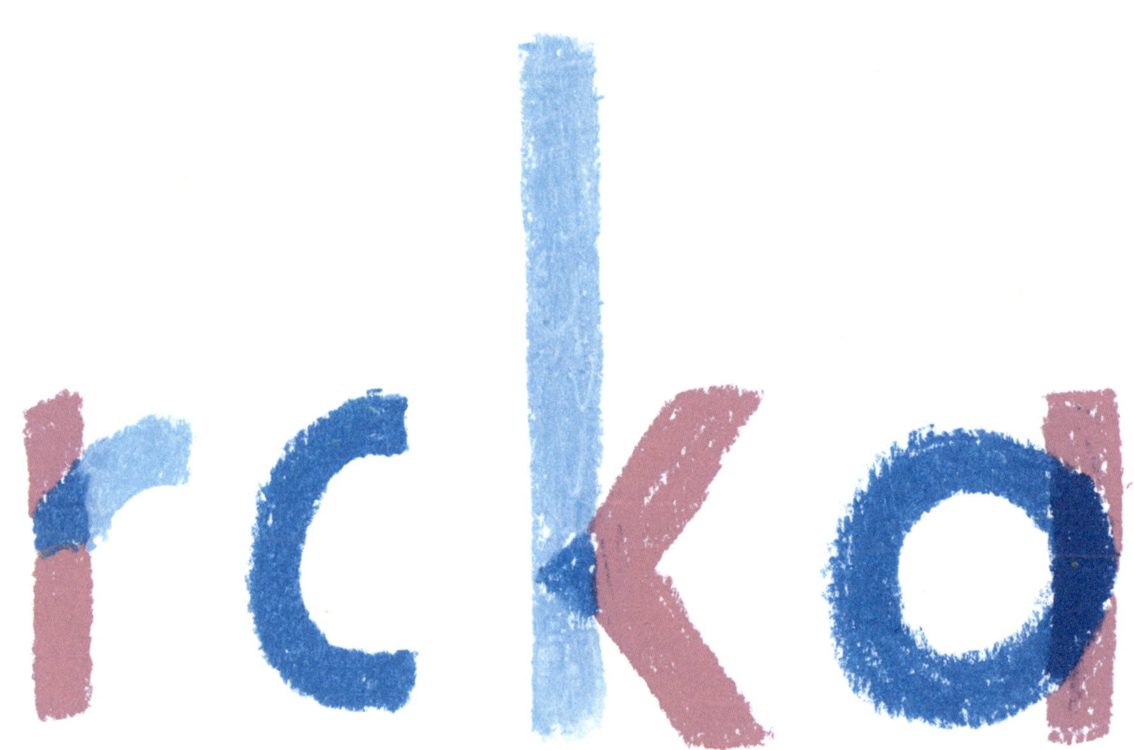
rcka

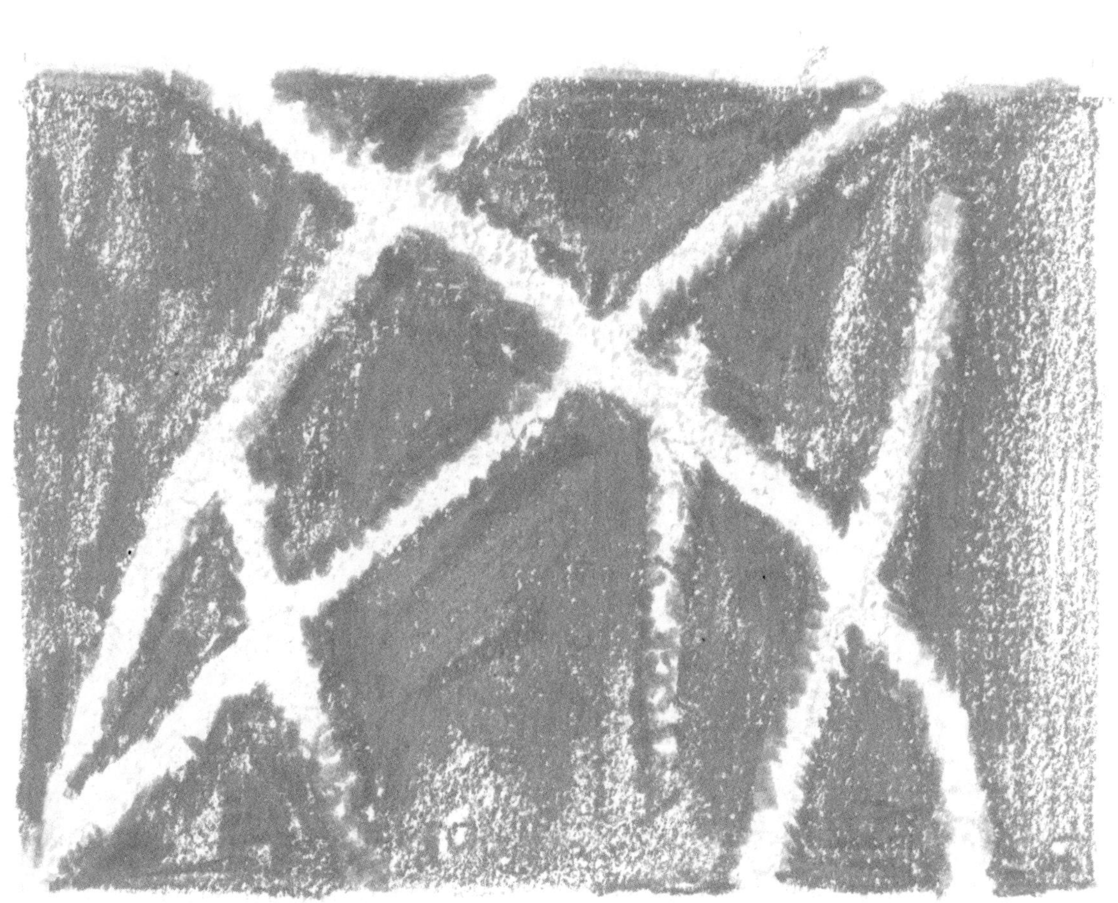

London &on
&on&on&
on & on&on&
on&on
&on&
on&on&on
&on&on
&on&on&
on&on
&on&on
&on&on&on
&on &on&on&

MERCEDES
BENZ

Iphgenia Baal

Semina No 8

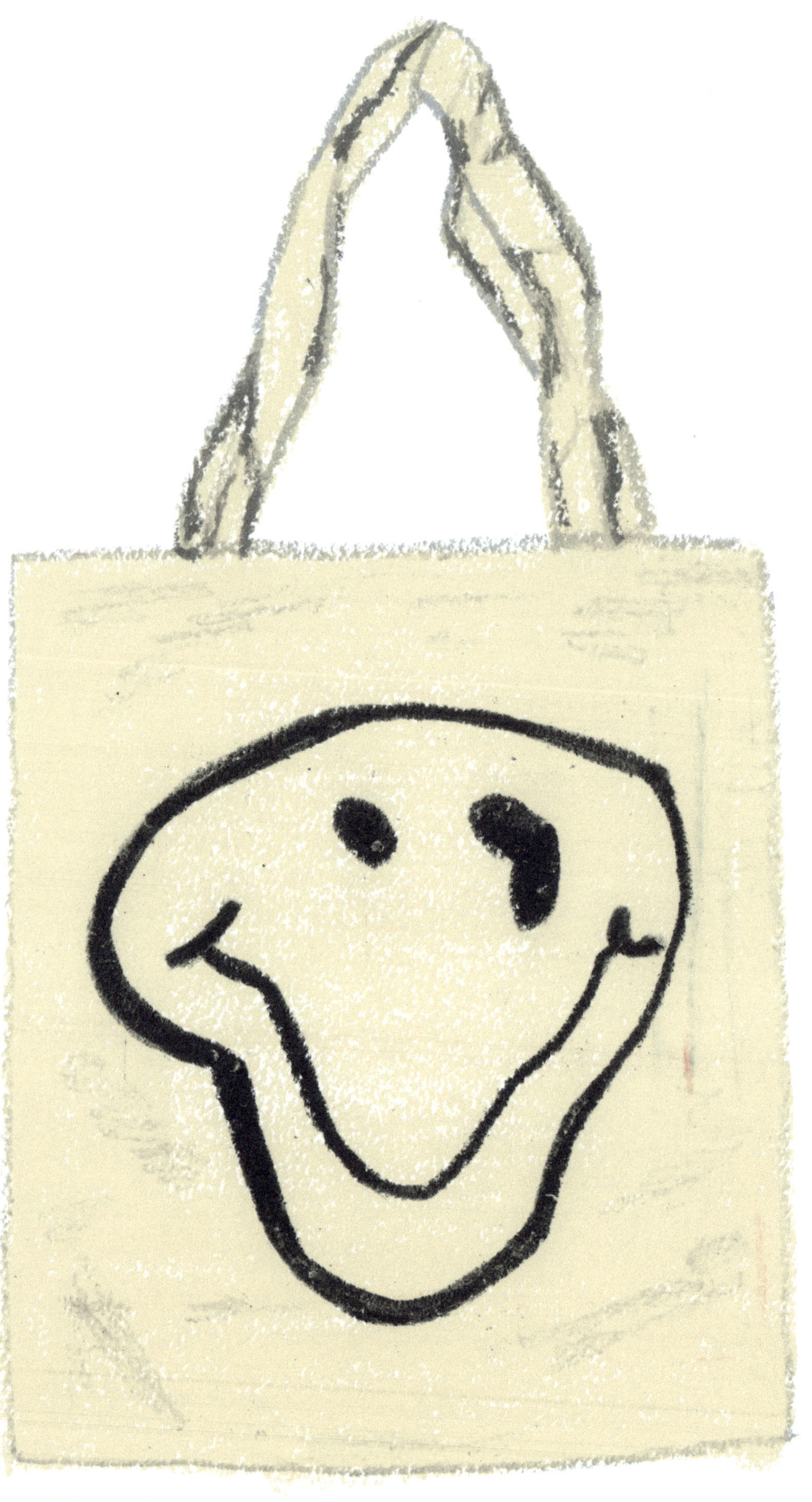

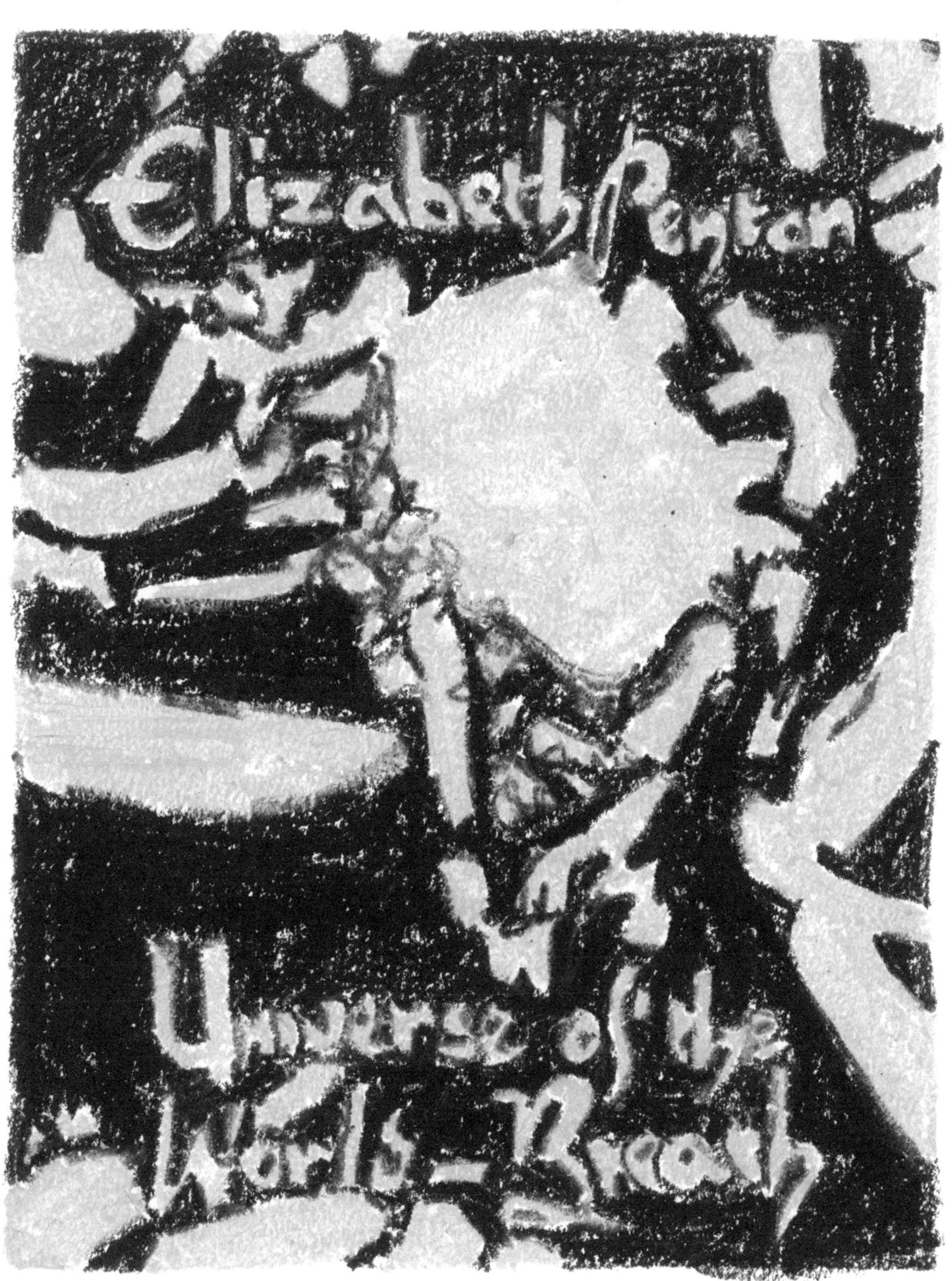
Élizabeth Renton
Universe of the
Worlds - Breath

THE INCUBATED GIRL

by

Sarah L. [illegible]

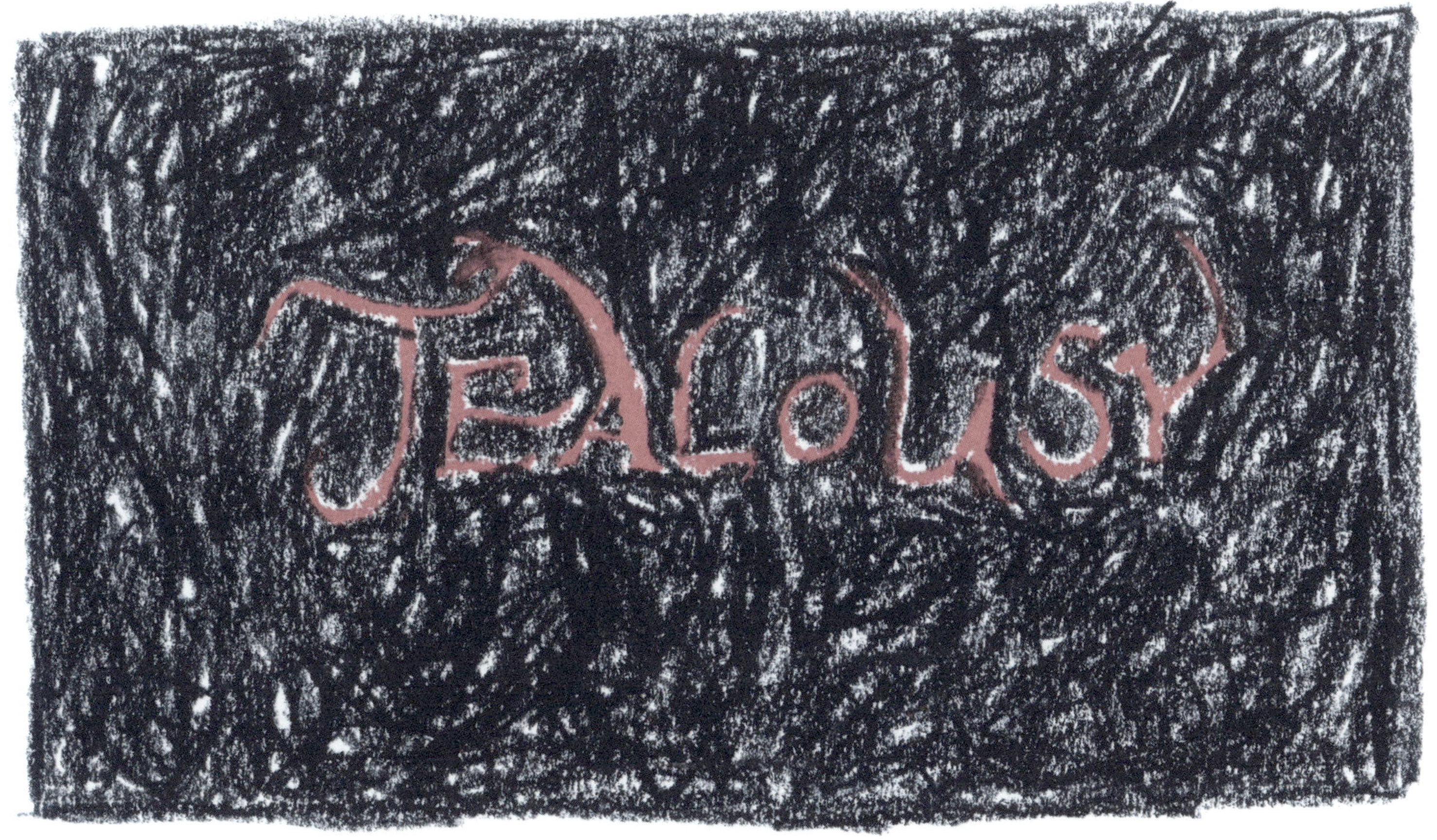
JEALOUSY

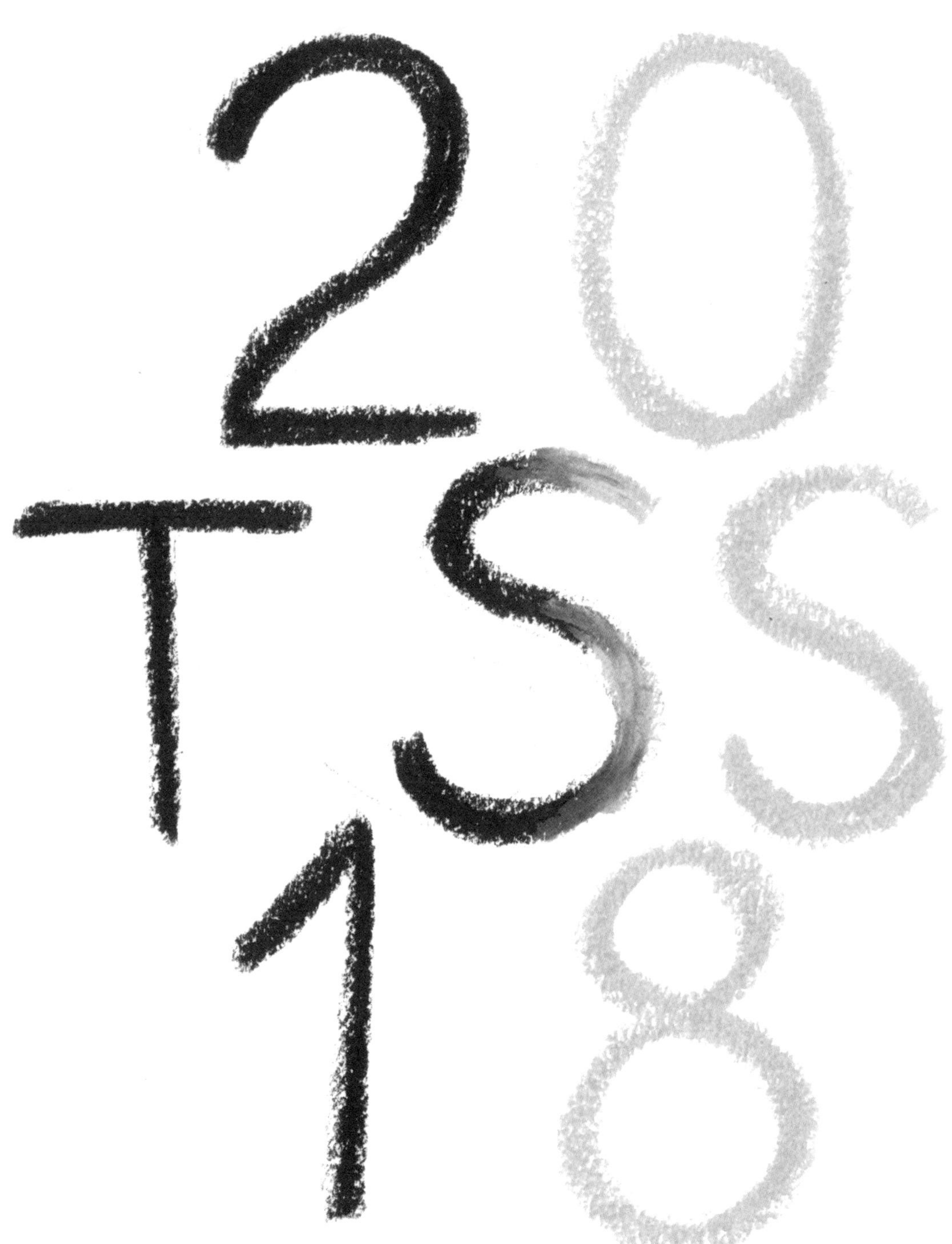
20
TSS
18

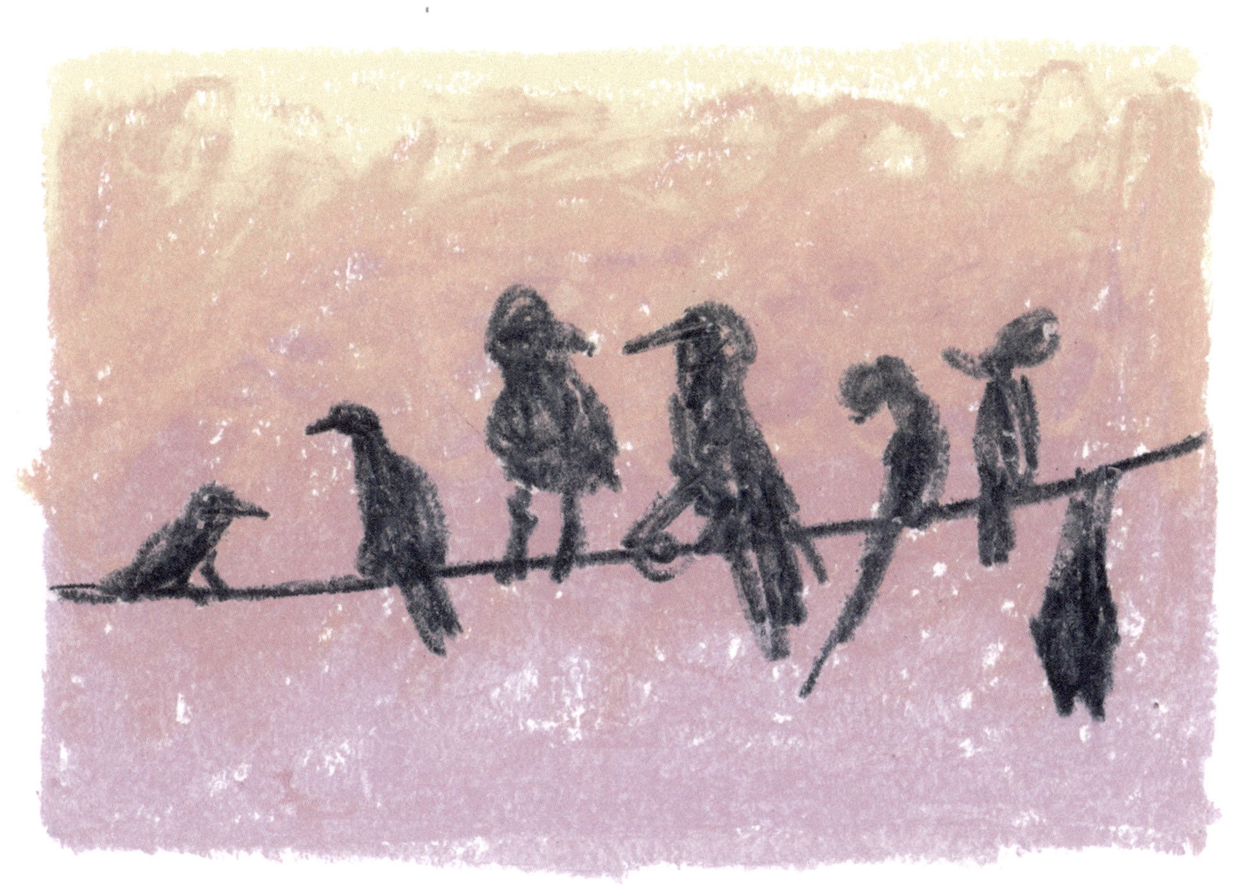

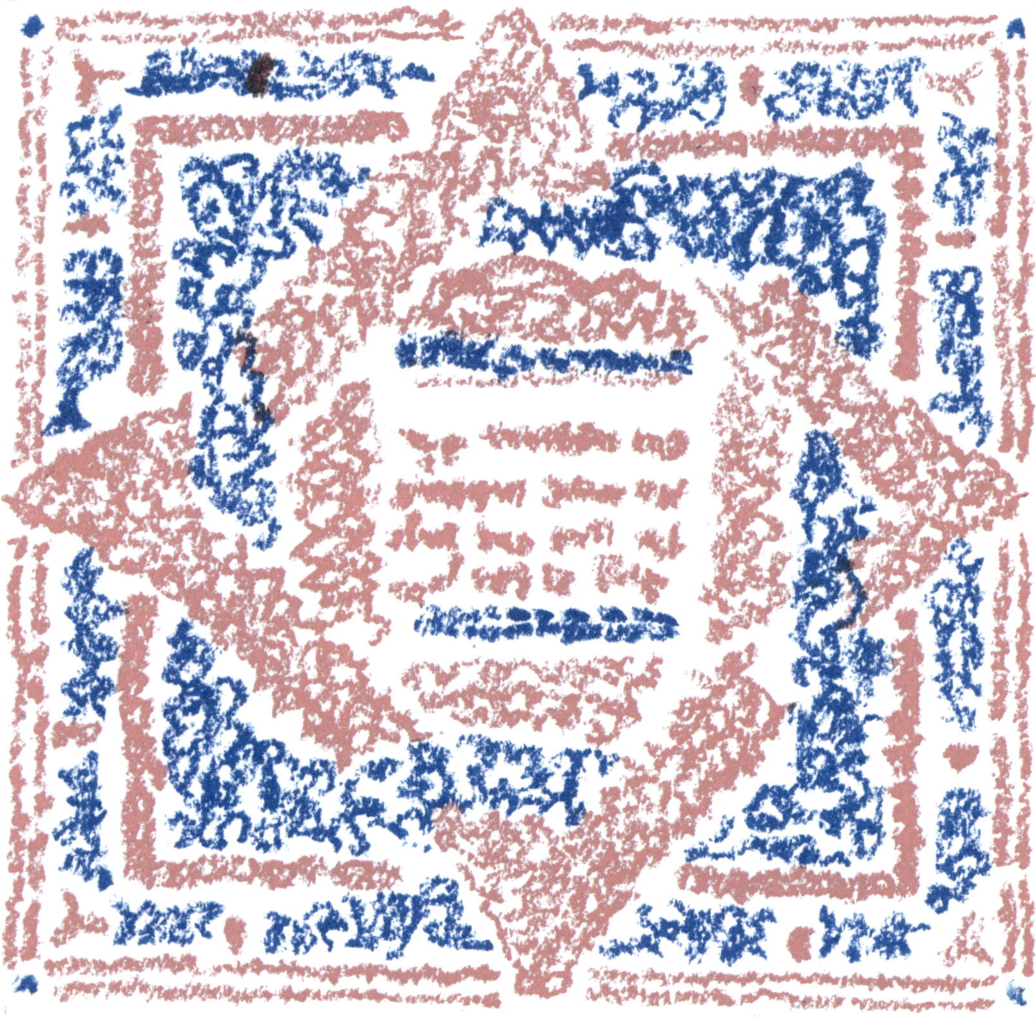

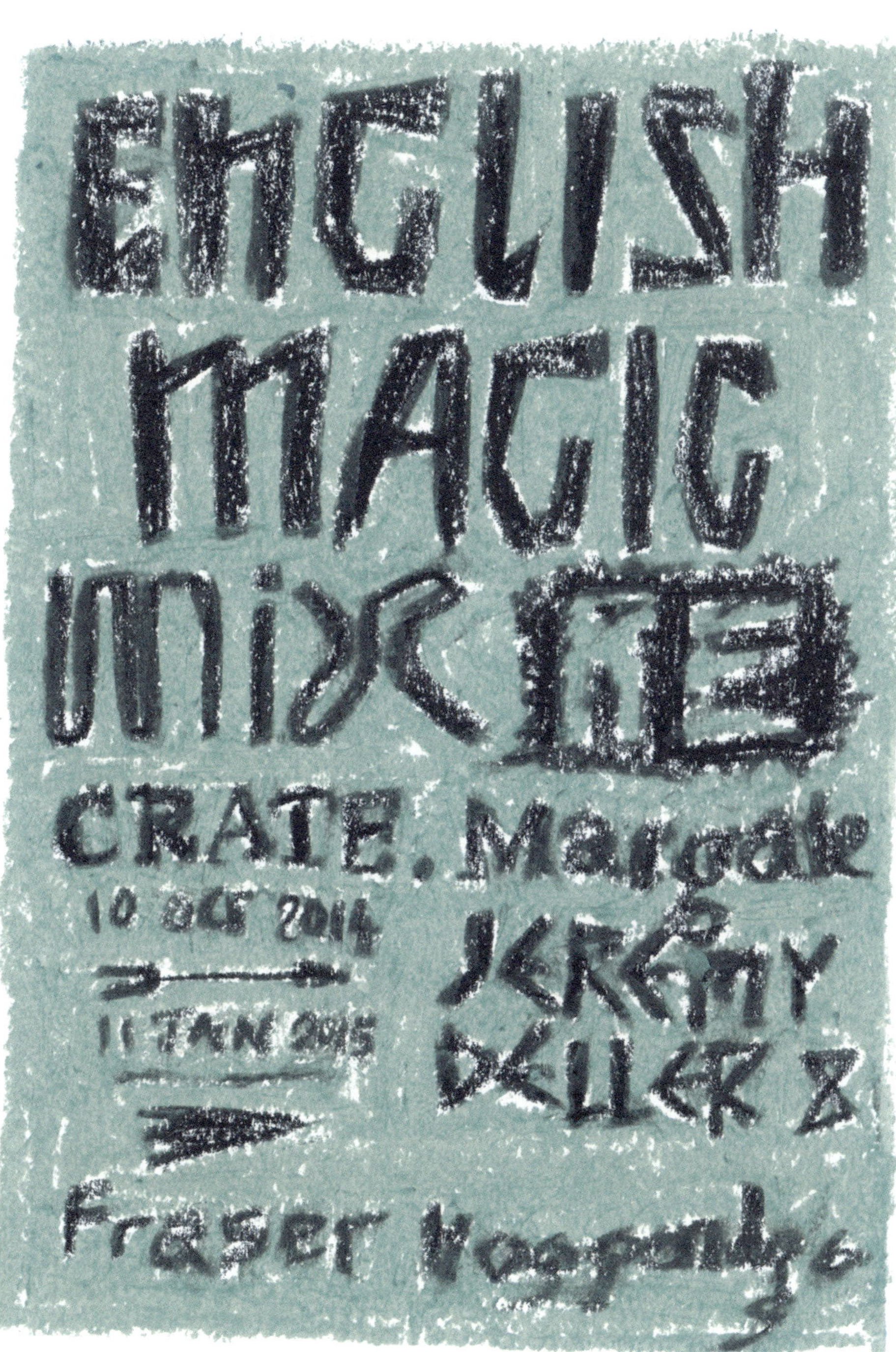
ENGLISH
MAGIC
MIX
CRATE. Margate
10 OCT 2014
11 JAN 2015
JEREMY
DELLER &
Fraser Muggeridge

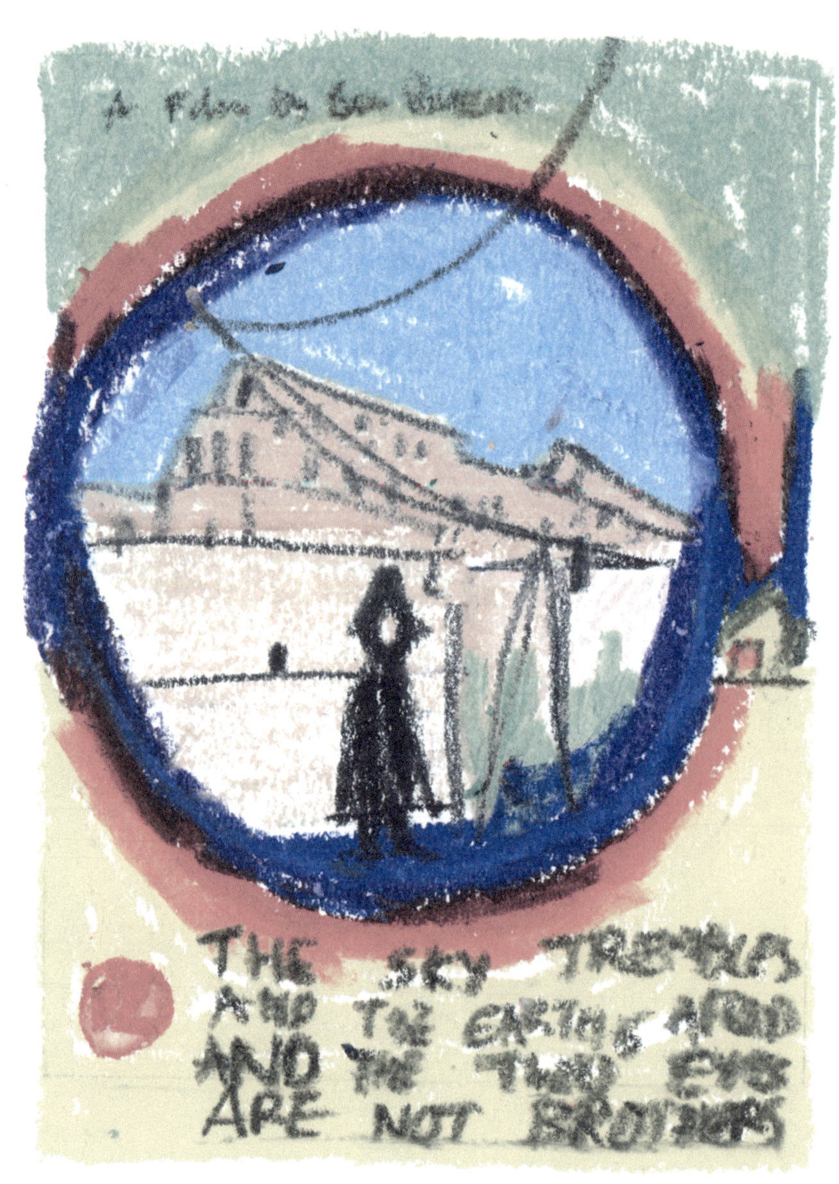
A Film by Ben Rivers
THE SKY TREMBLES
AND THE EARTH IS AFRAID
AND THE TWO EYES
ARE NOT BROTHERS

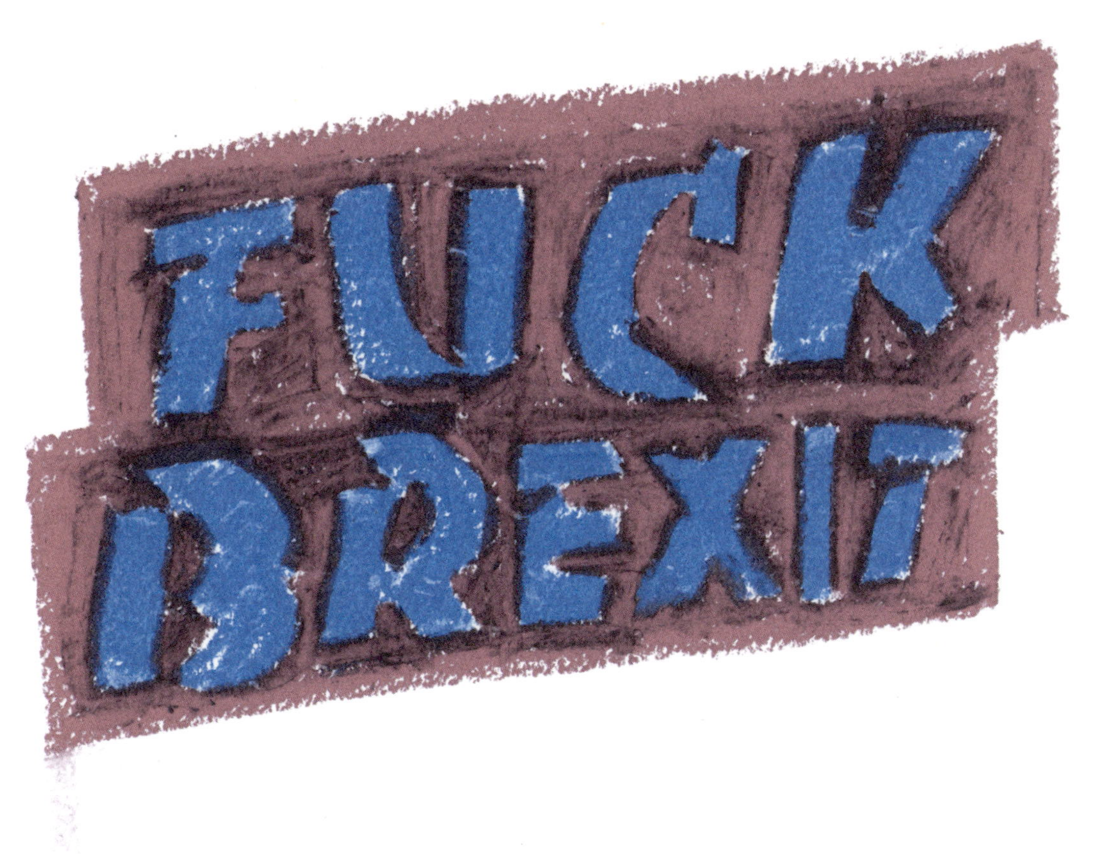
FUCK
BREXIT

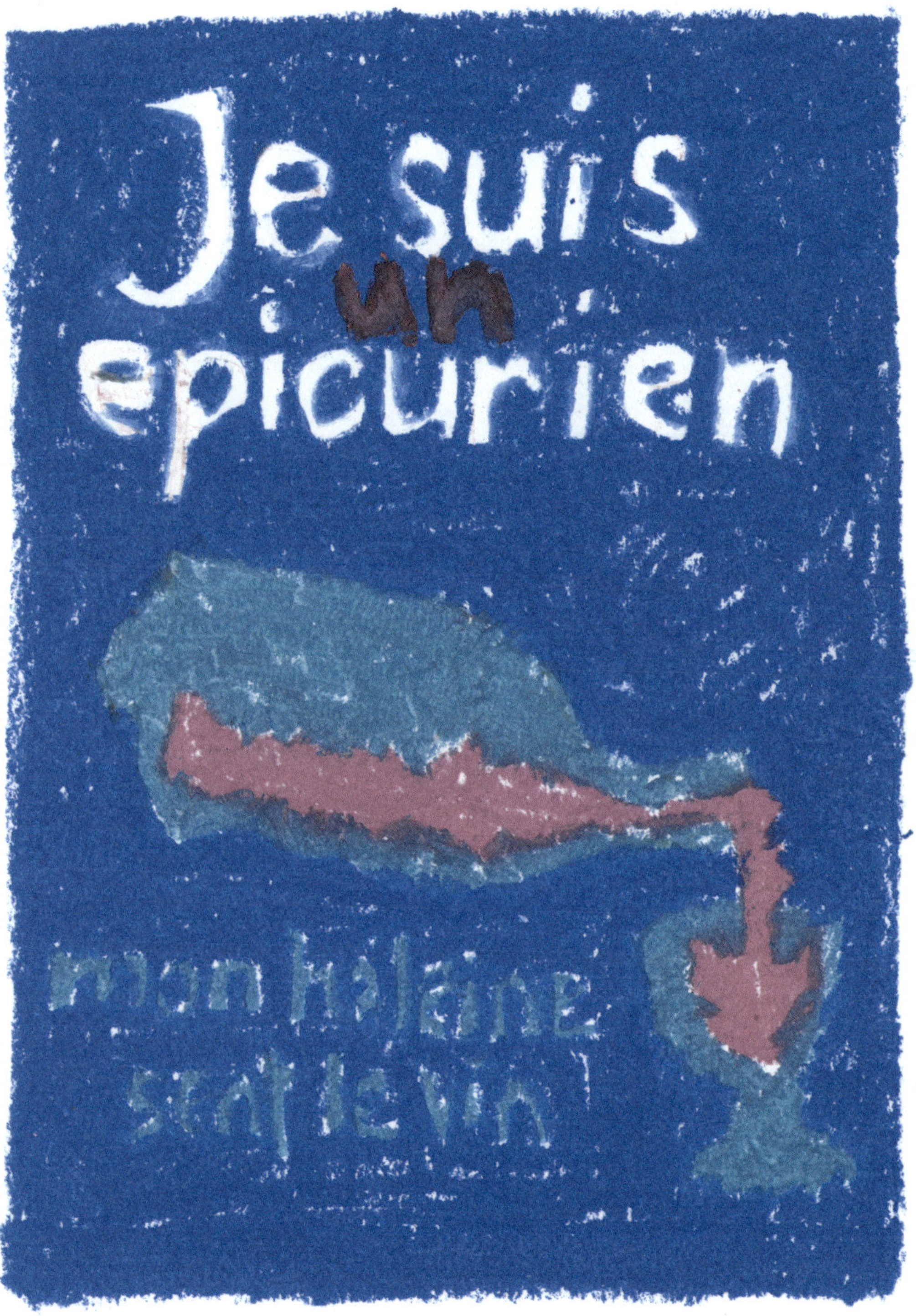

Je suis un epicurien

mon halaine
sent le vin

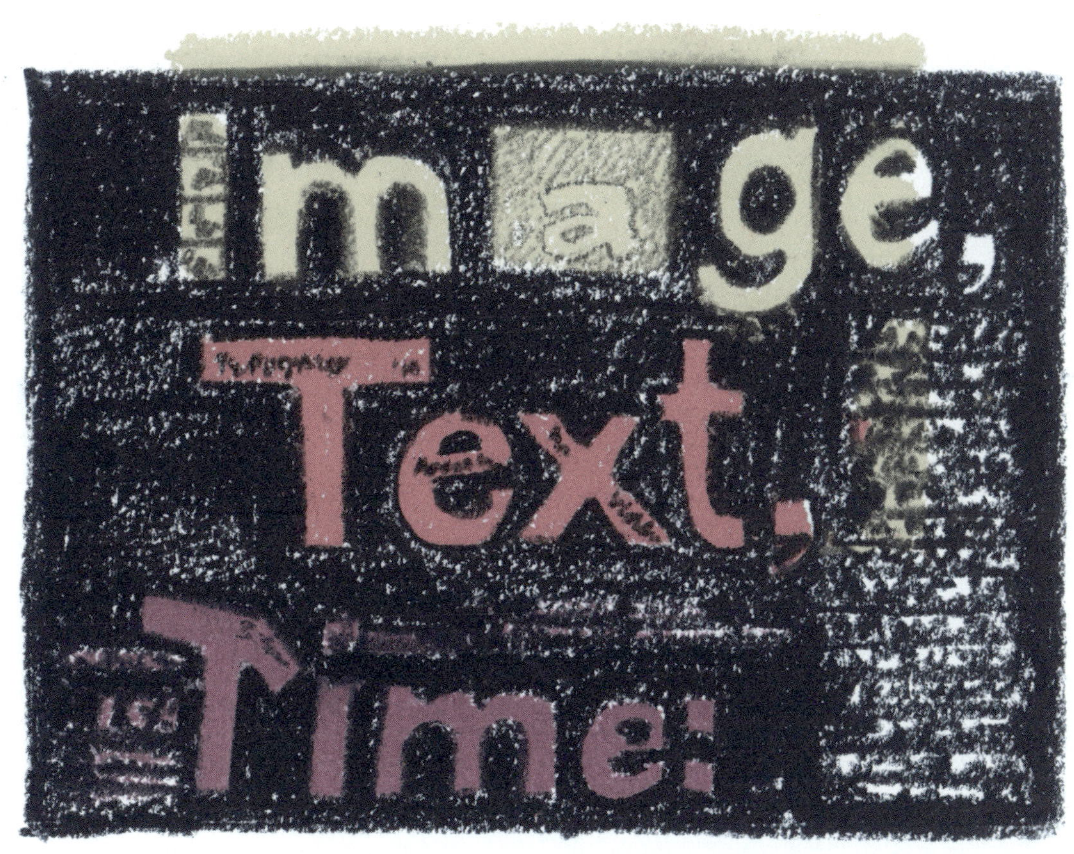
Image,
Text,
Time:

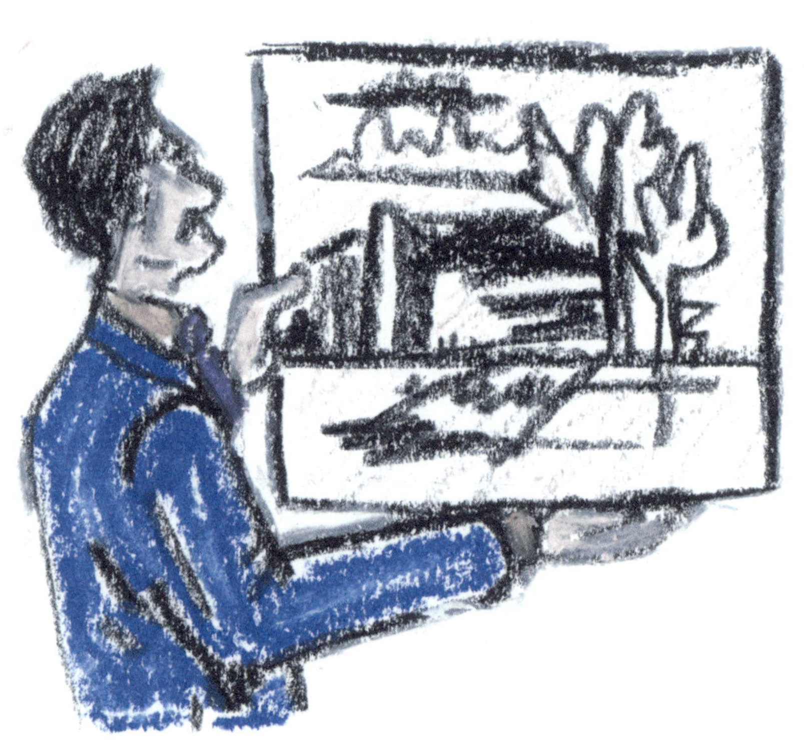

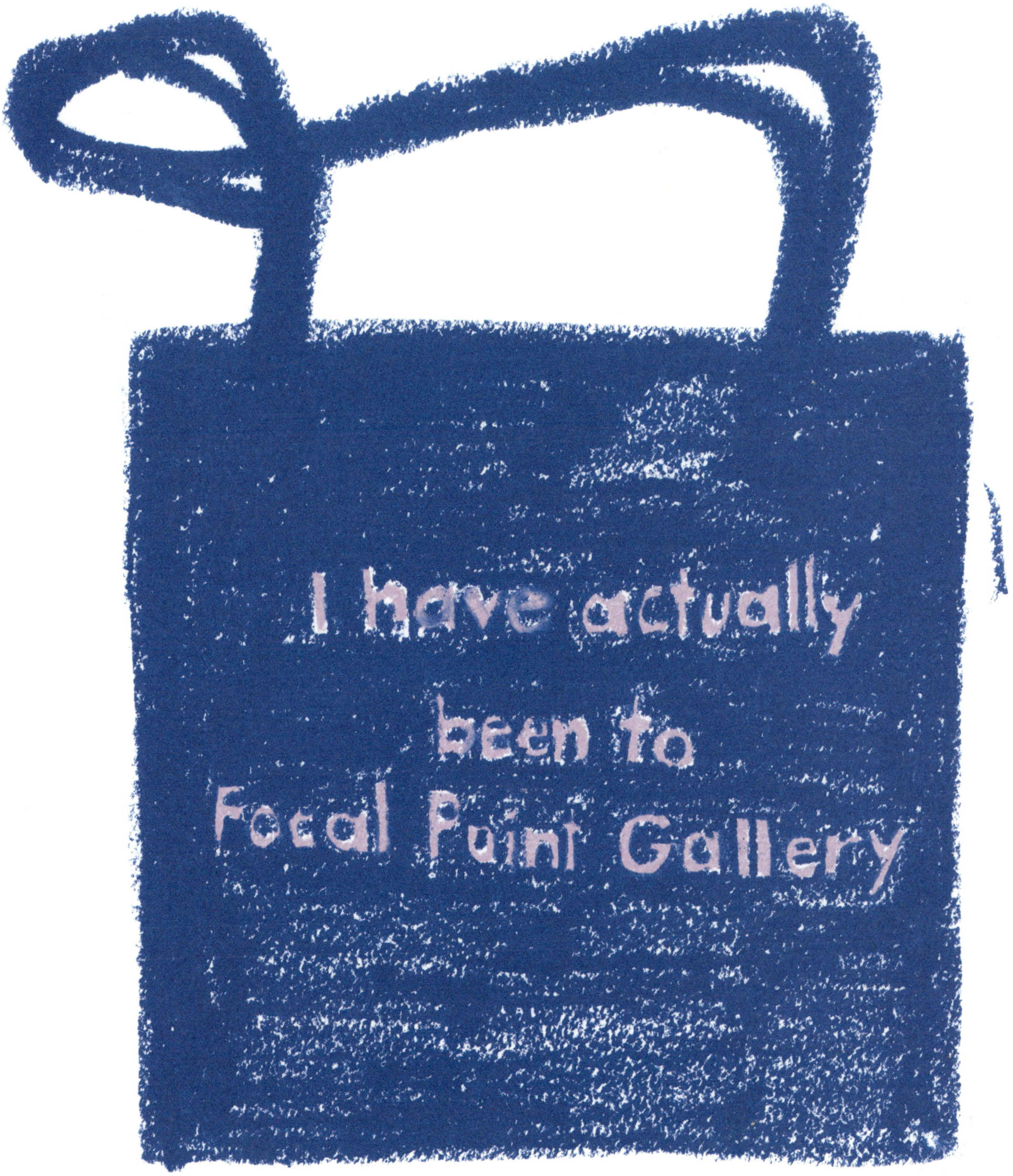

I have actually
been to
Focal Point Gallery

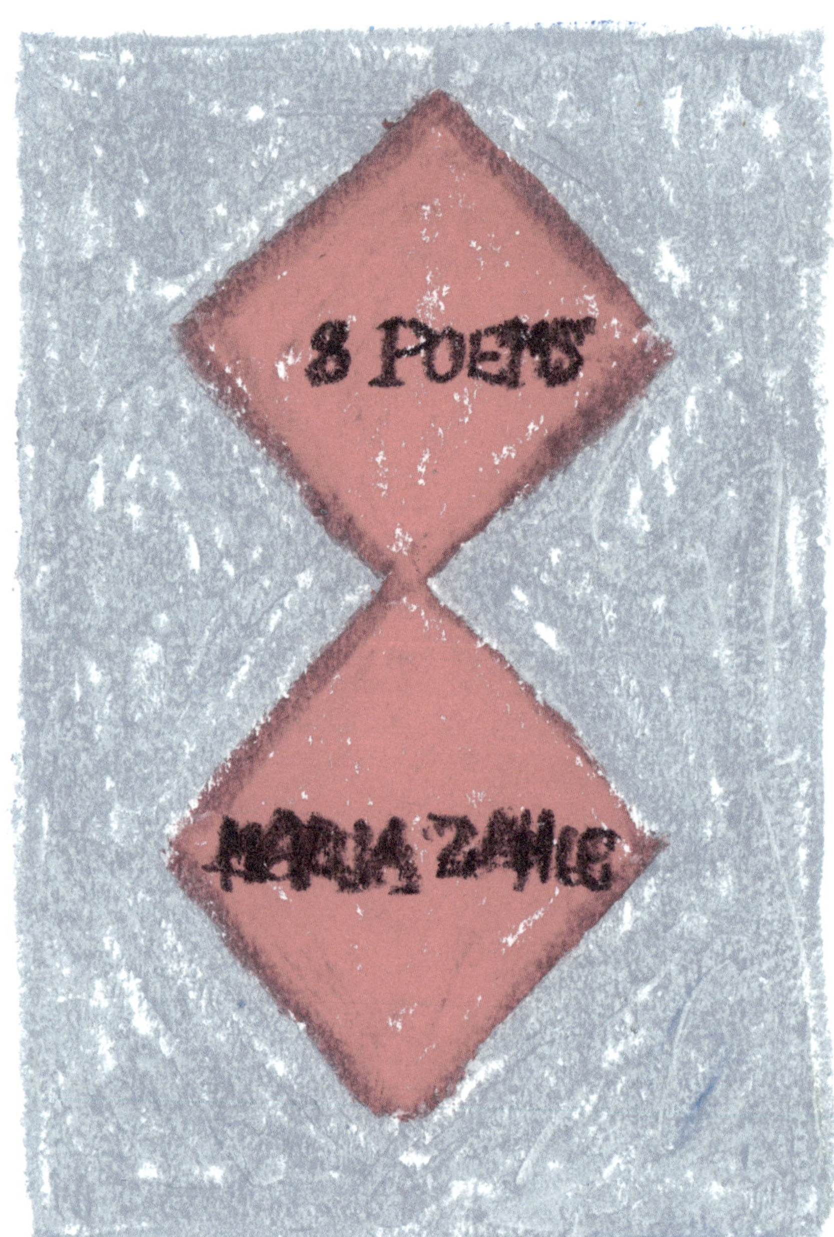
8 POEMS
MARIA ZAHLE

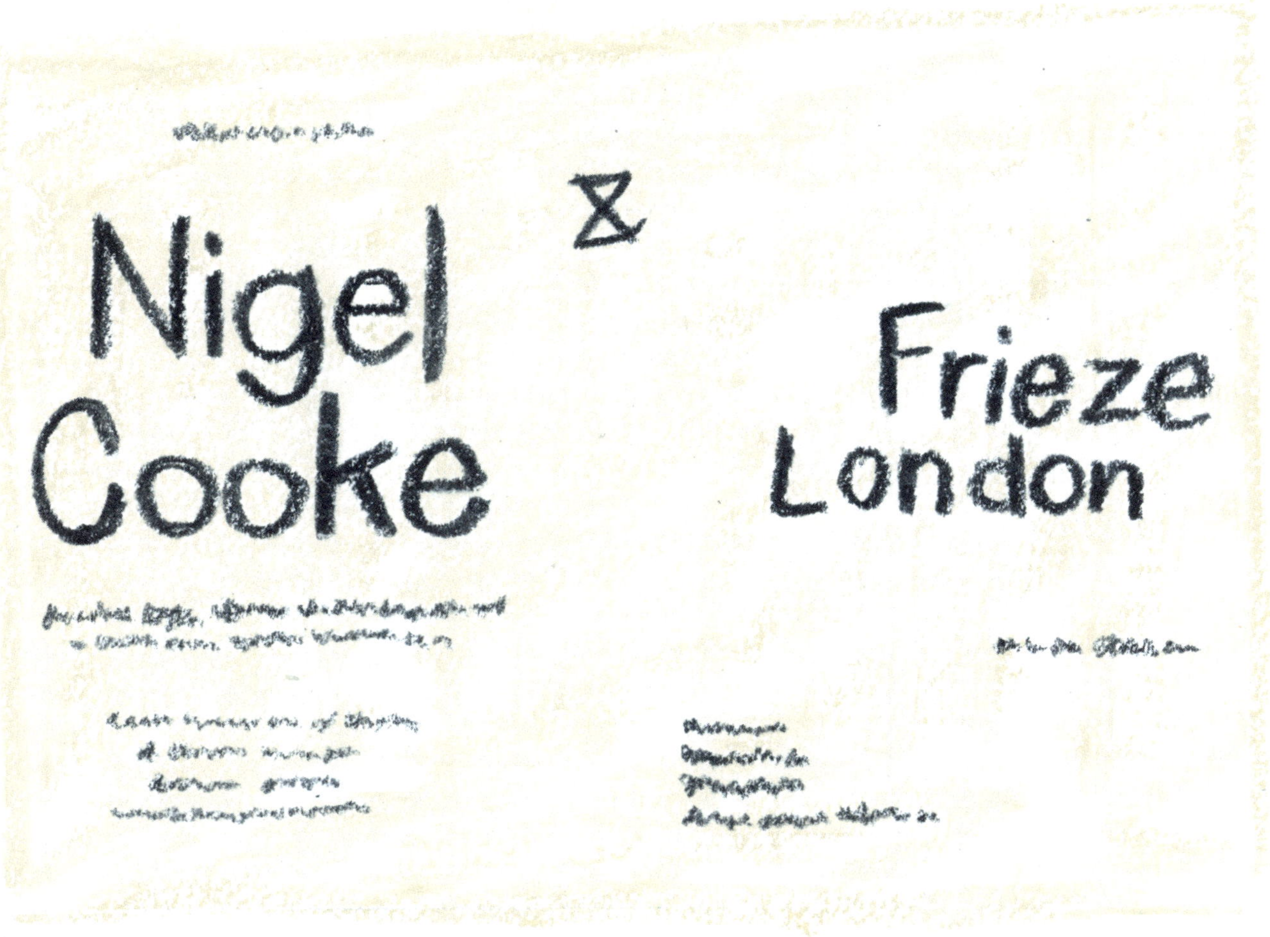

Nigel
Cooke

&

Frieze
London

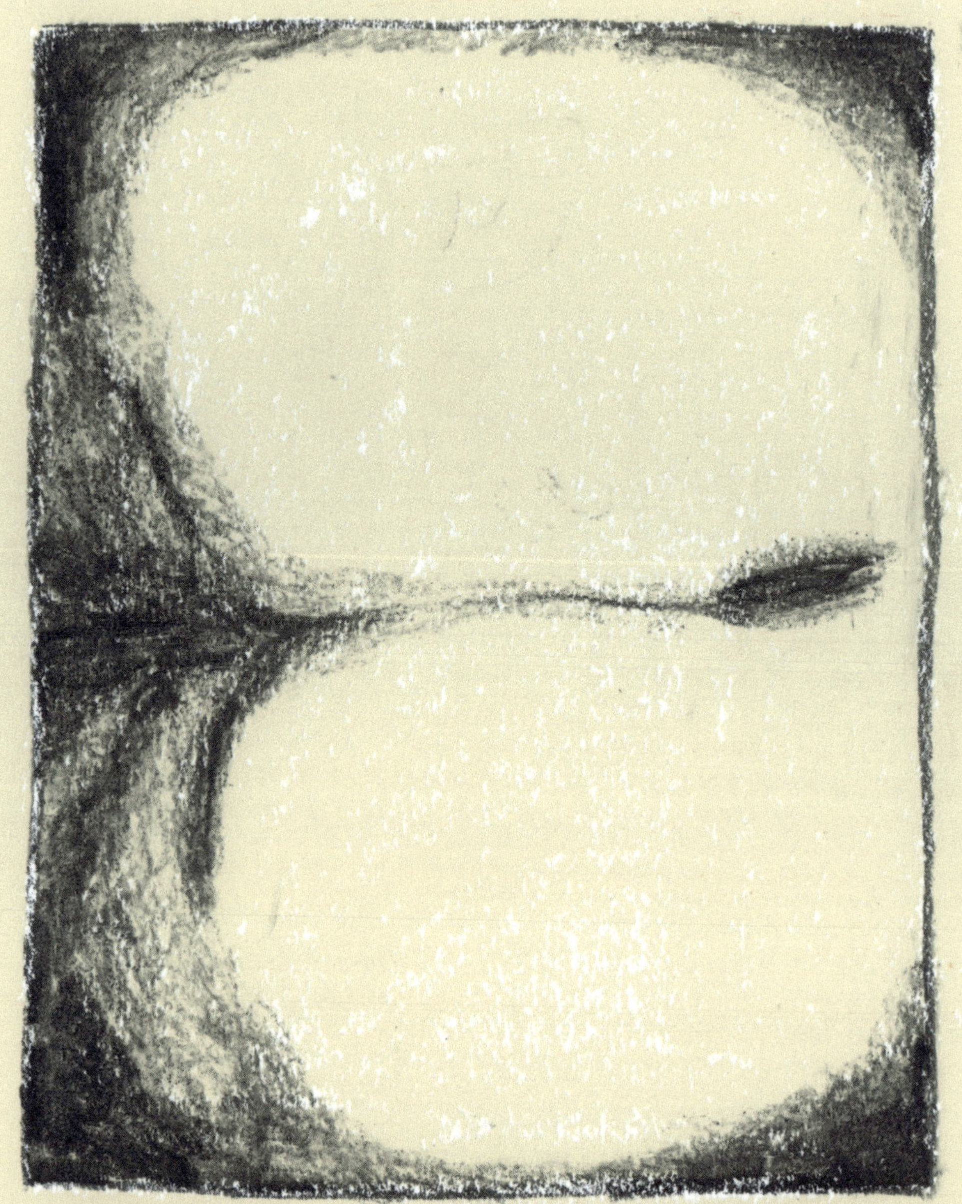

BUBBLE ENTENDRE

Mark Waugh

Semma No. 3

I LOOK GOOD, I KNOW

I CAN'T HEAR,

I CAN'T SEE

BUT I LOOK GOOD

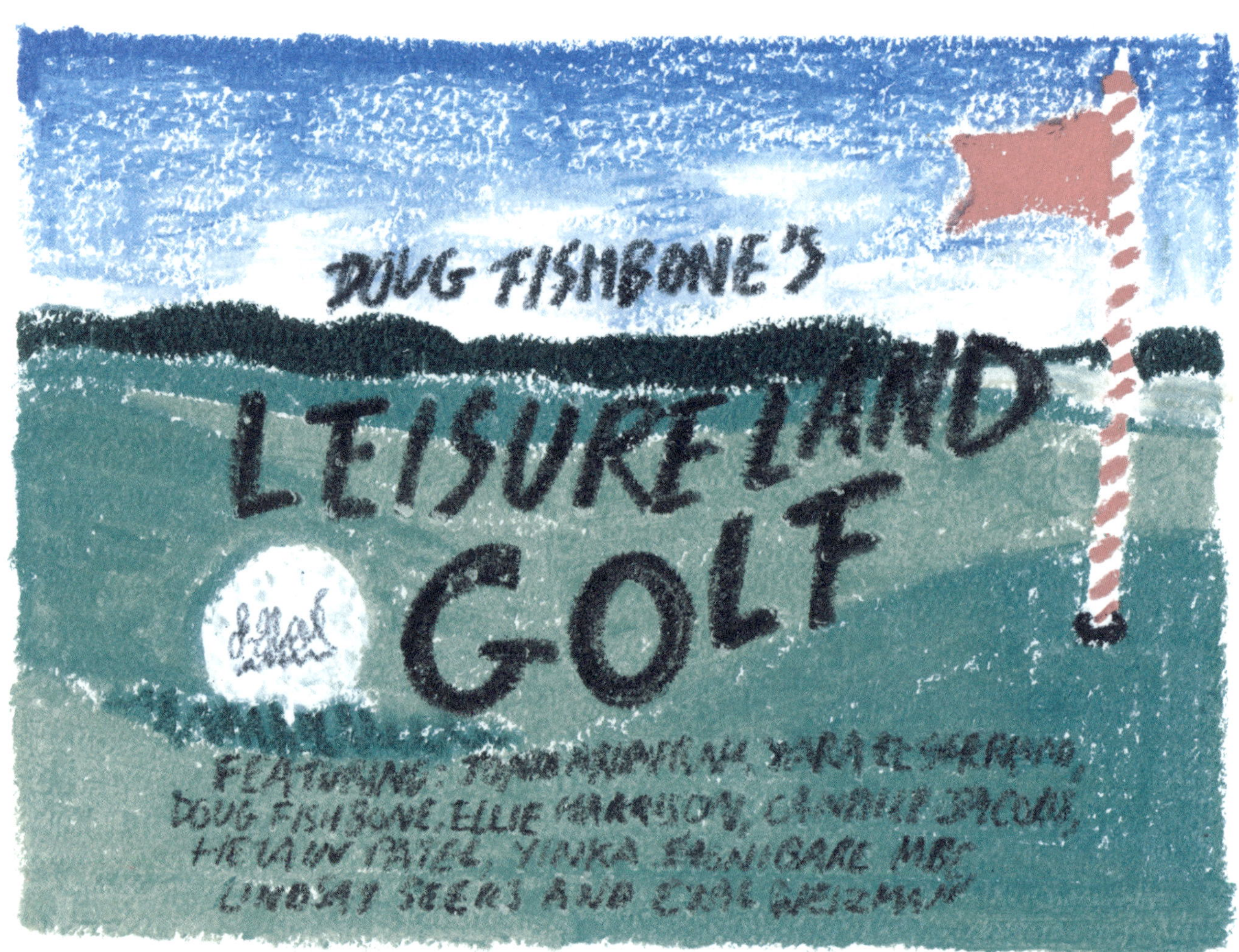
DOUG FISHBONE'S
LEISURELAND
GOLF
FEATURING:
DOUG FISHBONE, ELLIE HARRISON,
HETAIN PATEL, YINKA SHONIBARE MBE
LINDSAY SEERS AND

VOICE
SCORES.
FACSIMILES.

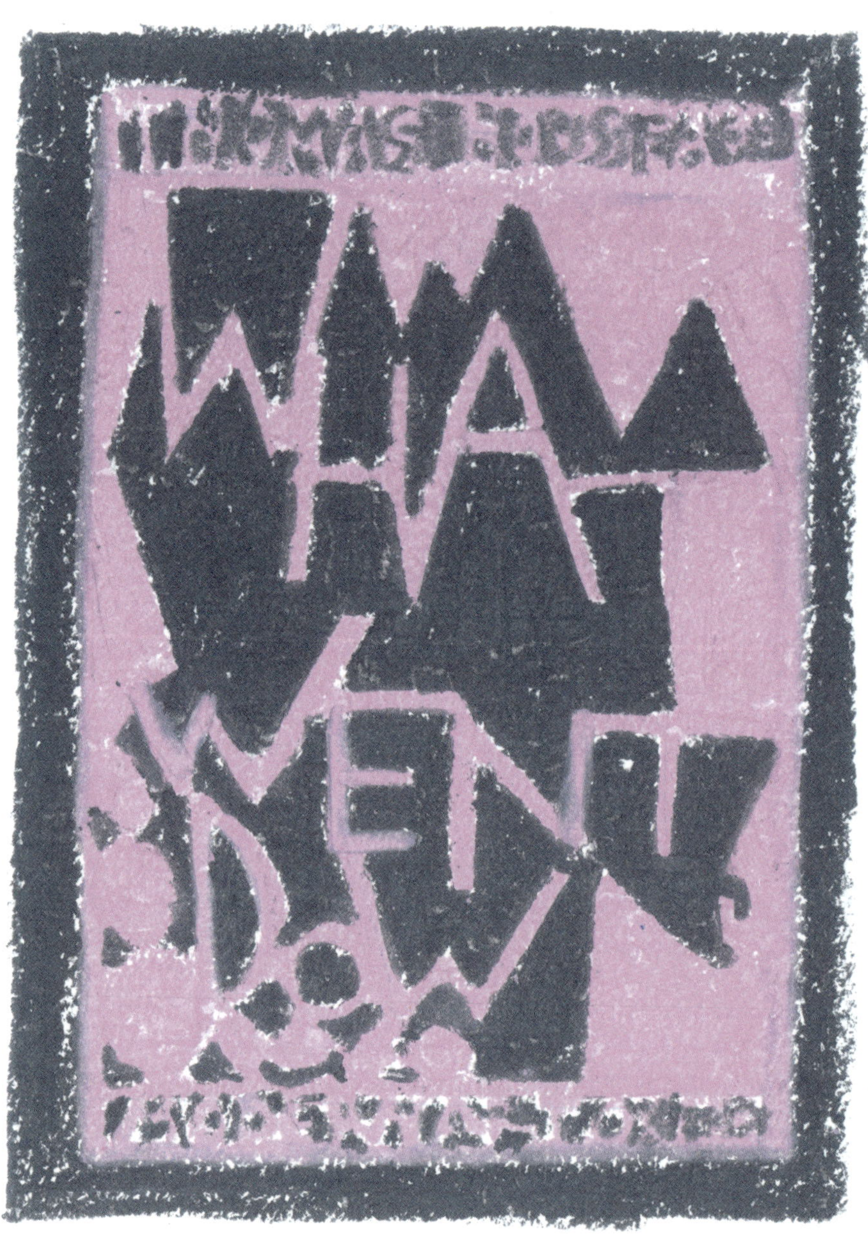

MICHAEL
JACKSON
and other

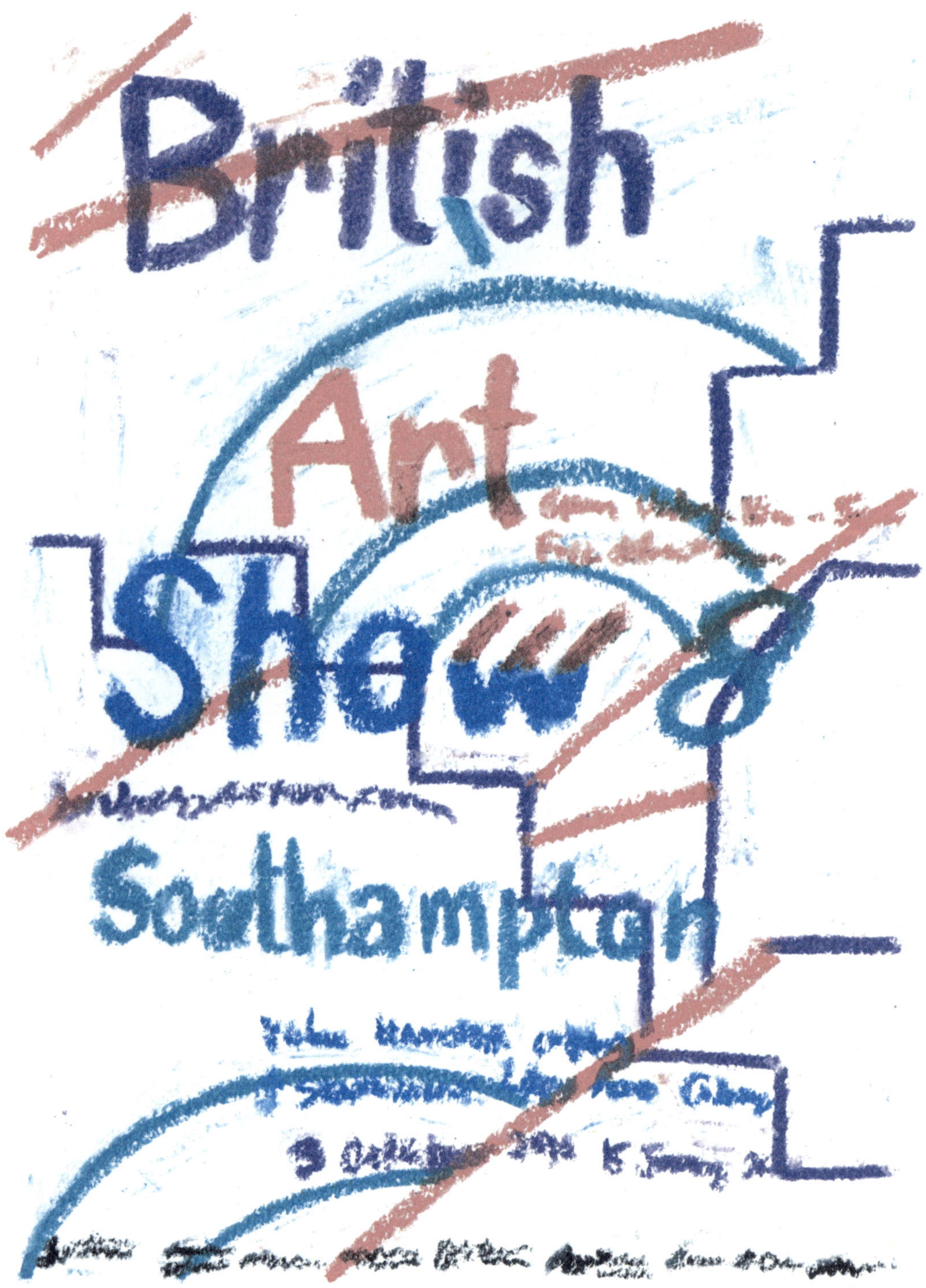
British
Art
Show 8
Southampton

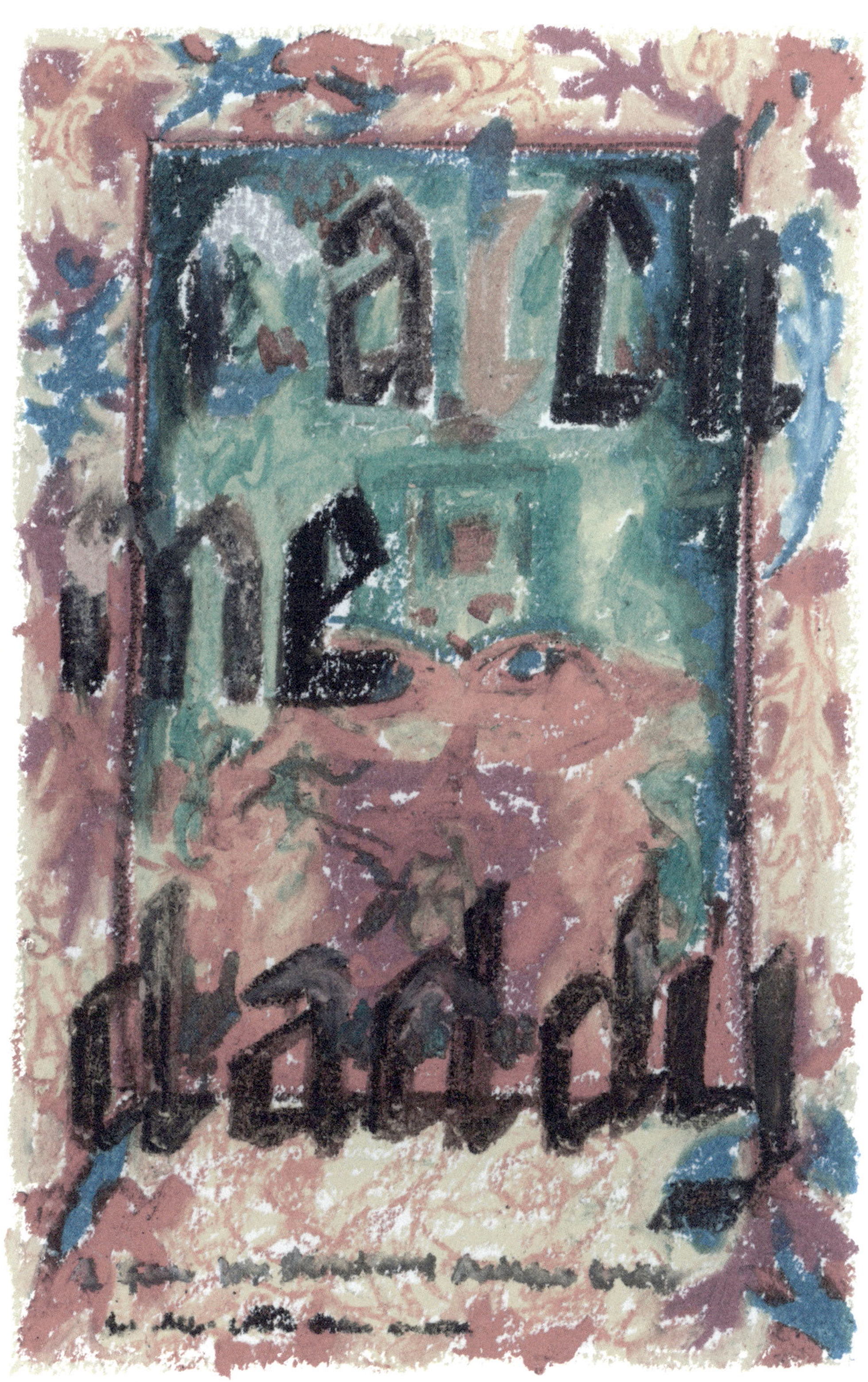
catch
me
daddy

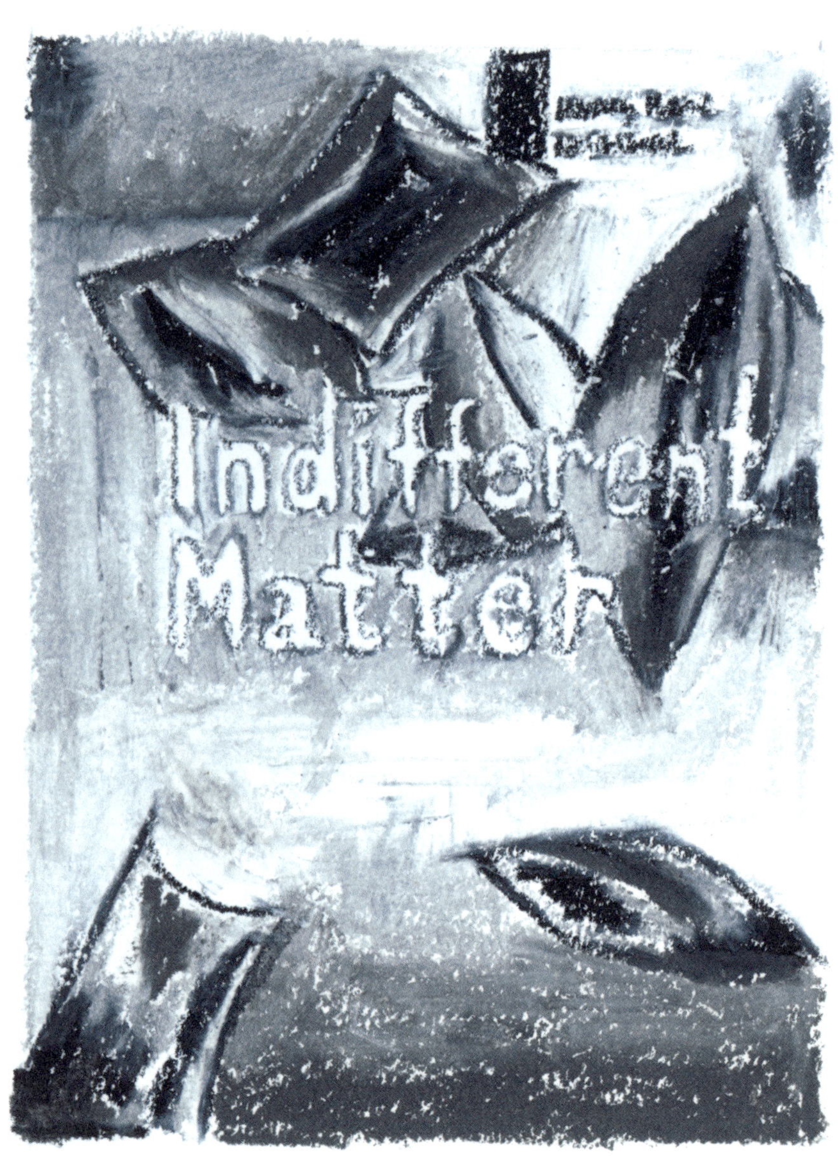
Indifferent
Matter

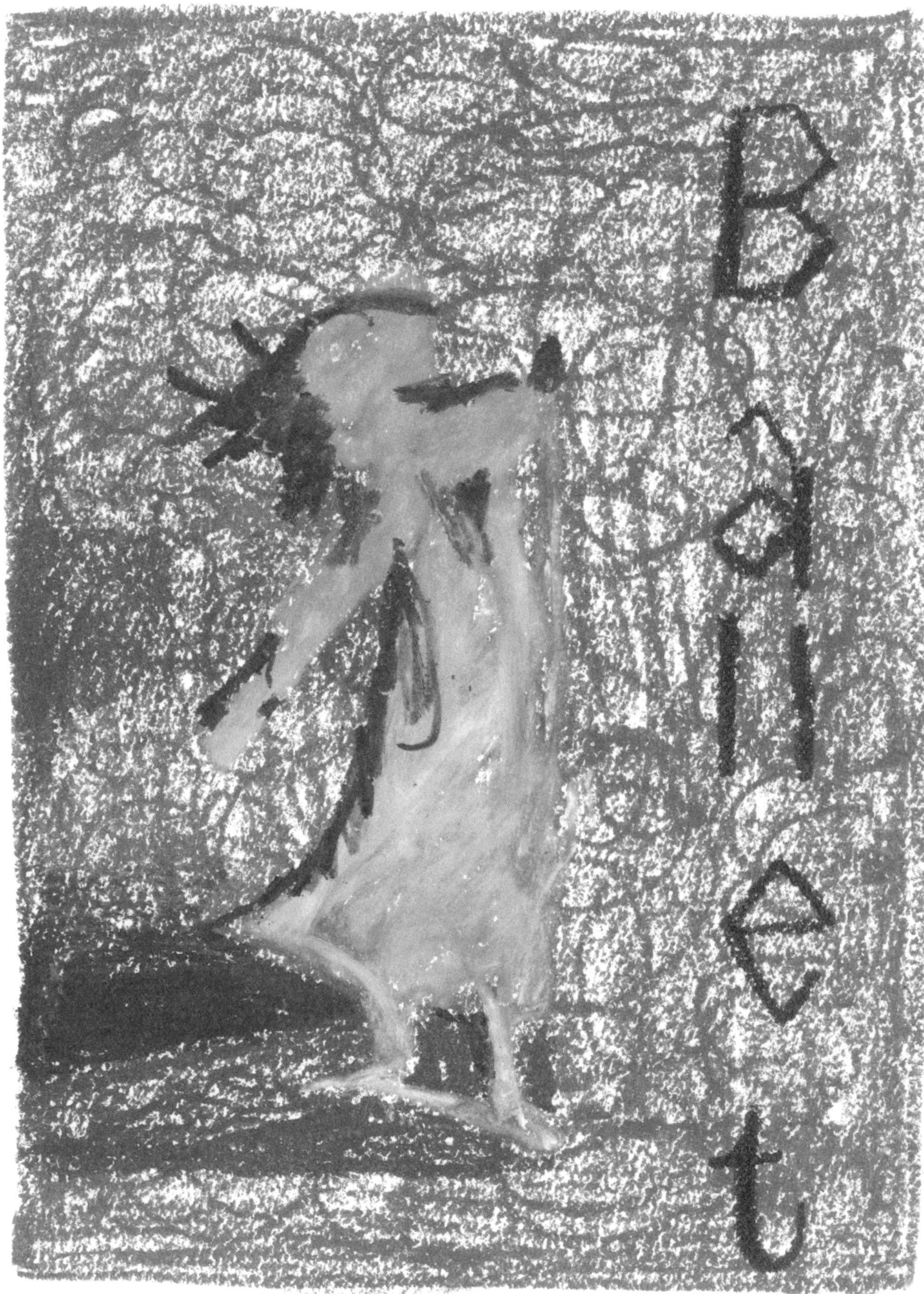
Ballet

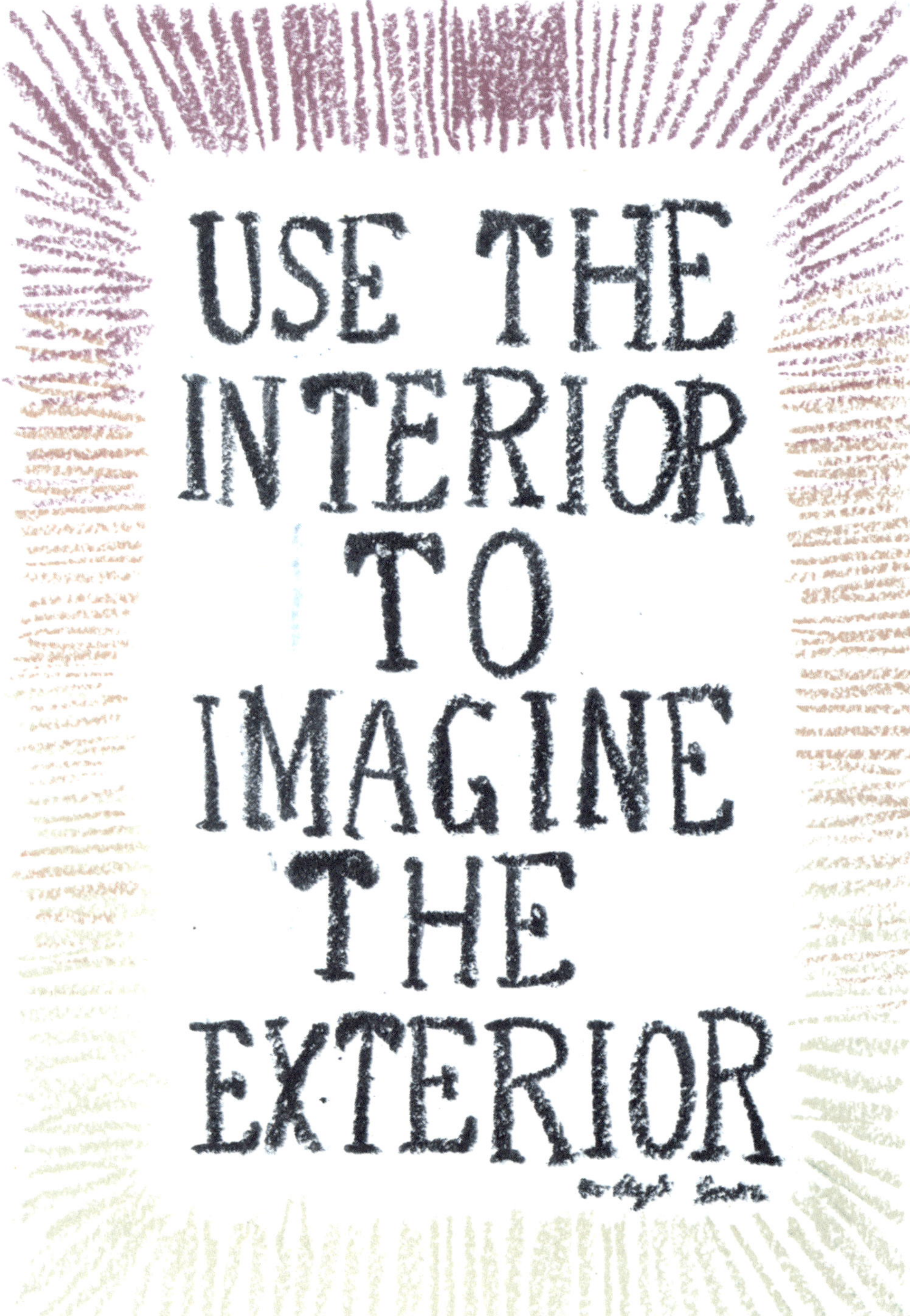
USE THE
INTERIOR
TO
IMAGINE
THE
EXTERIOR

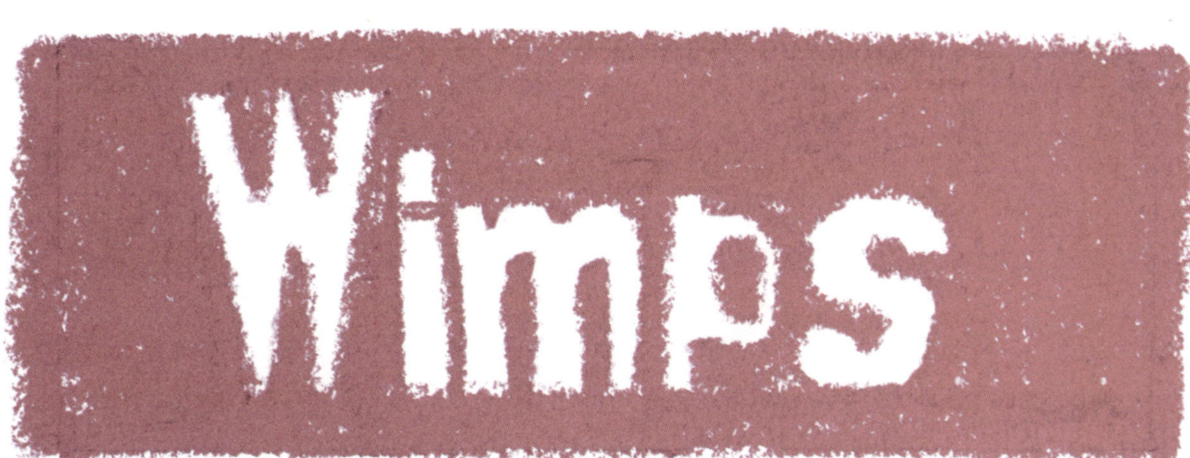
Wimps

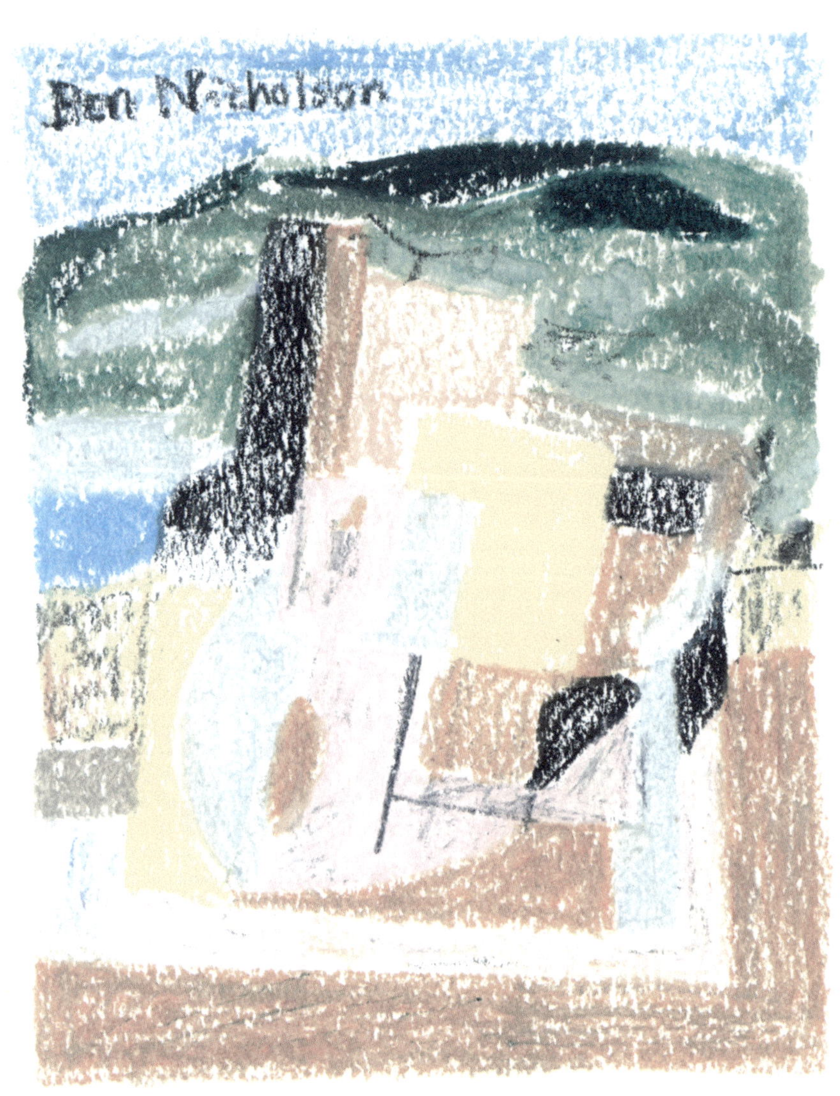
Ben Nicholson

SUCK
NO
MORE

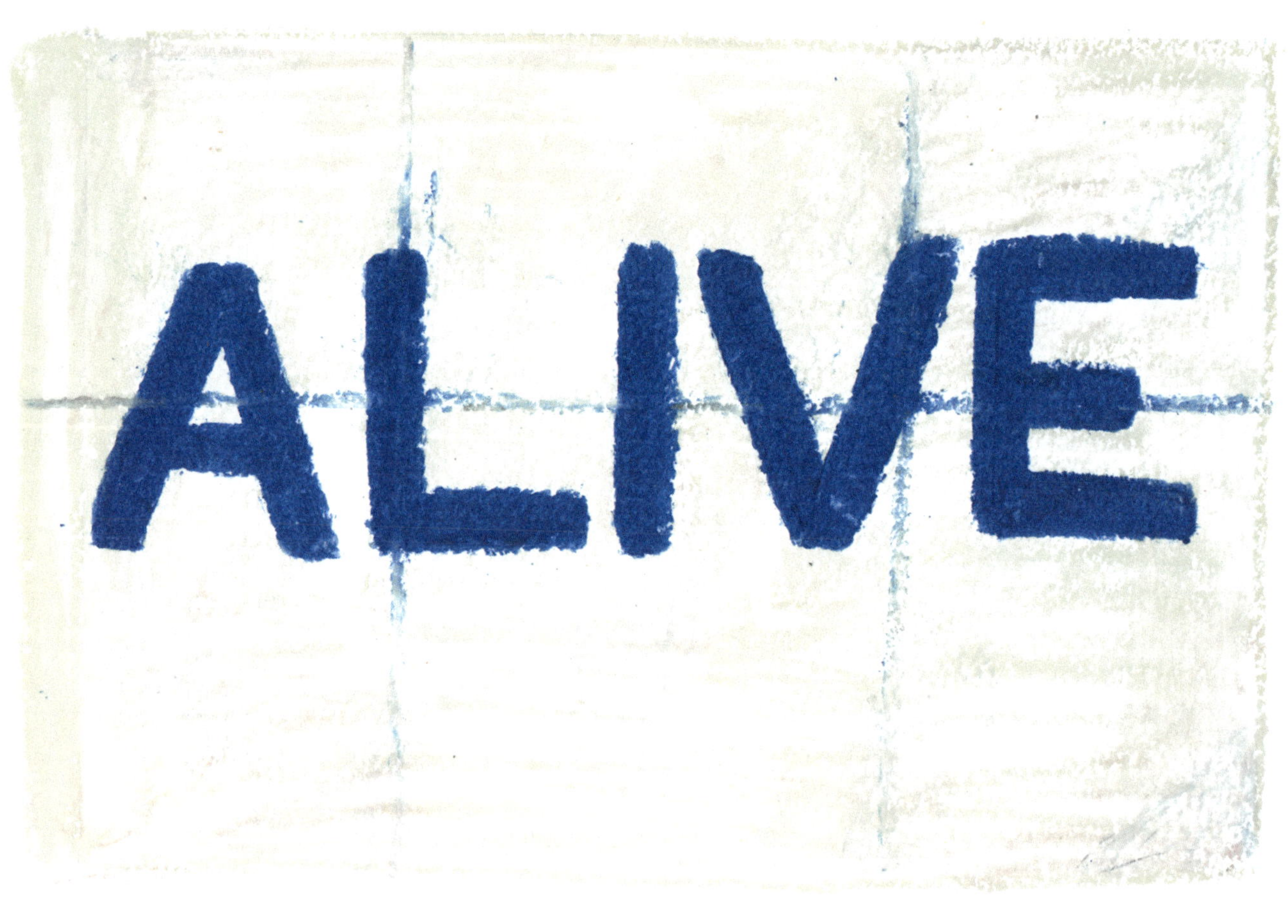
ALIVE

TOM OF FINLAND

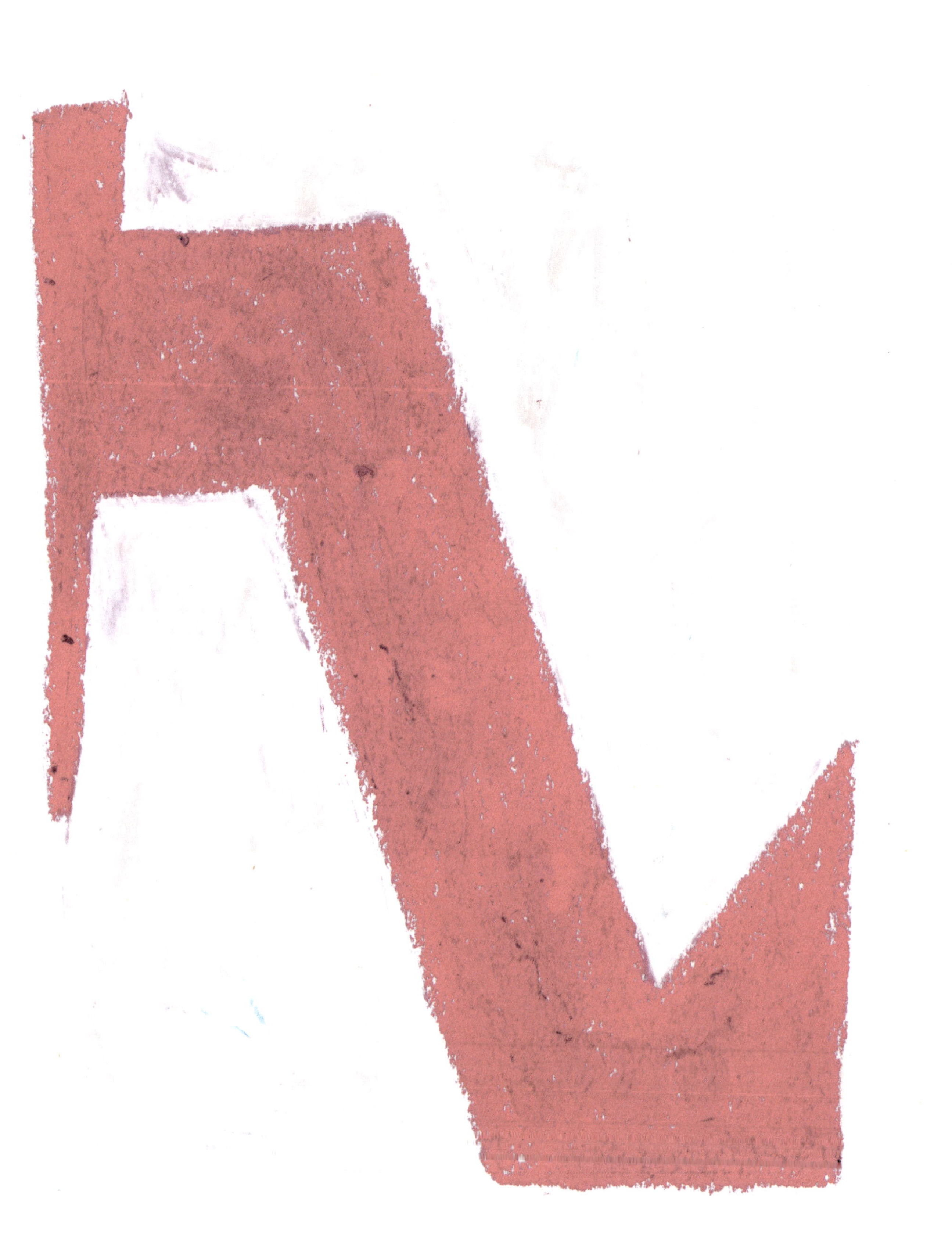

What is the City But the People?

THURSDAY
29 JUNE 2017
6.30PM

PICCADILLY
GARDENS

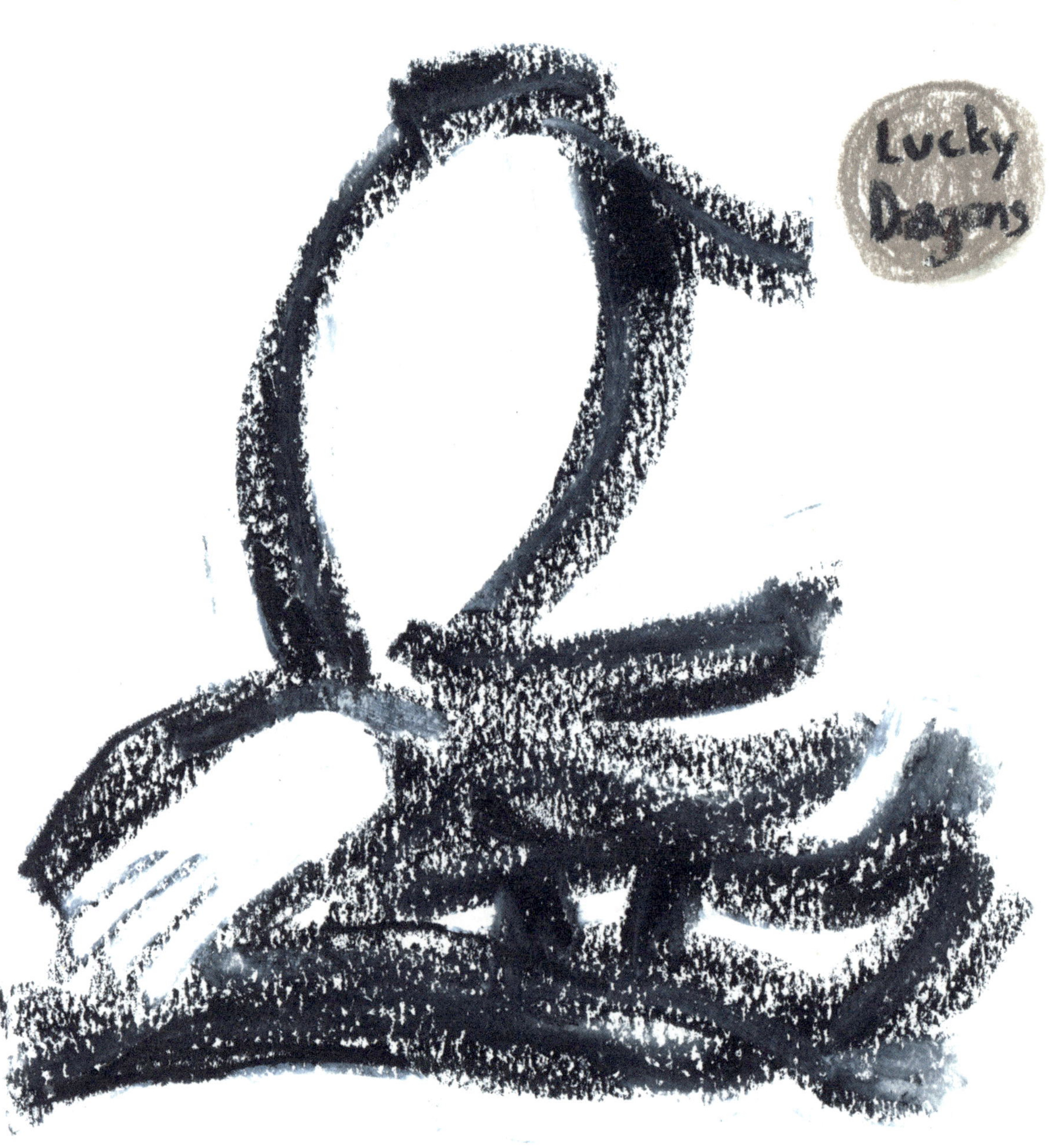
Lucky
Dragons

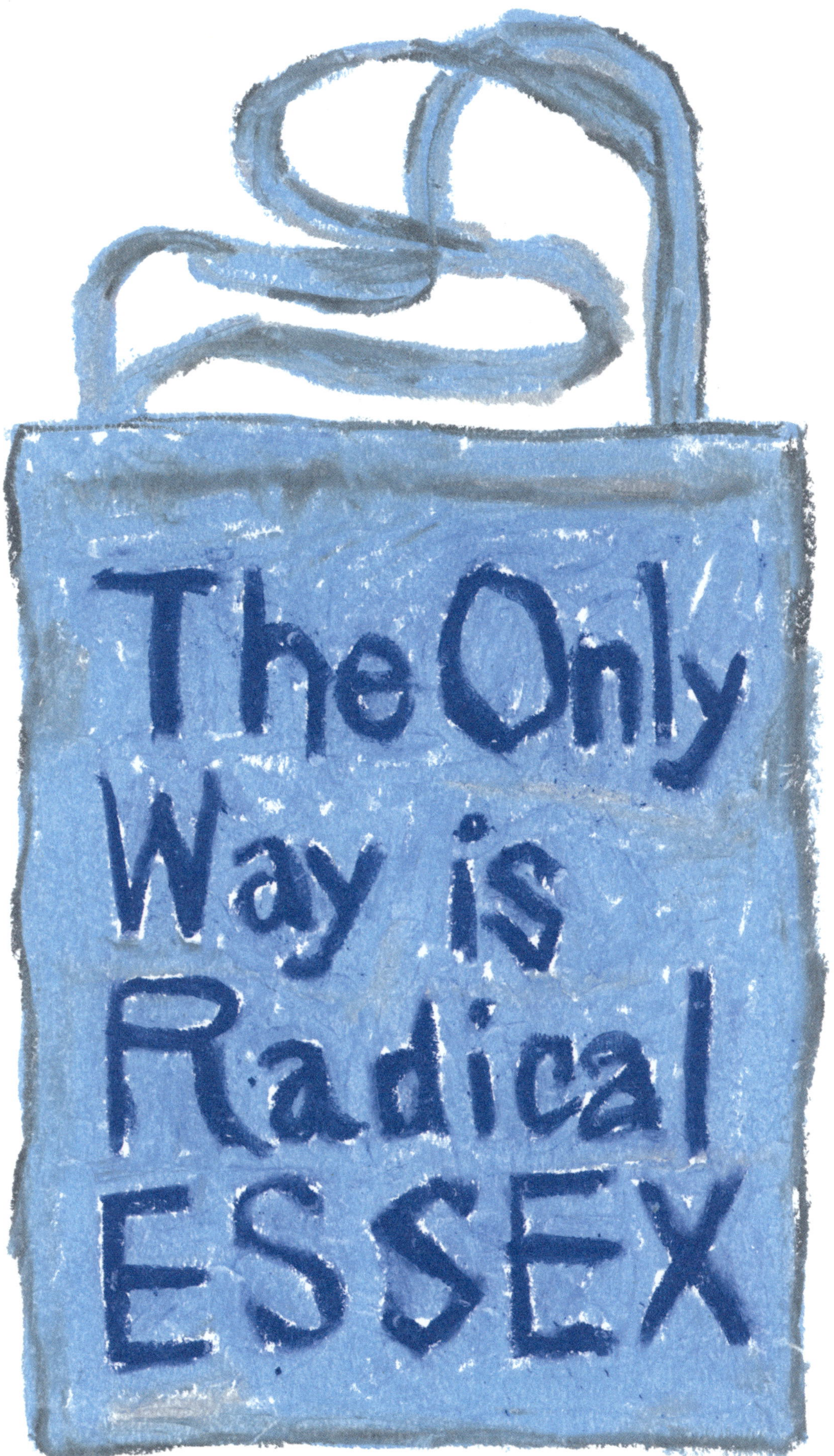
The Only
Way is
Radical
ESSEX

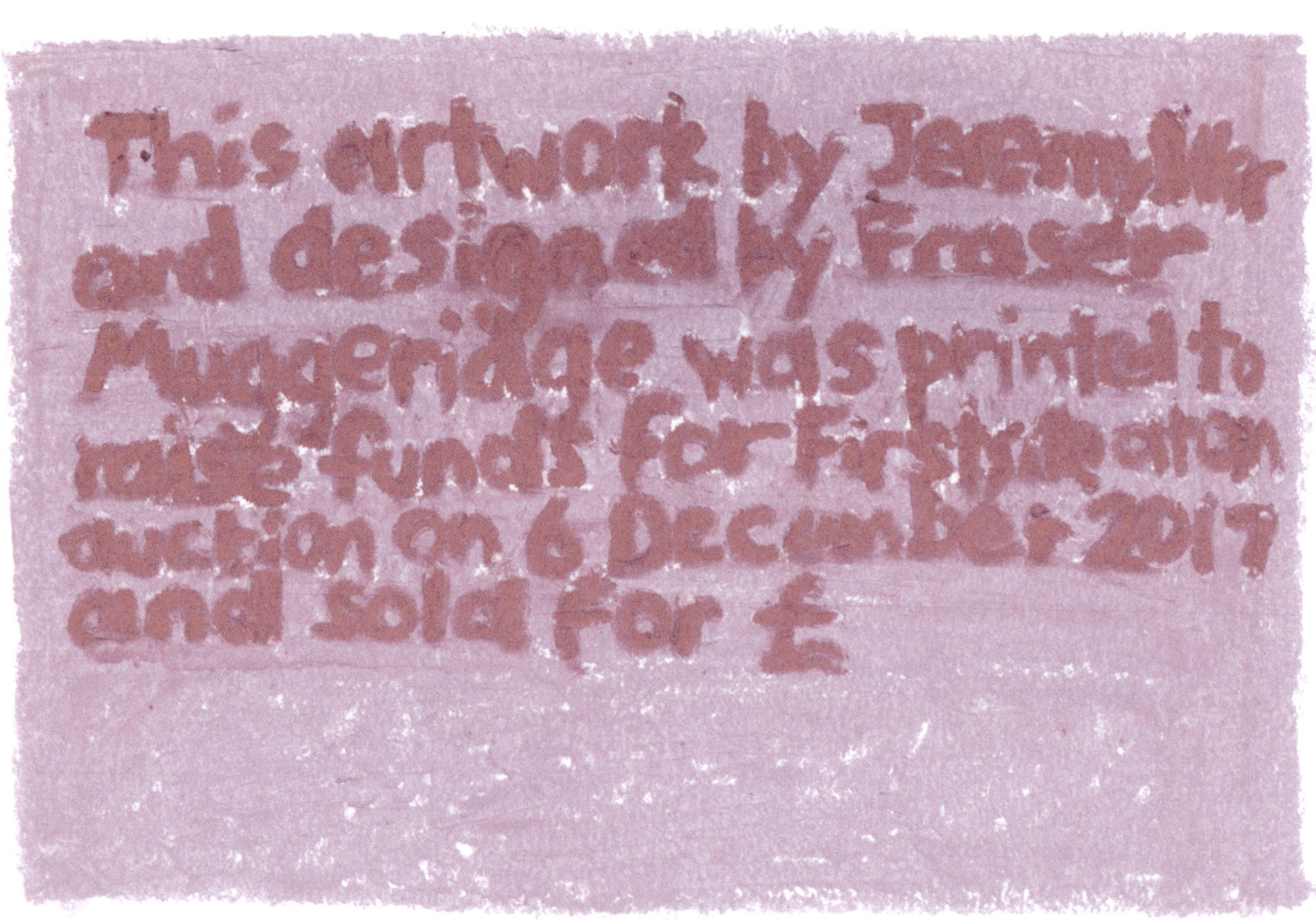
This artwork by Jeremy Deller
and designed by Fraser
Muggeridge was printed to
raise funds for Firstsite at an
auction on 6 December 2017
and sold for £

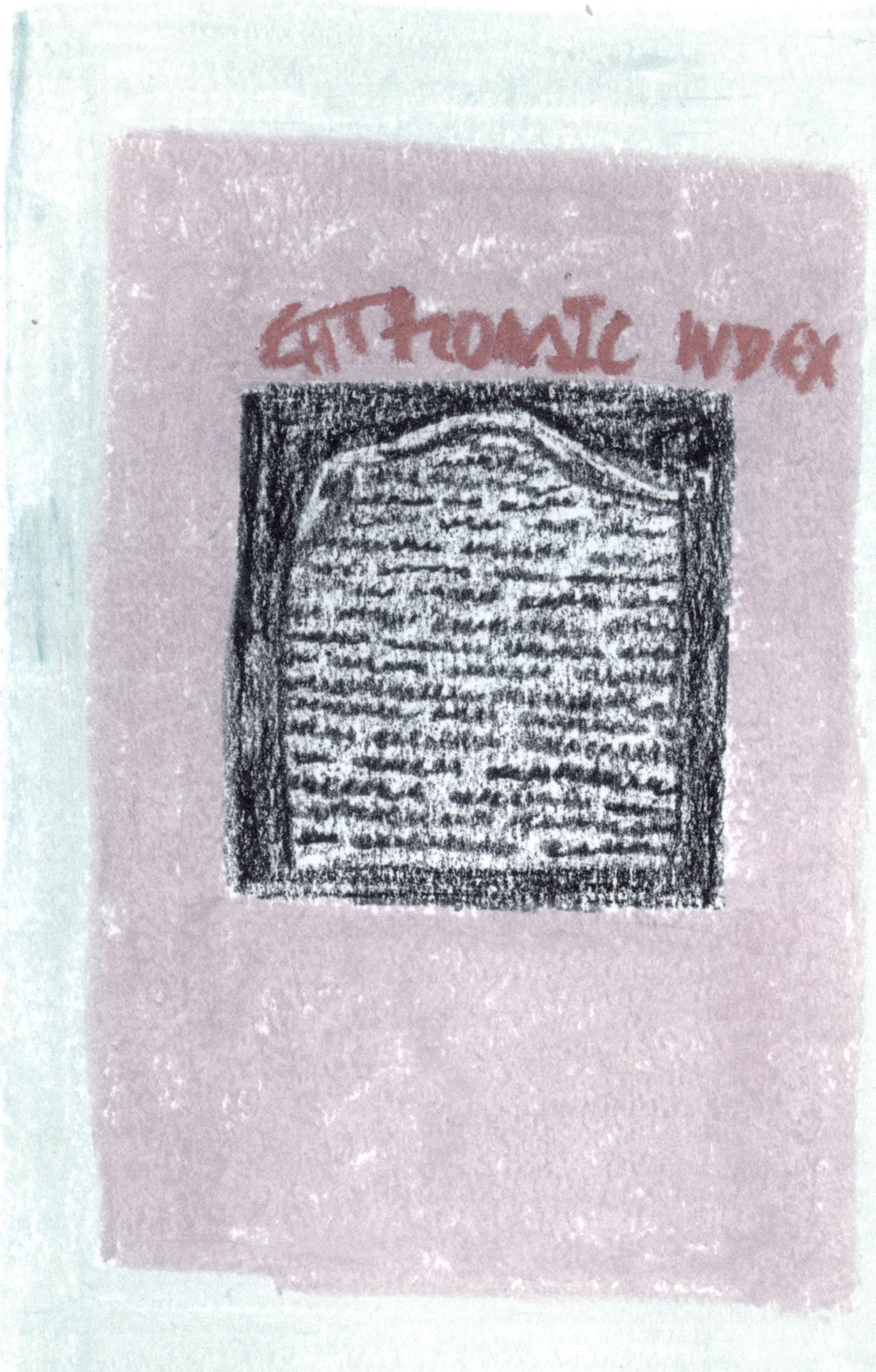
CHTHONIC INDEX

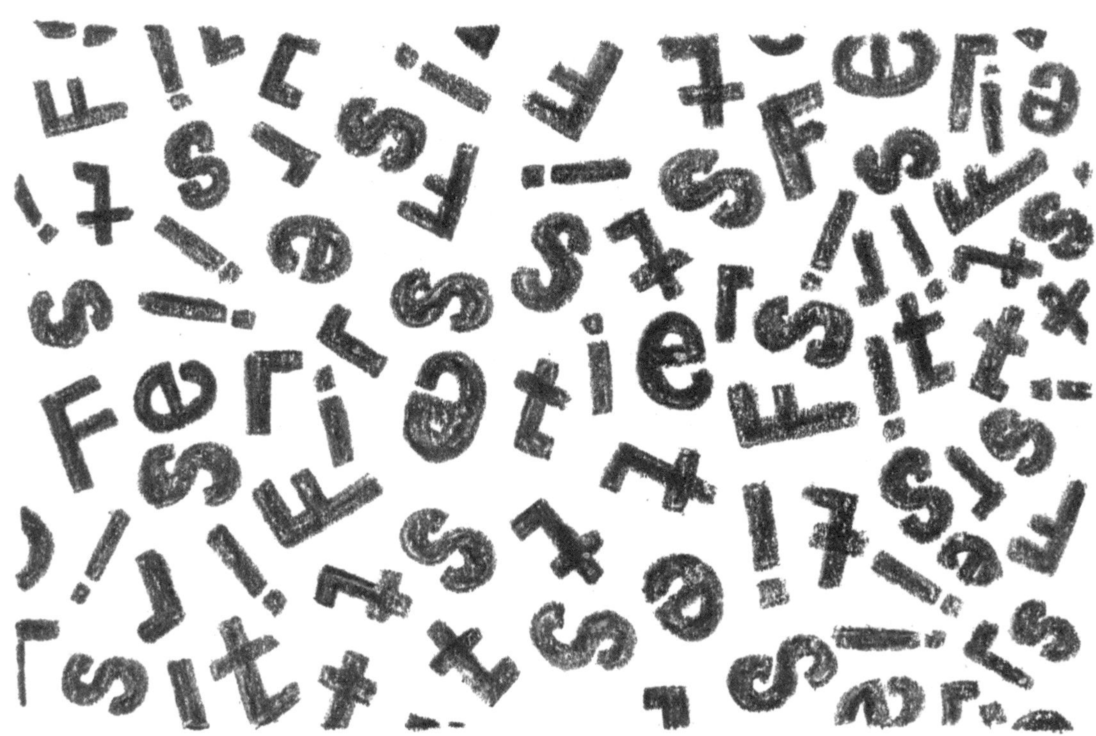

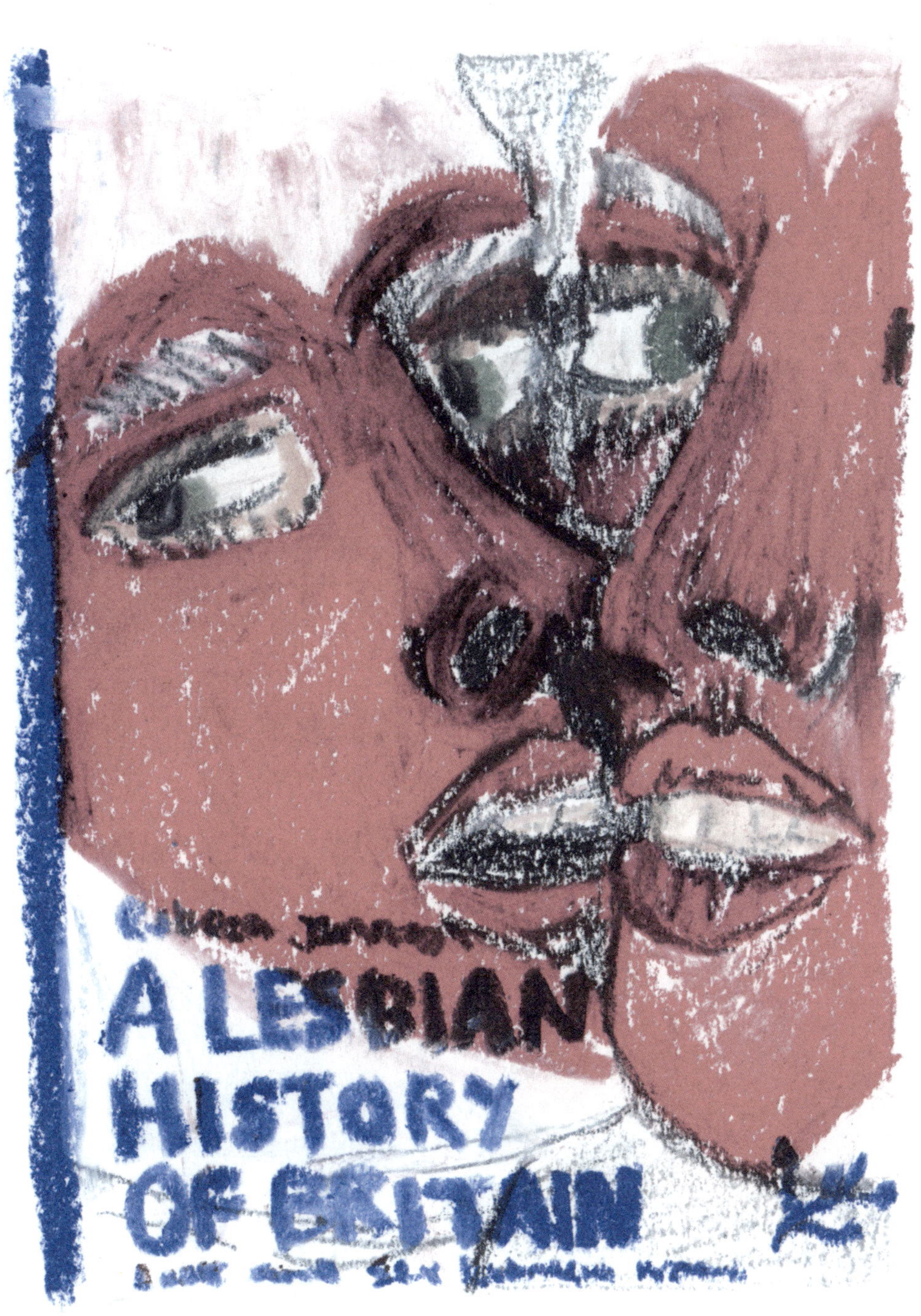
A LESBIAN
HISTORY
OF BRITAIN

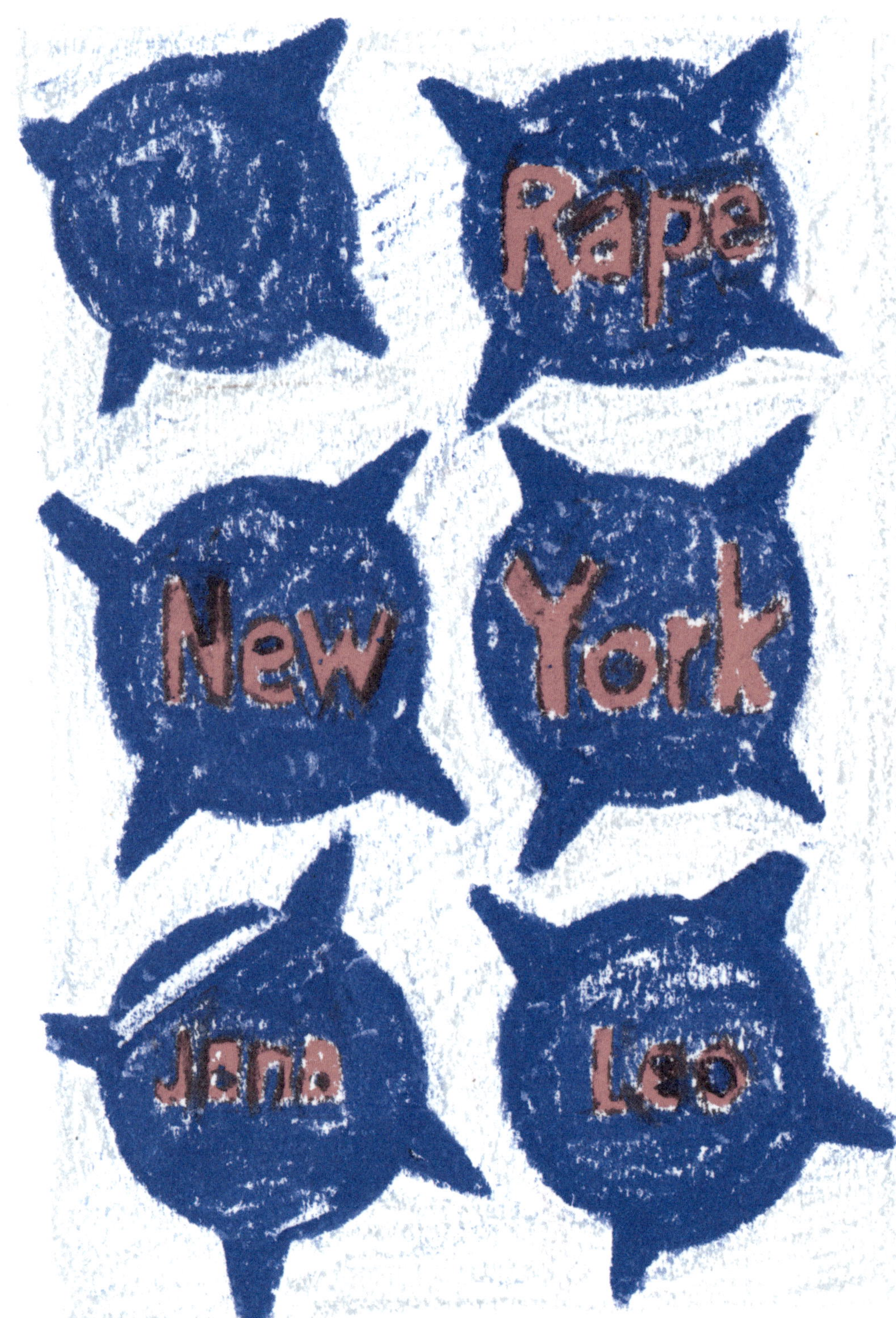
Rape
New
York
Jana
Leo

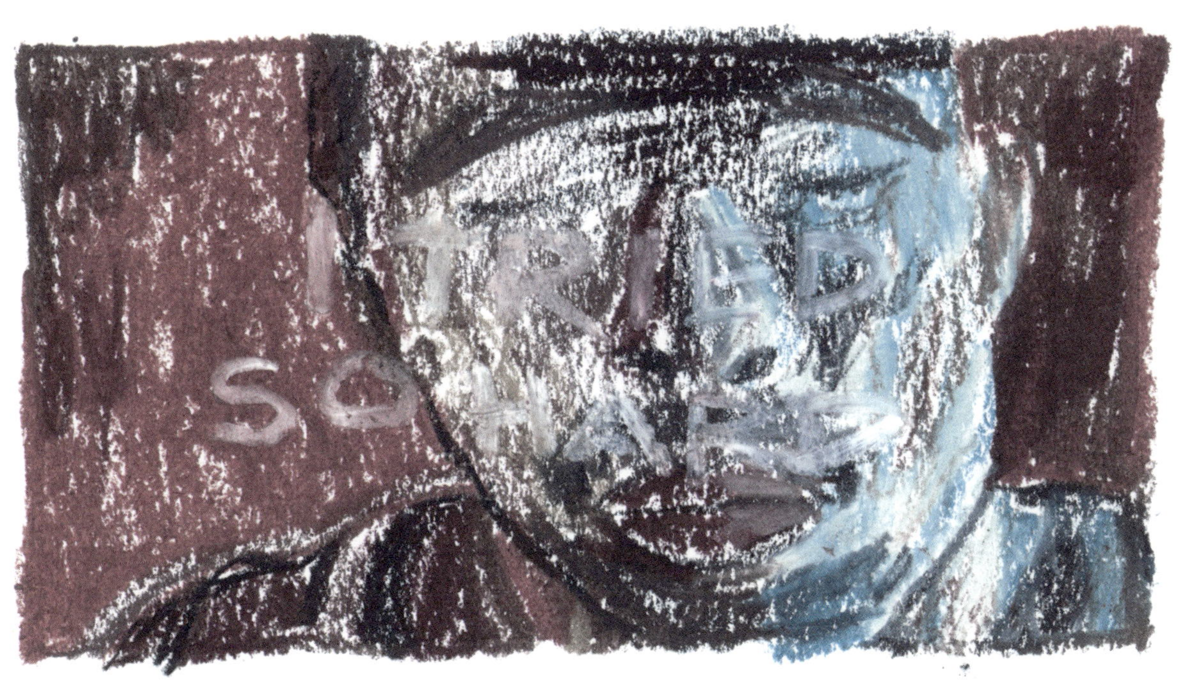
I TRIED
SO HARD

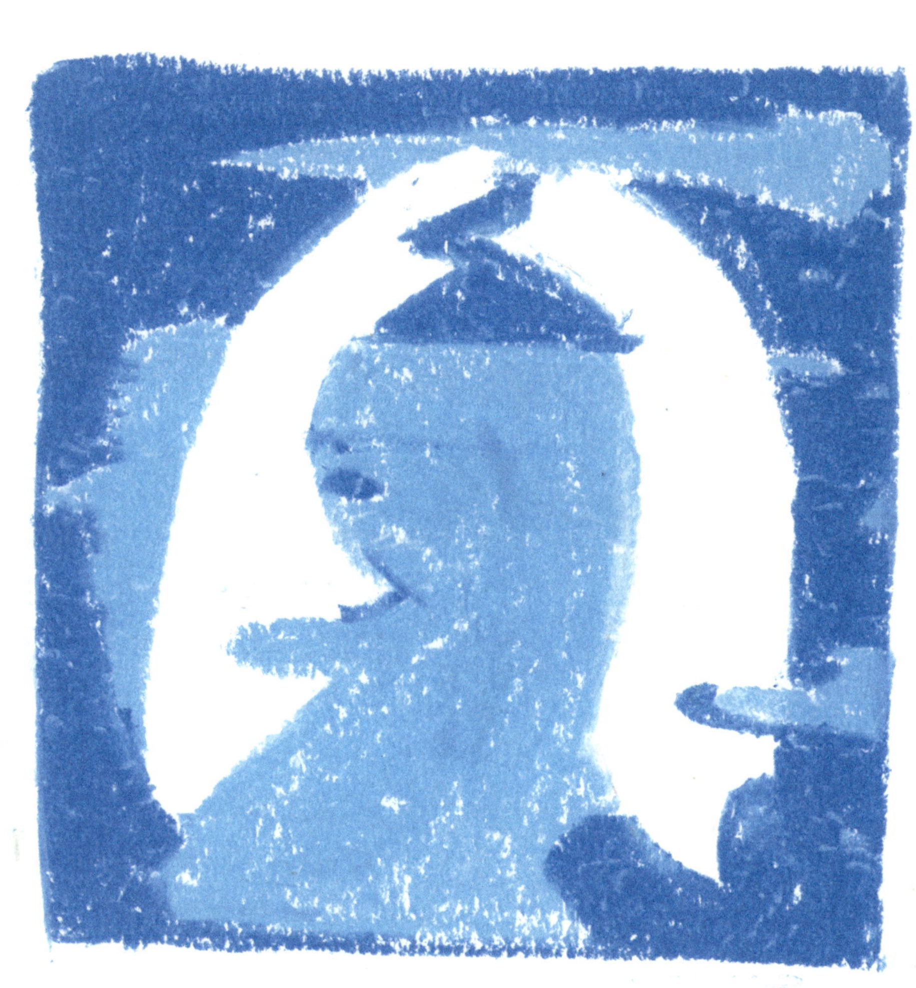

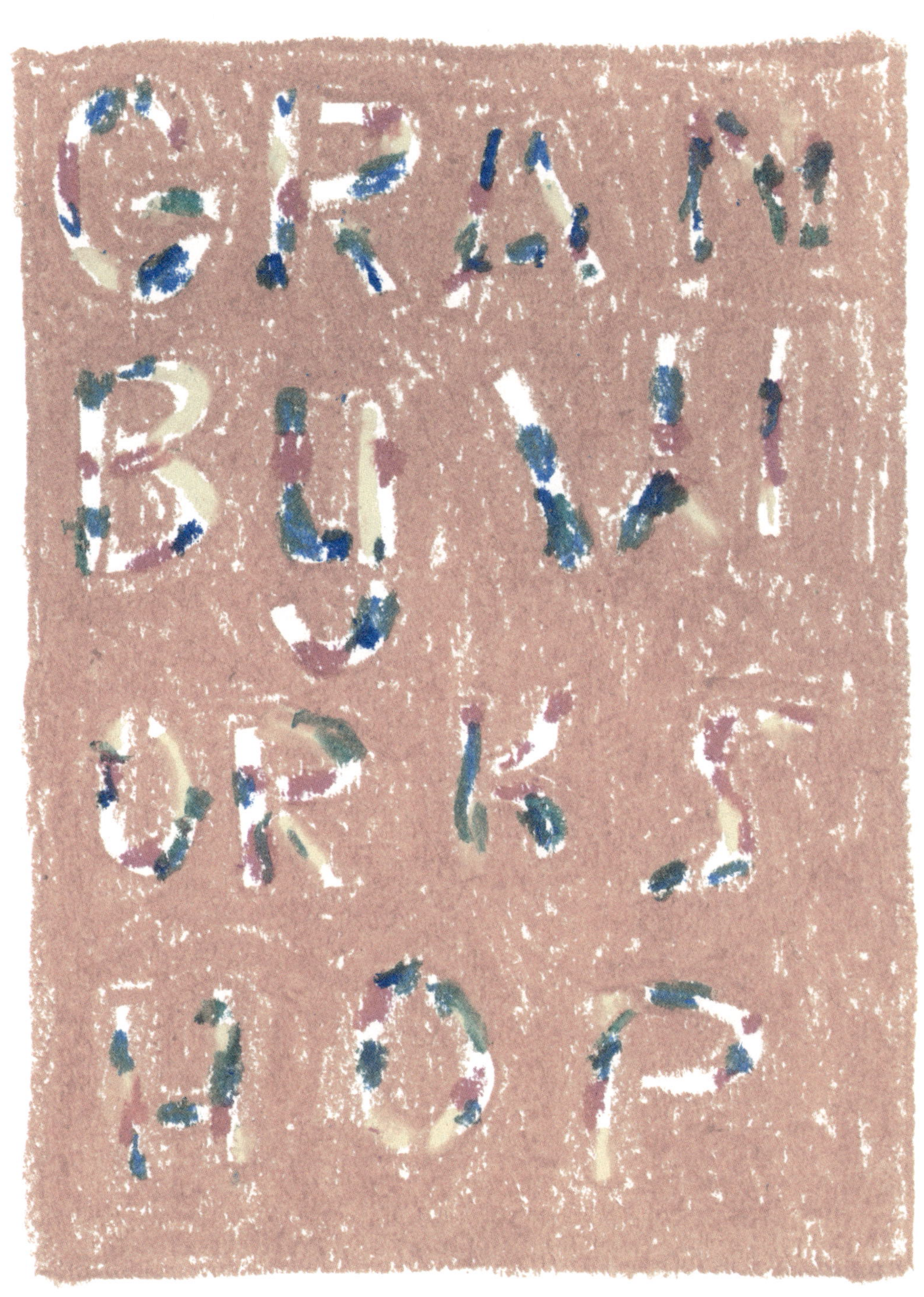
GRAM
ORKS
HOP

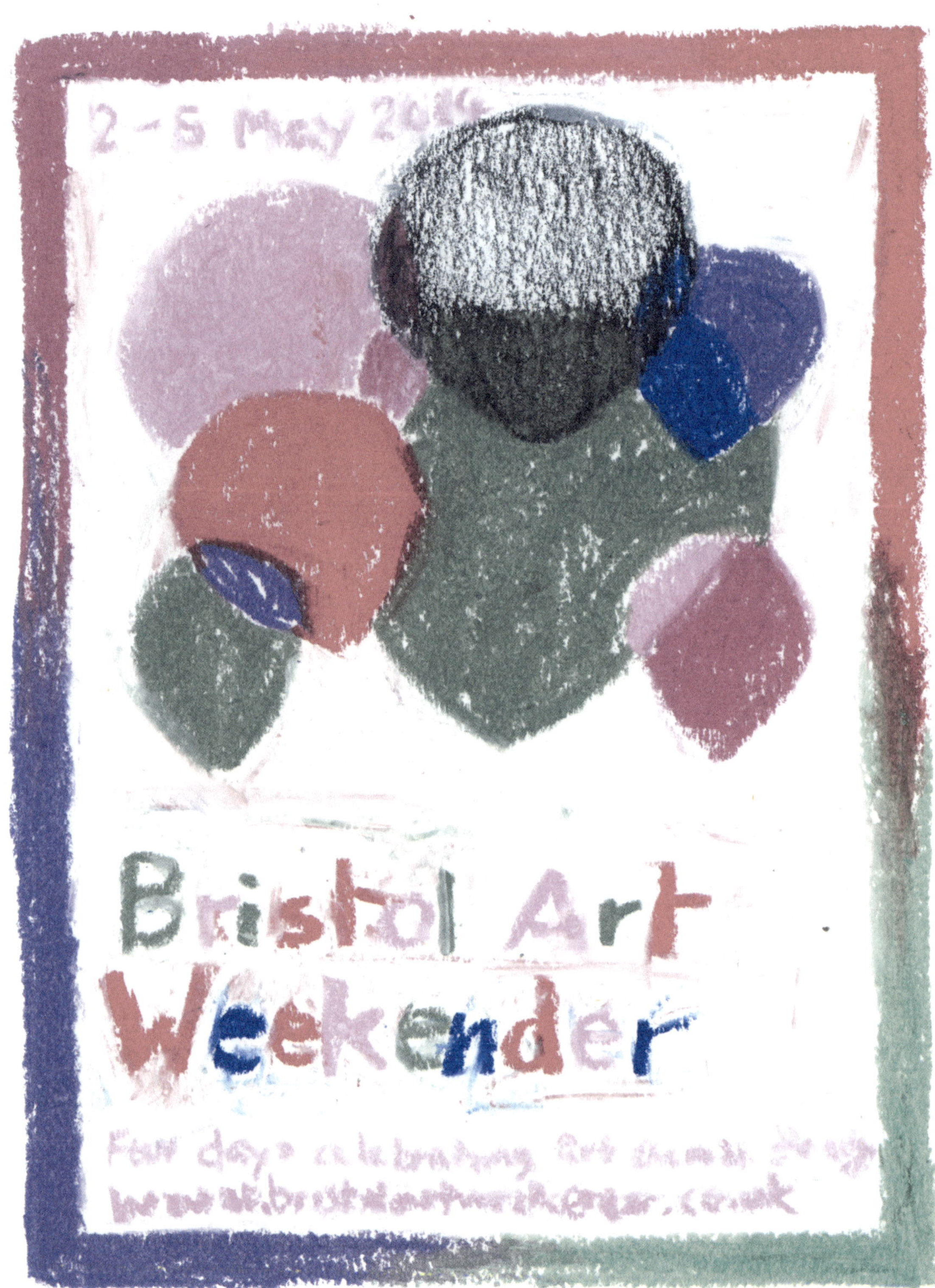
2 - 5 May
Bristol Art
Weekender

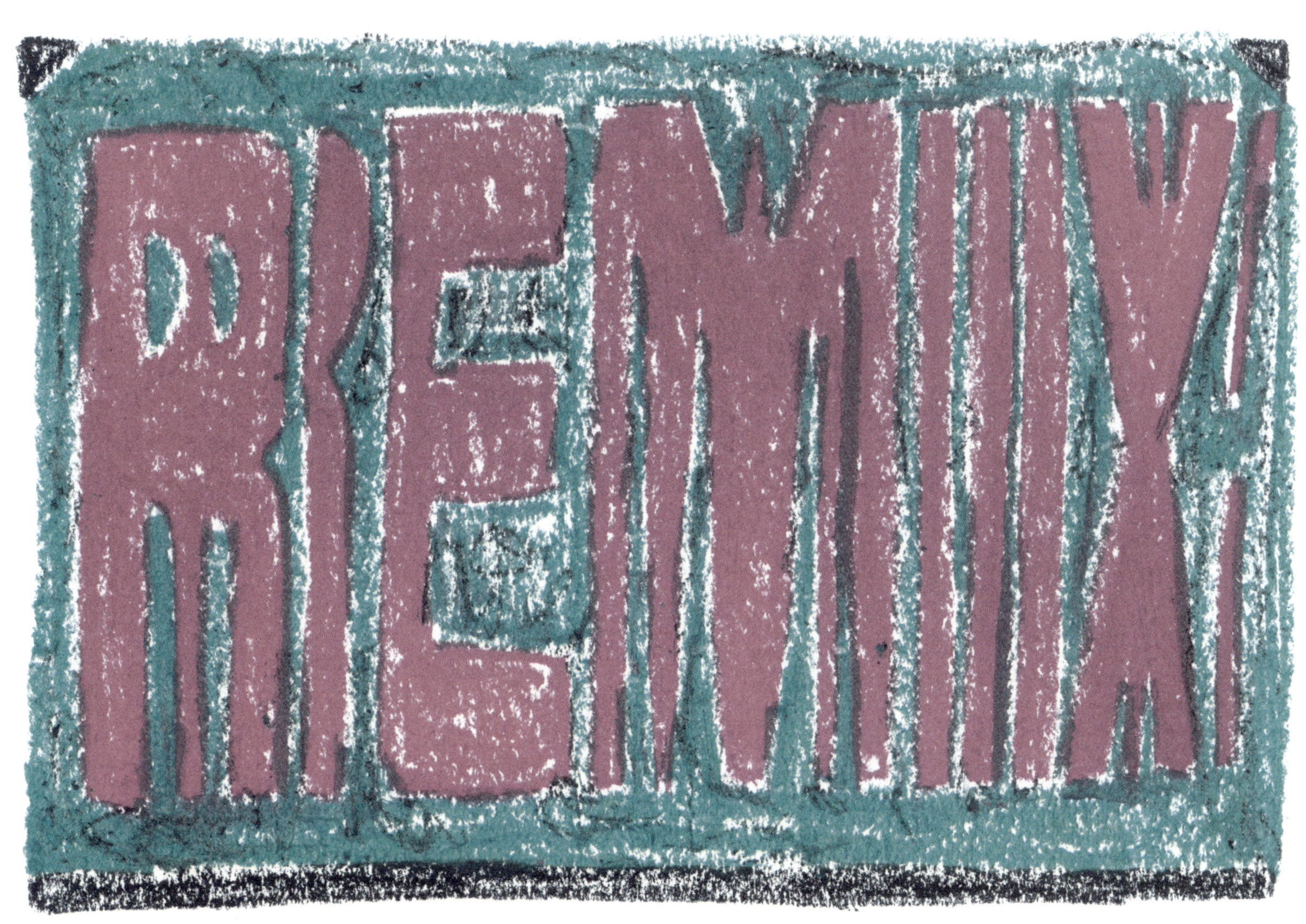
REMIX

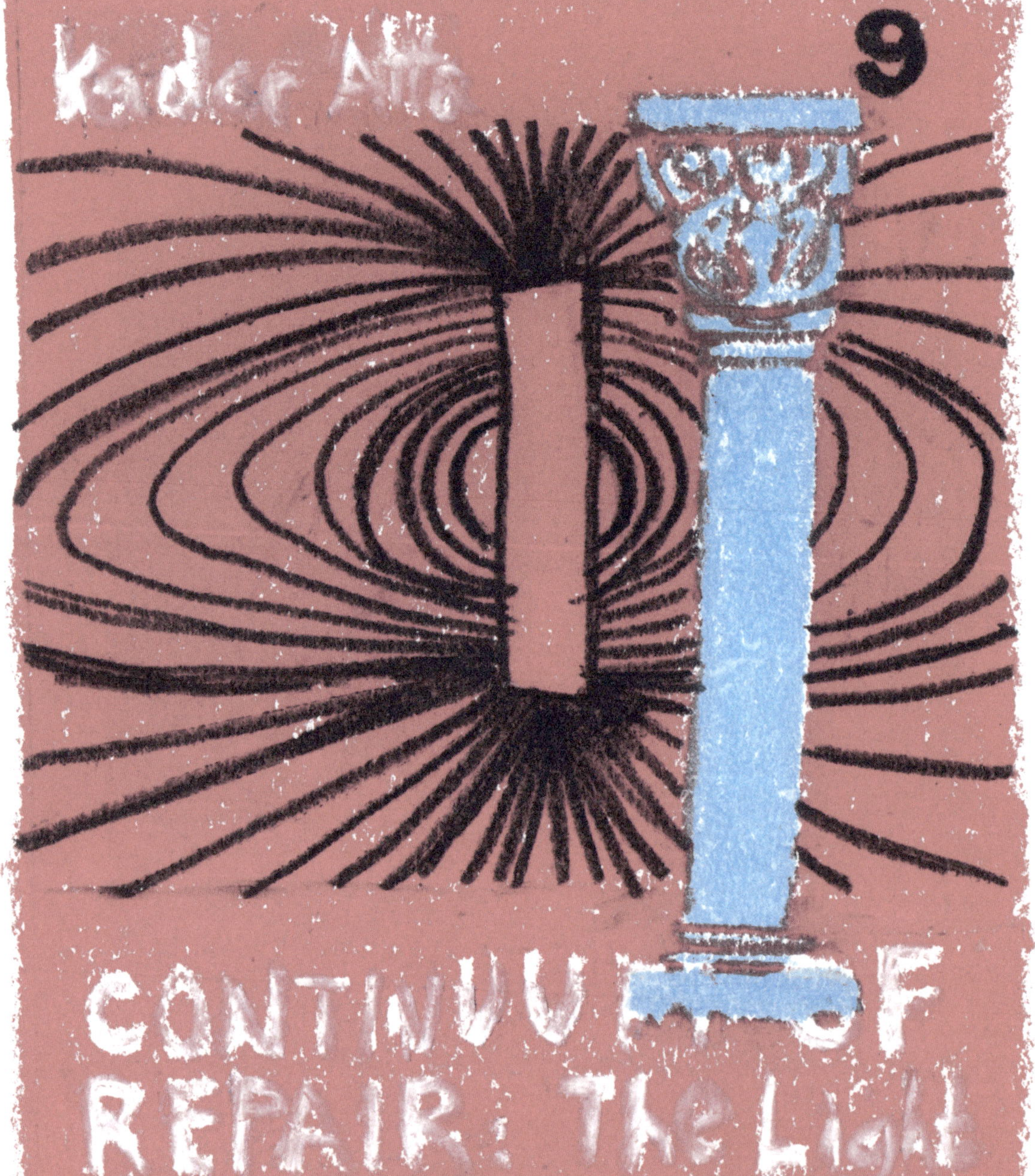
Kader Attia
9
CONTINUUM OF
REPAIR: The Light
of Jacob's Ladder

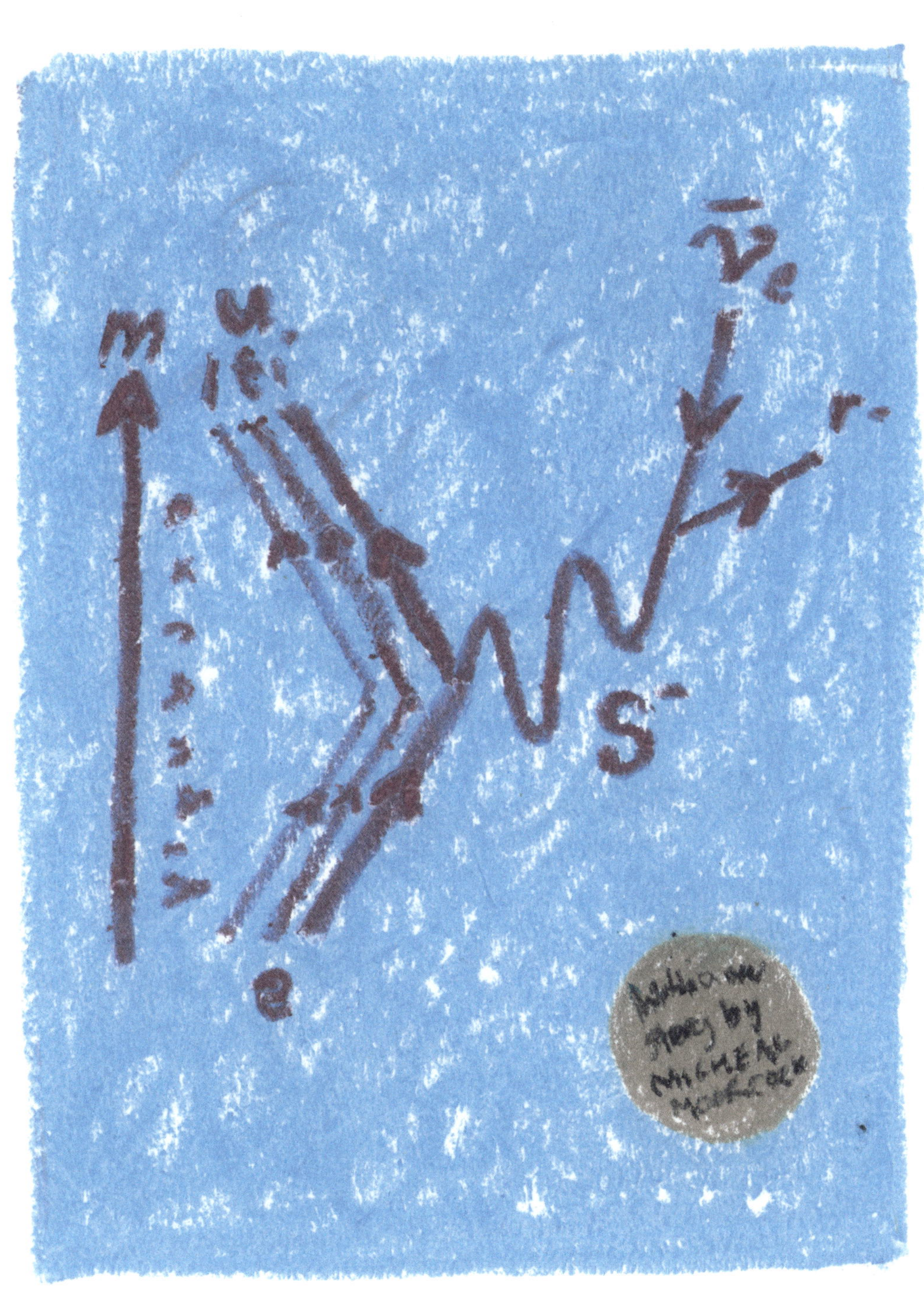
m
u
e
S⁻
$\bar{\nu}_e$
r⁻

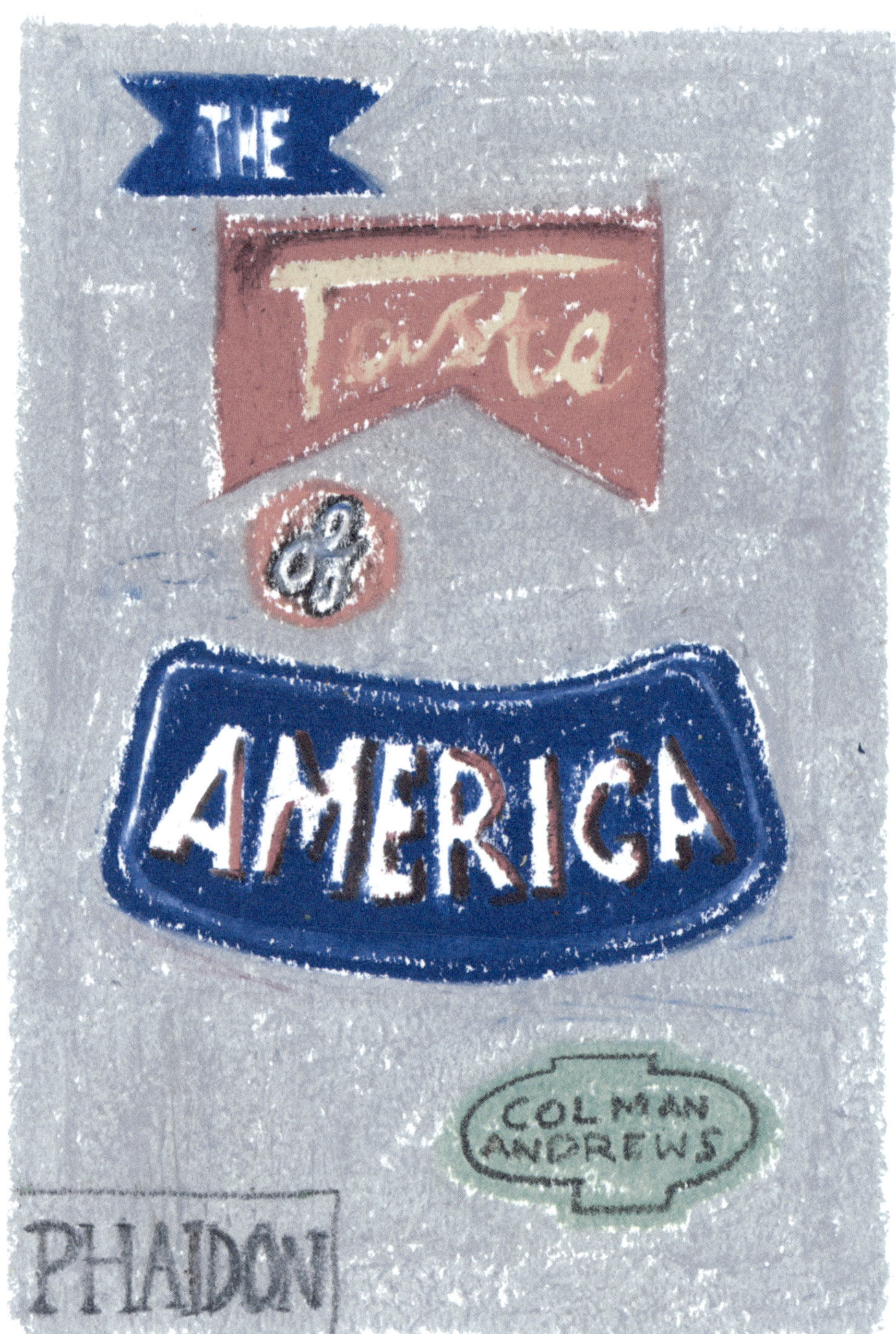
THE
Taste
of
AMERICA
COLMAN ANDREWS
PHAIDON

PLEASE
DO NOT
PLACE
DRINKS
ON
VITRINES
OR
BOOKS.

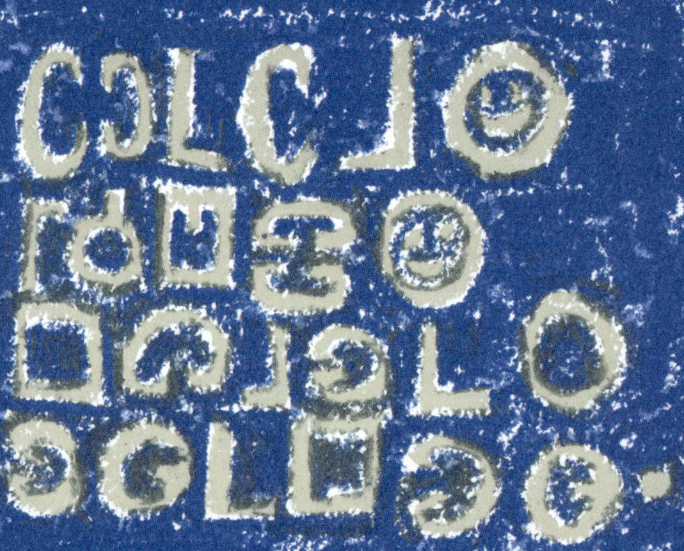

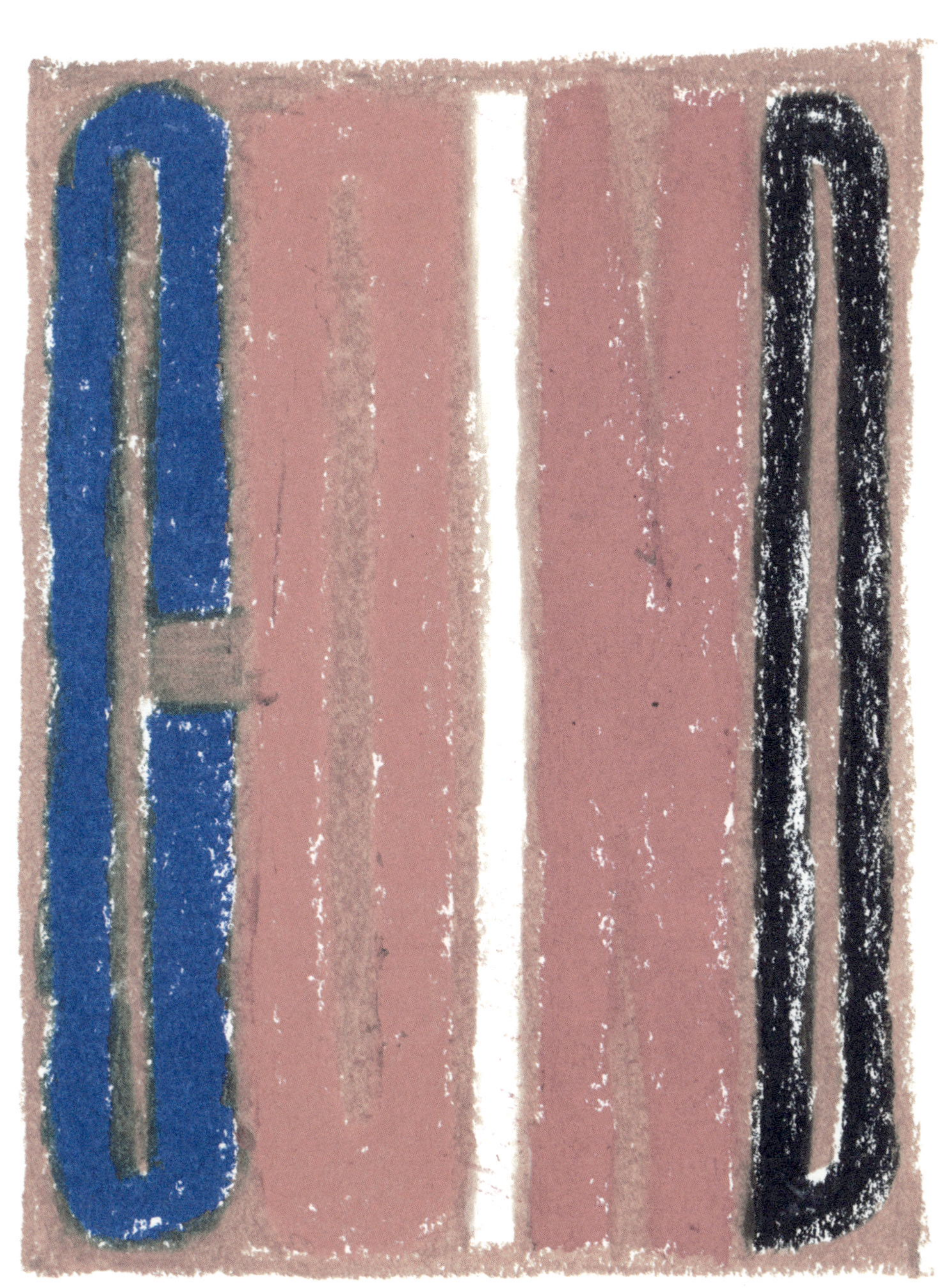

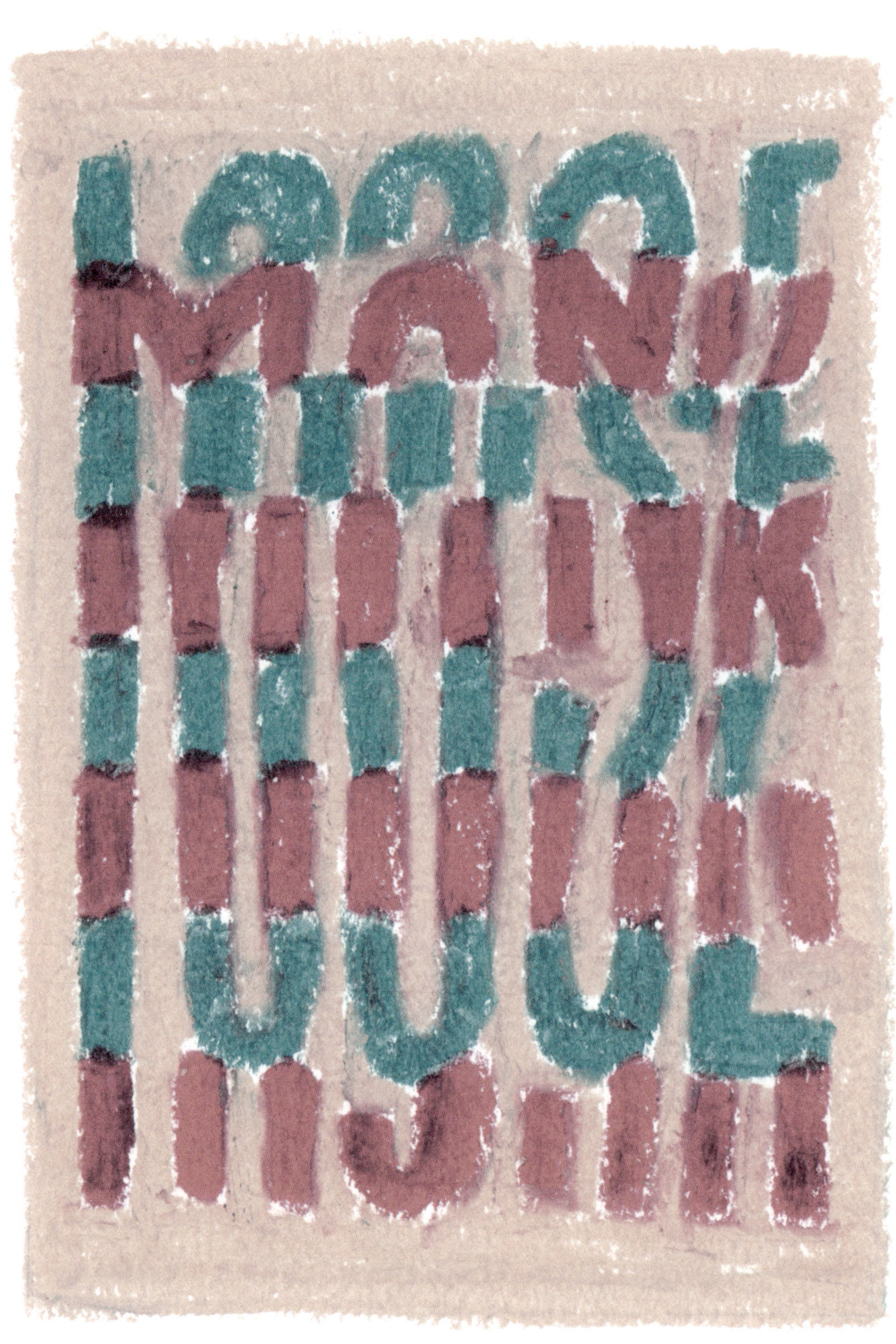

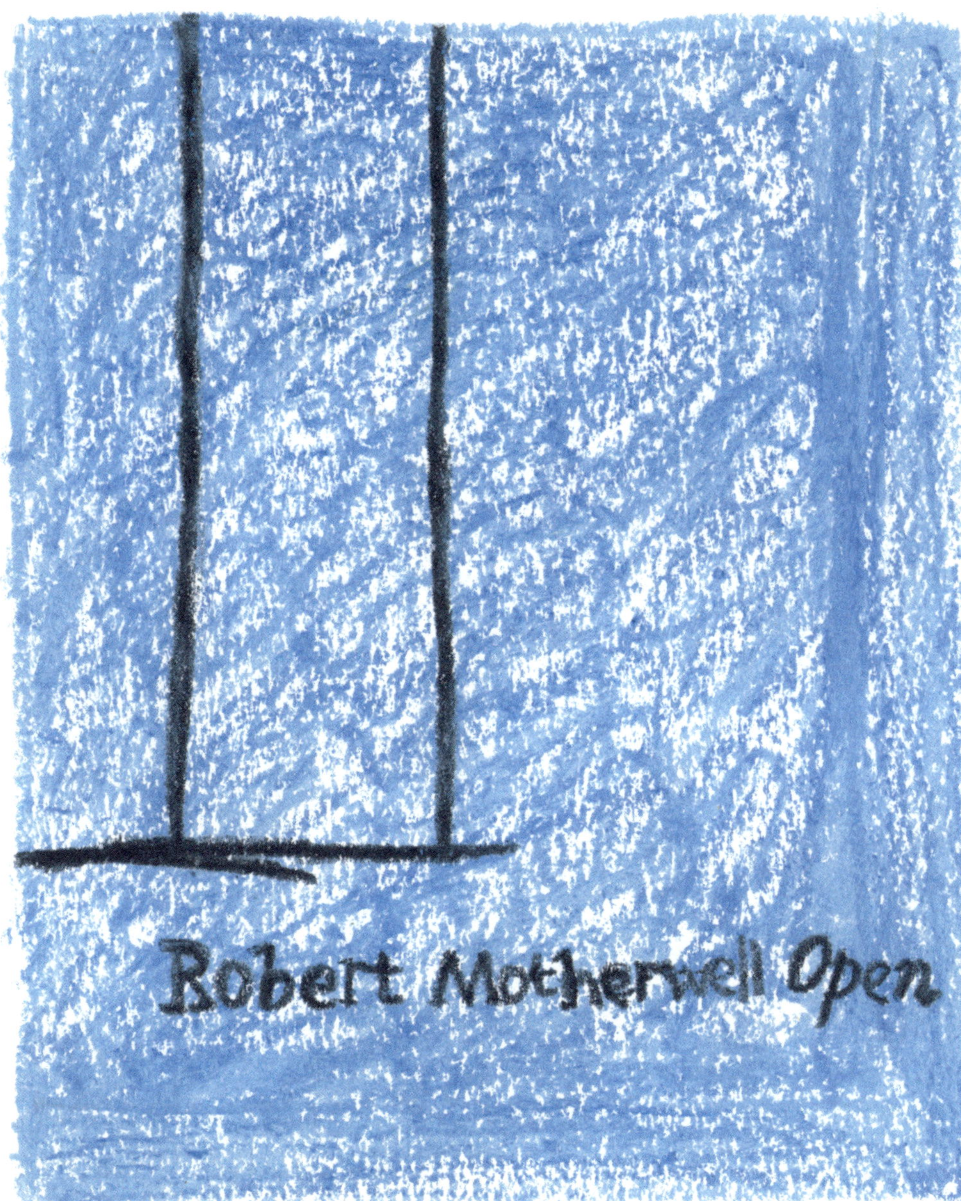
Robert Motherwell Open

Superabundant

A Celebration of [illegible]

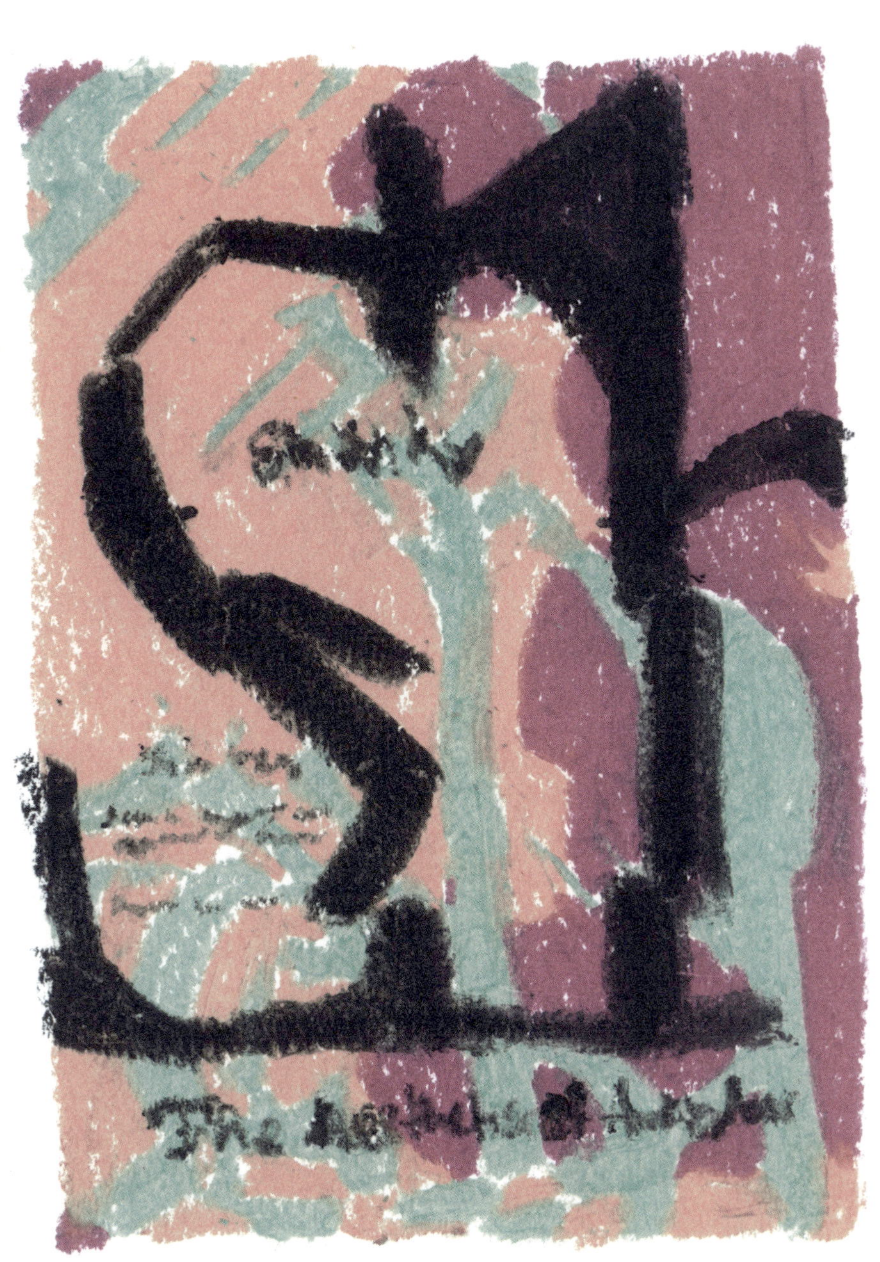

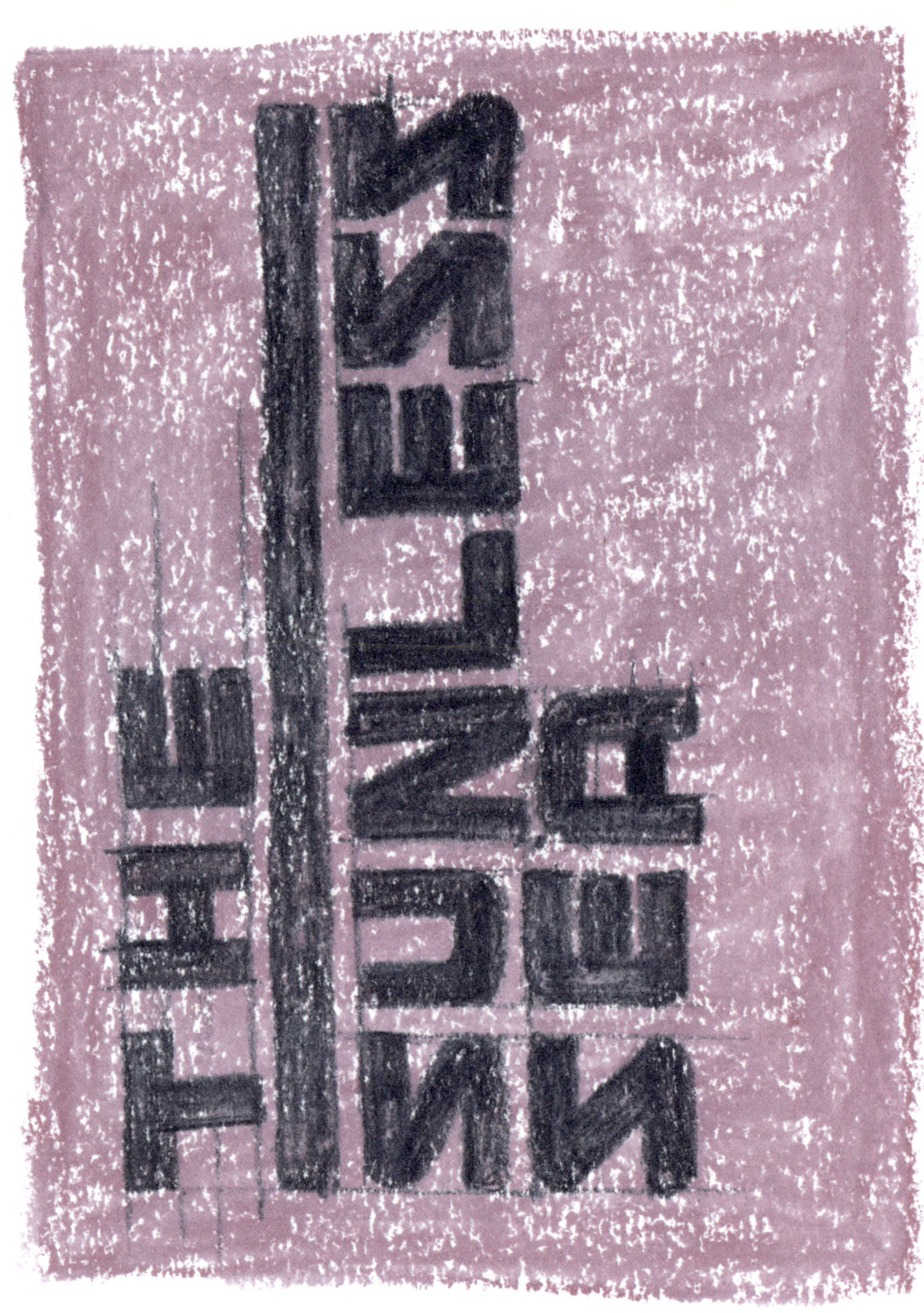
THE
SUNLESS
SEA

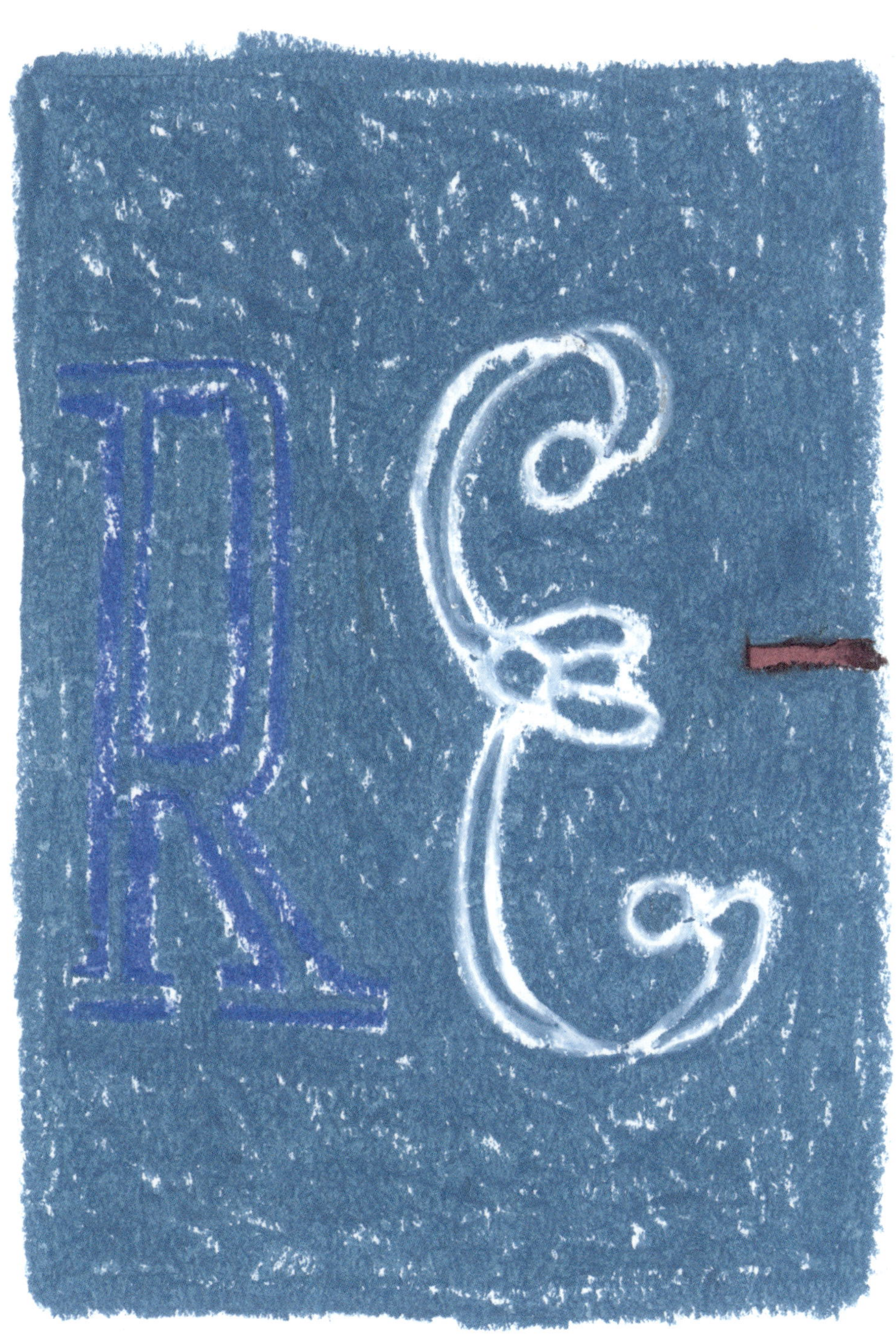
RE-

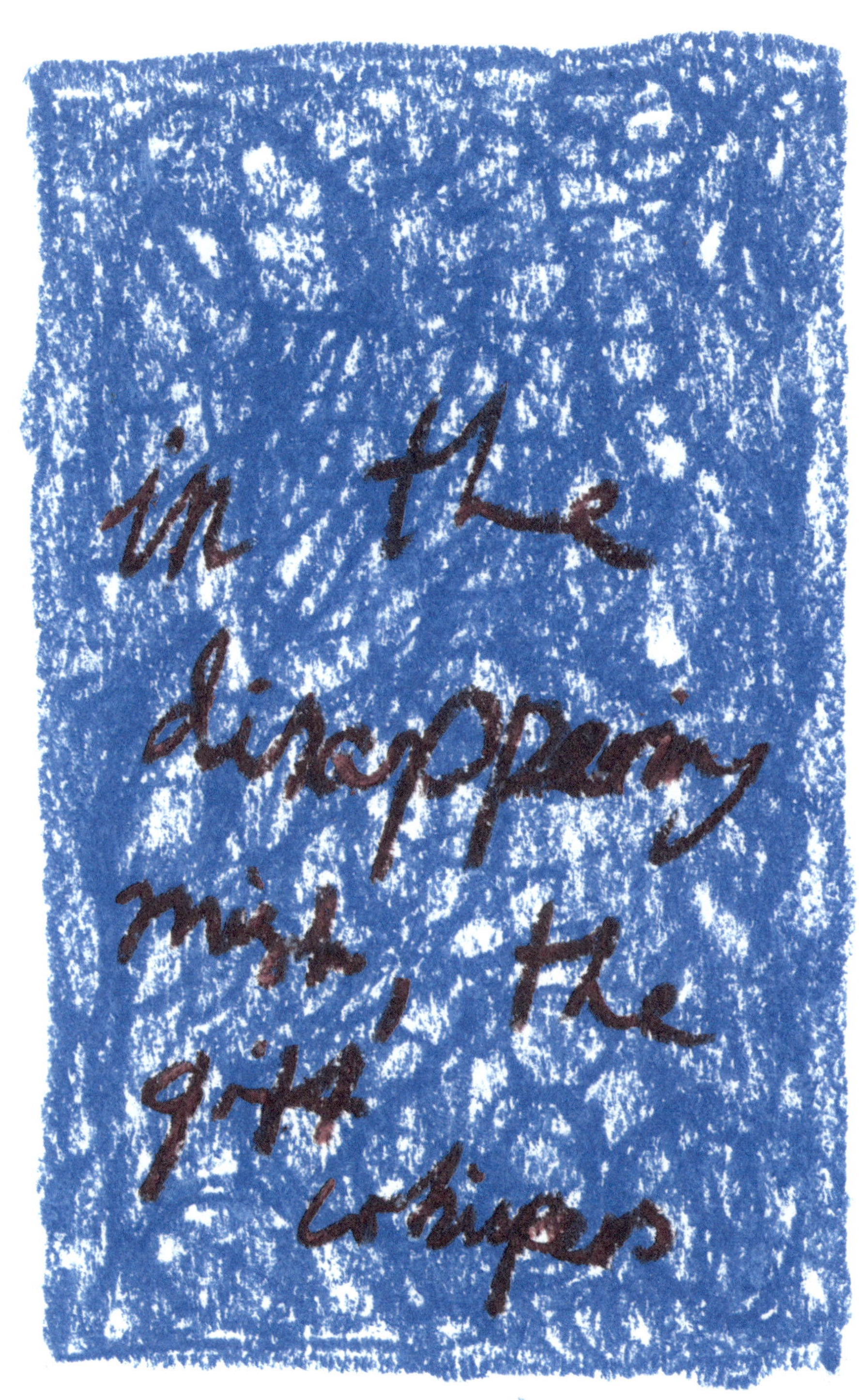
in the
disappearing
mist, the
gift
whispers

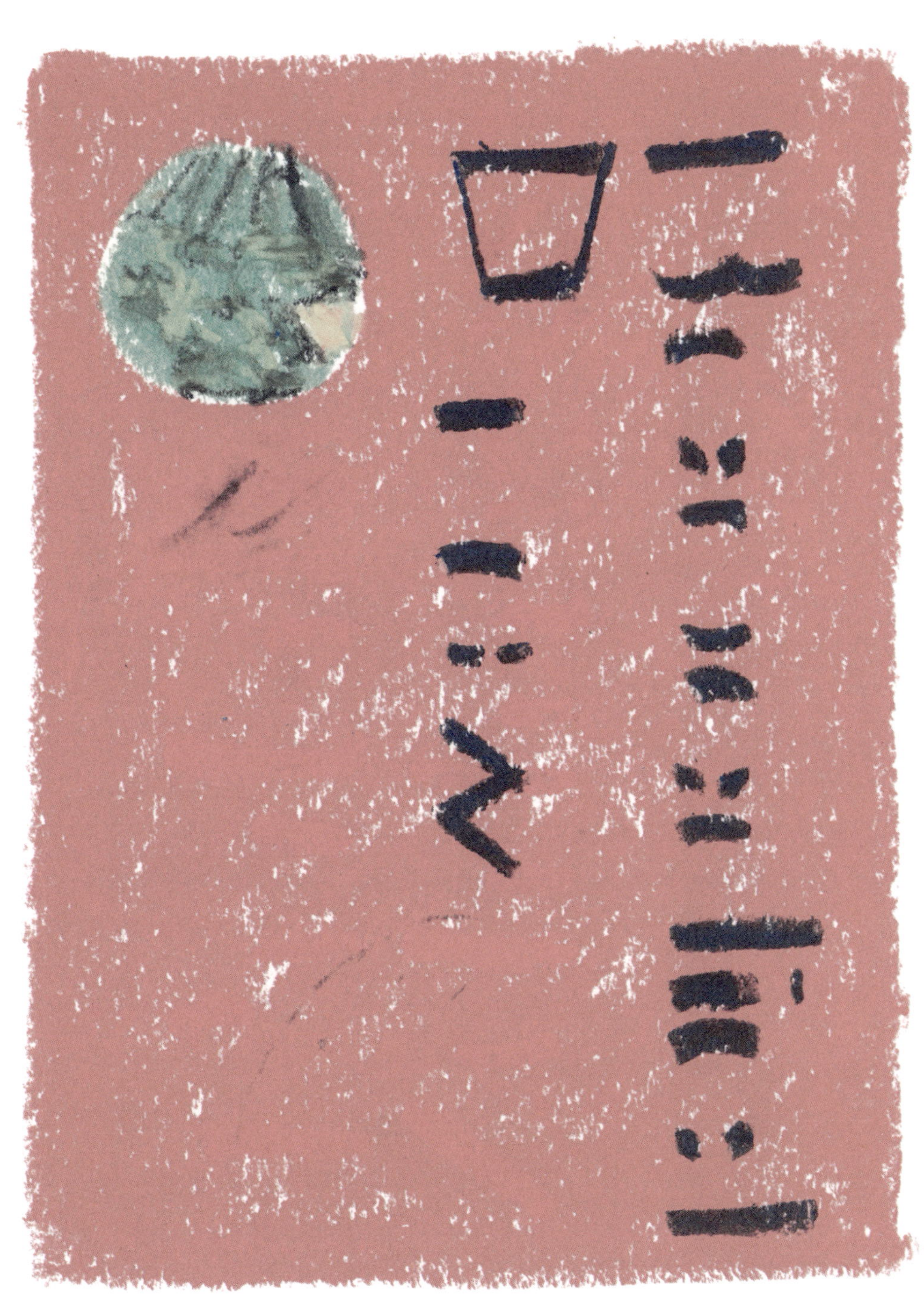

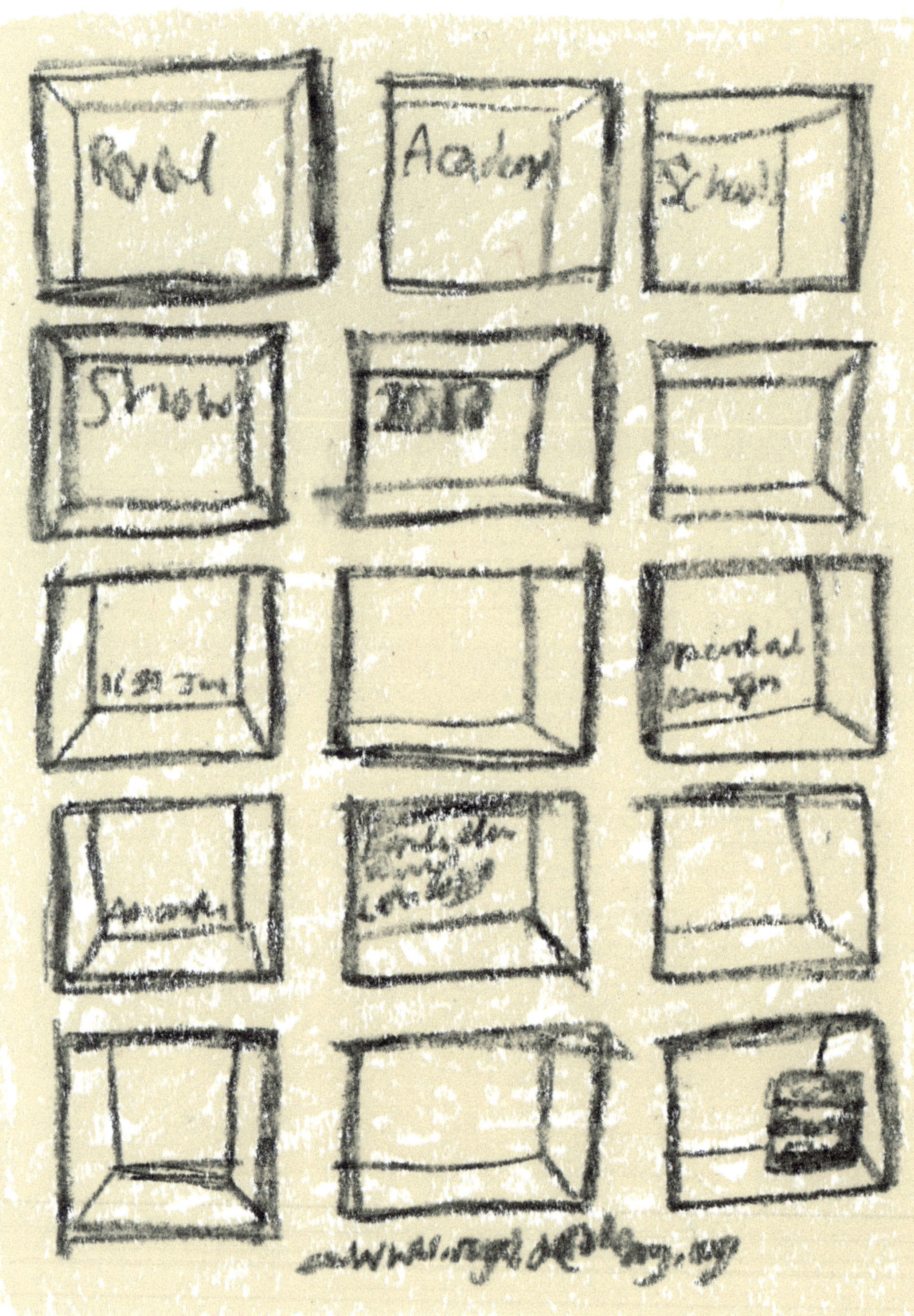
Royal
Academy
Schools
Show

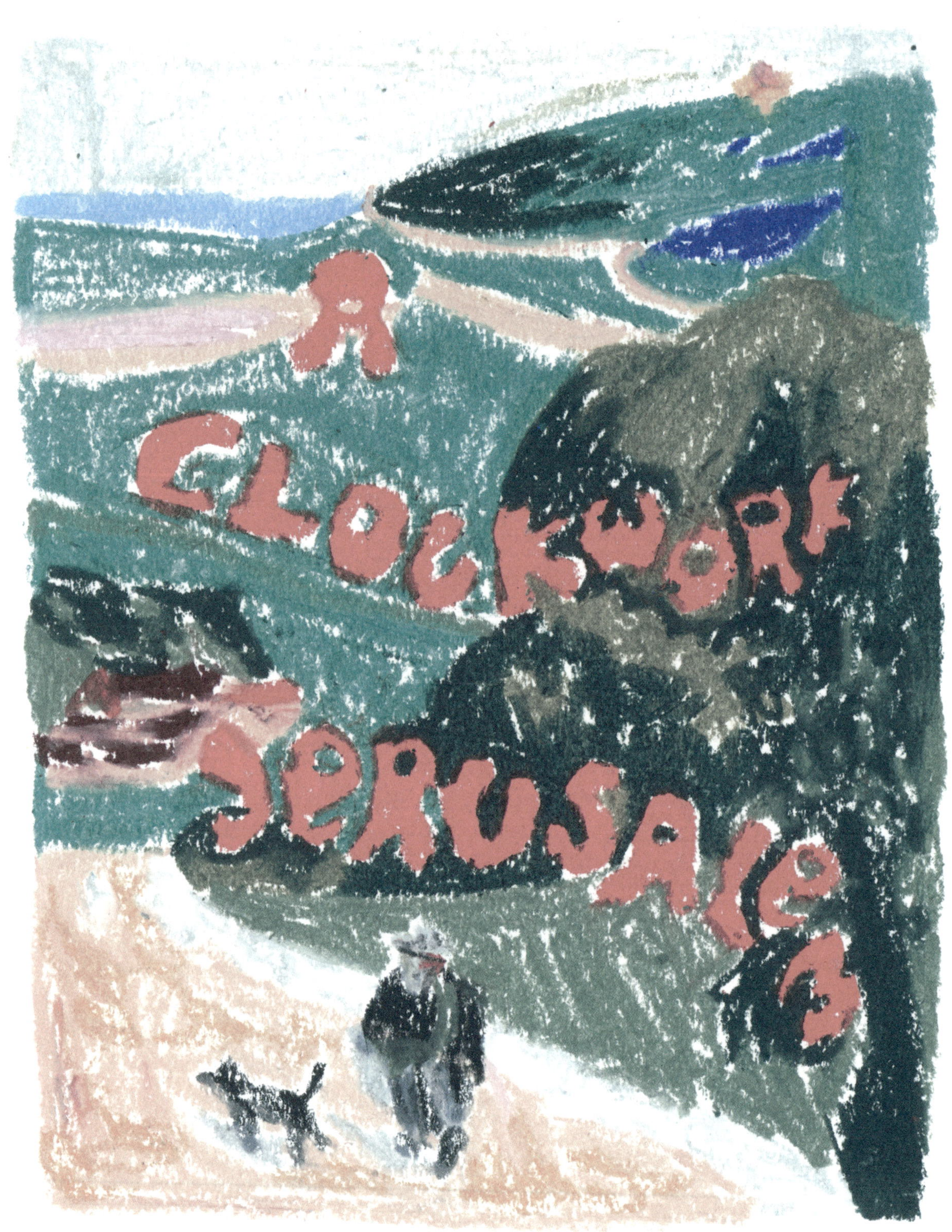
A
CLOCKWORK
JERUSALEM

Iggy Pop Life Class

Jeremy Deller

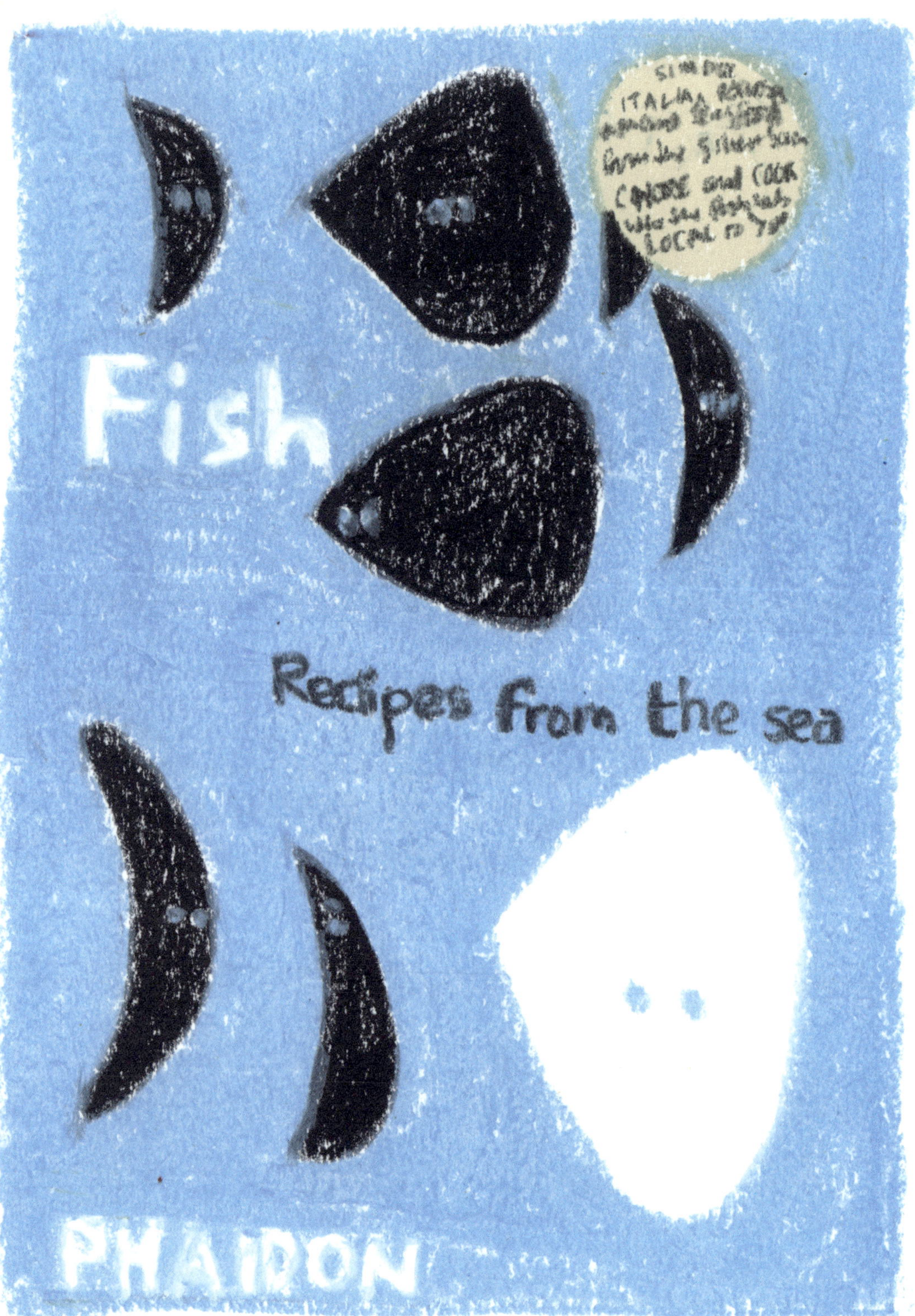
Fish
Recipes from the sea
PHAIDON

Citizen Cannes
Gilles Jacob
30 years

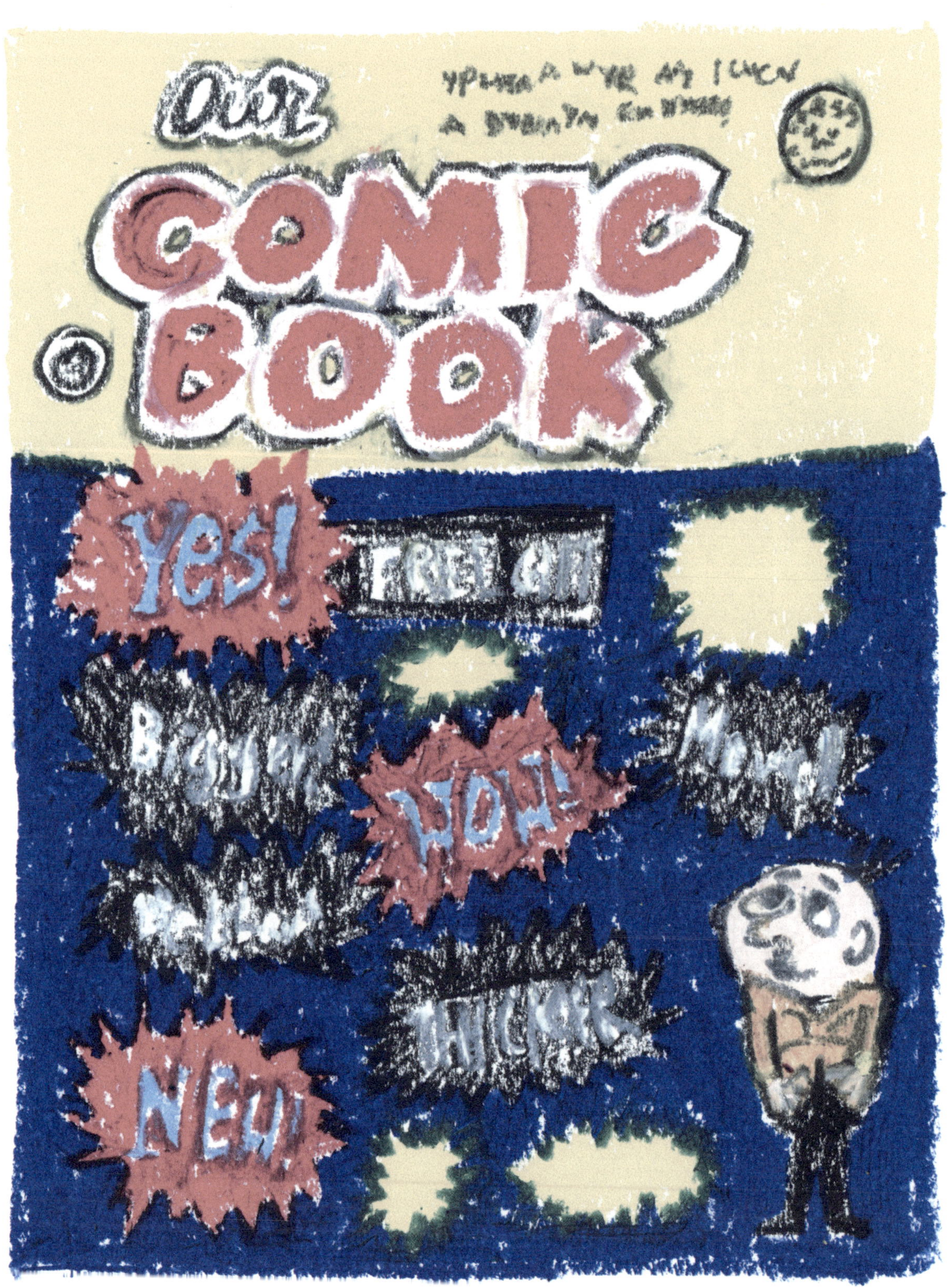
Our
COMIC BOOK
Yes!
WOW!
THICKER
NEW!

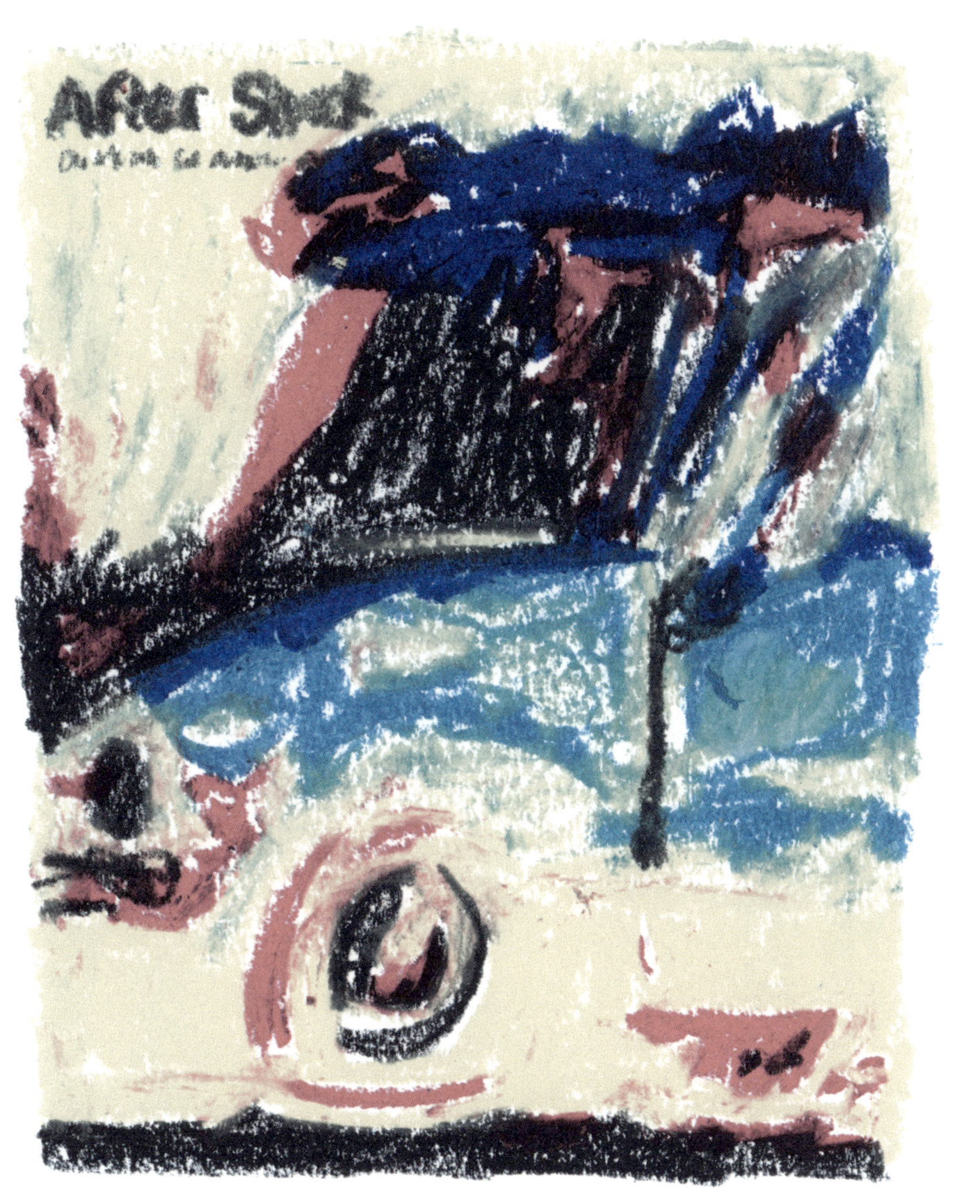
After Shock

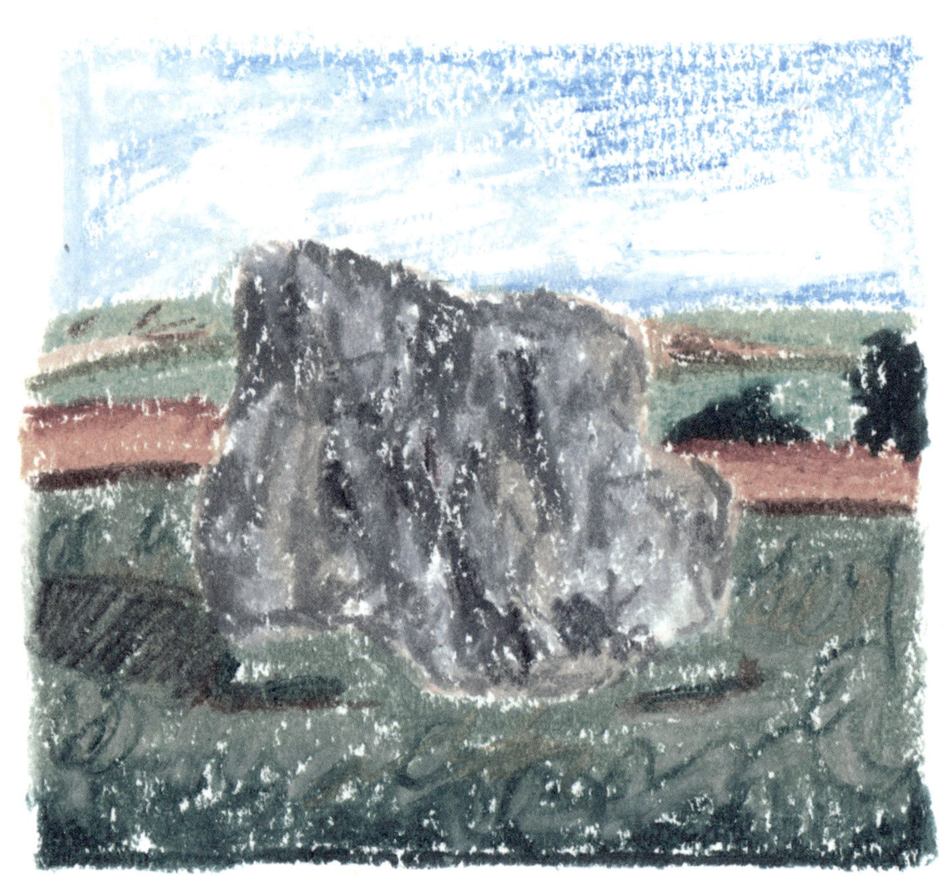

Profile of William Morris detected
on a standing stone at Avebury, Wiltshire
Jeremy Deller, 2018

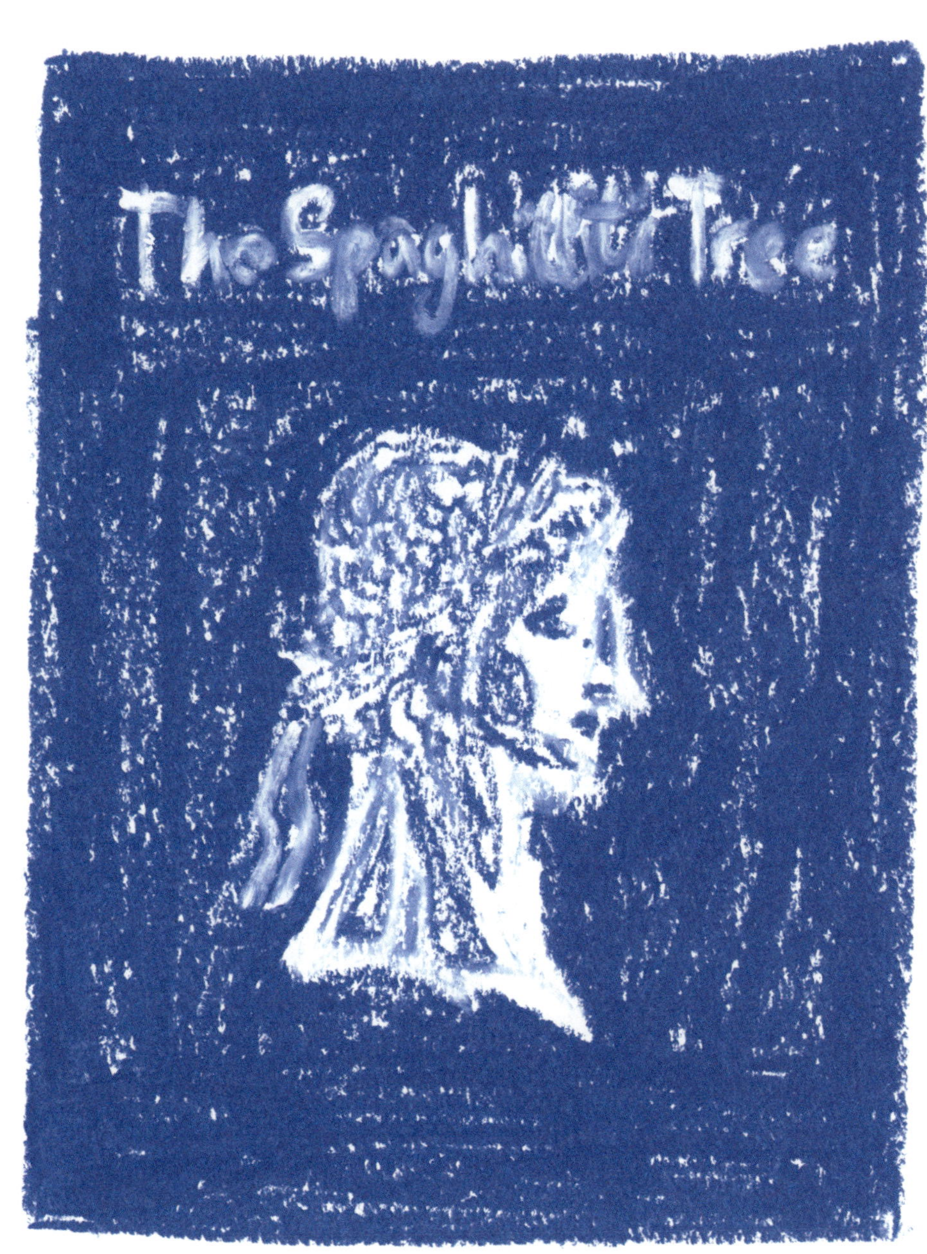
The Spaghetti Tree

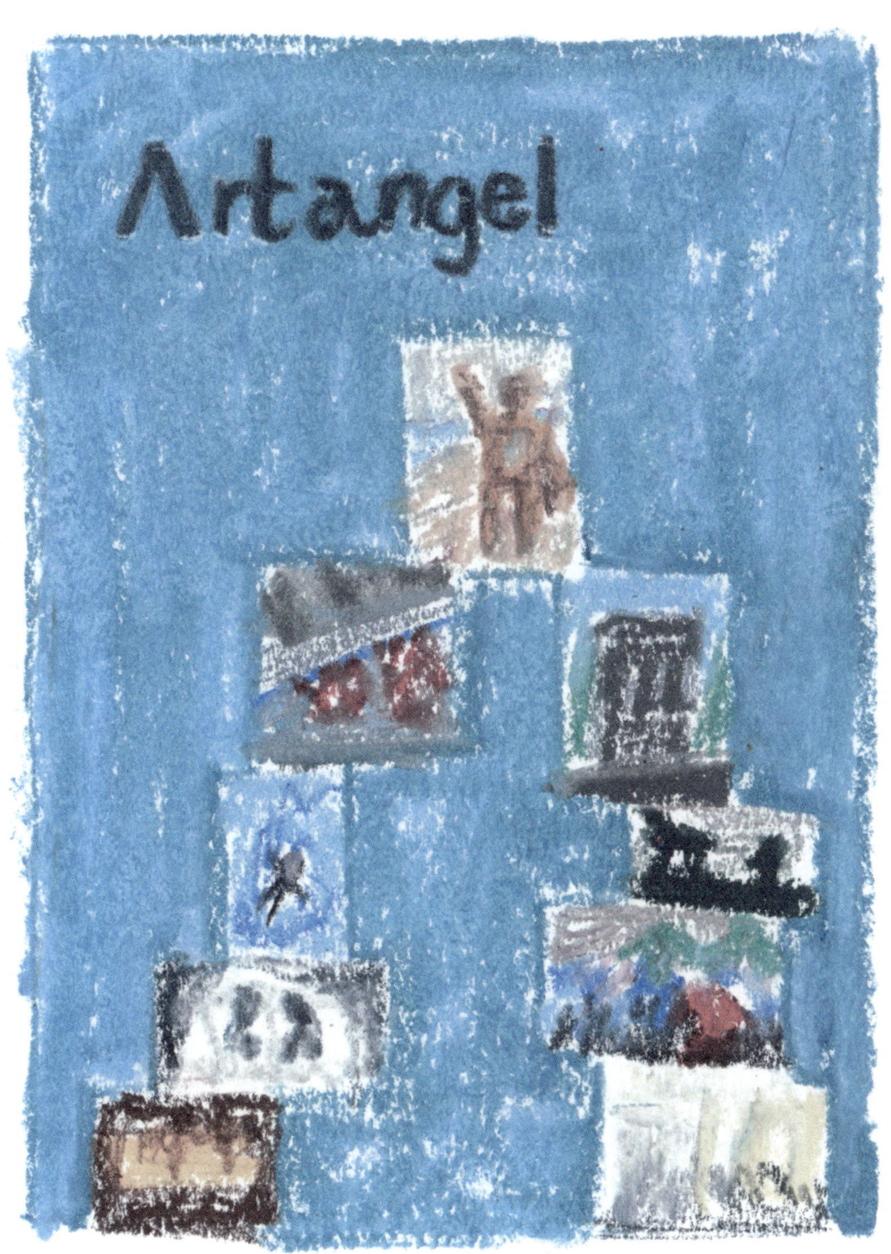
Artangel

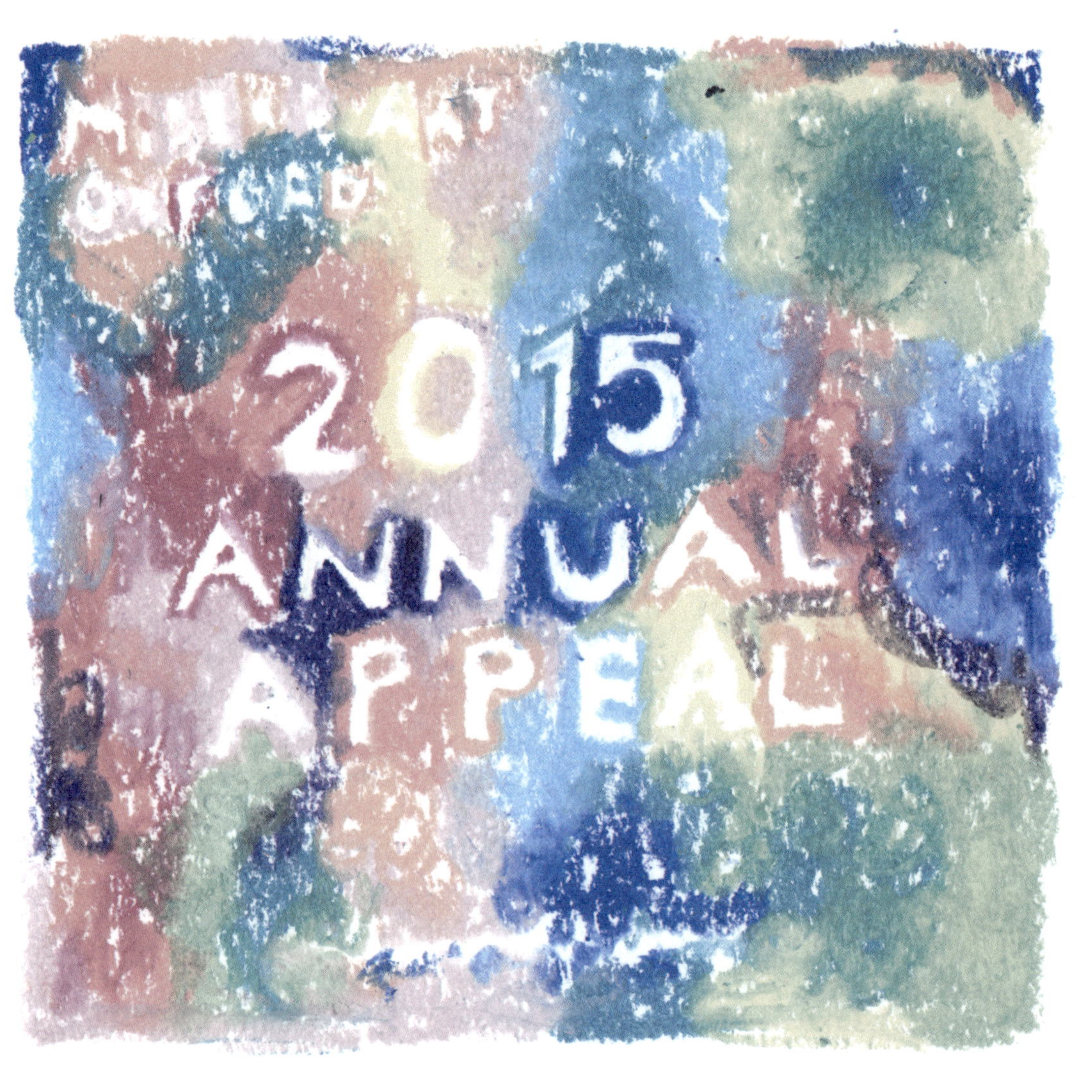
2015
ANNUAL
APPEAL

FONT BOOK

Fiona Banner

Lynn Valley 8

ZONE

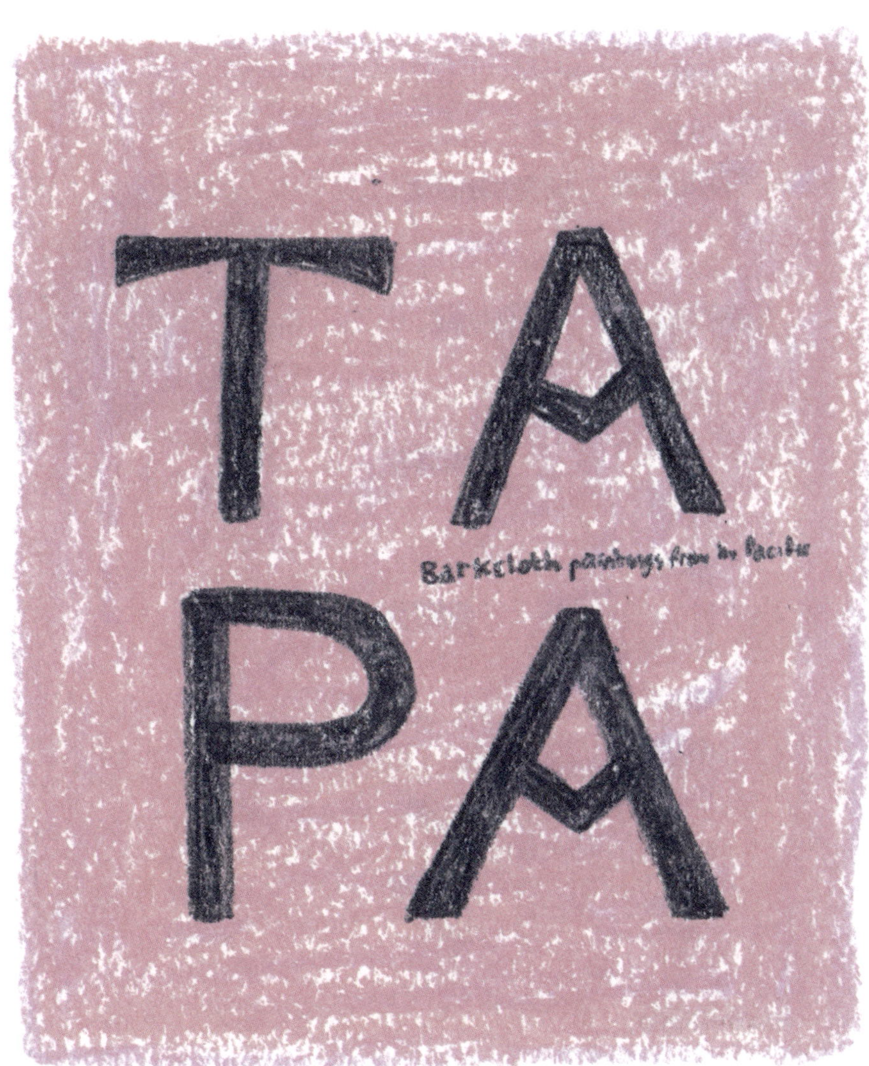
TA
PA
Barkcloth paintings from the Pacific

ARTON THE
UNDERGROUND

Oh, boy, what a wonderful city!

MAYOR OF LONDON

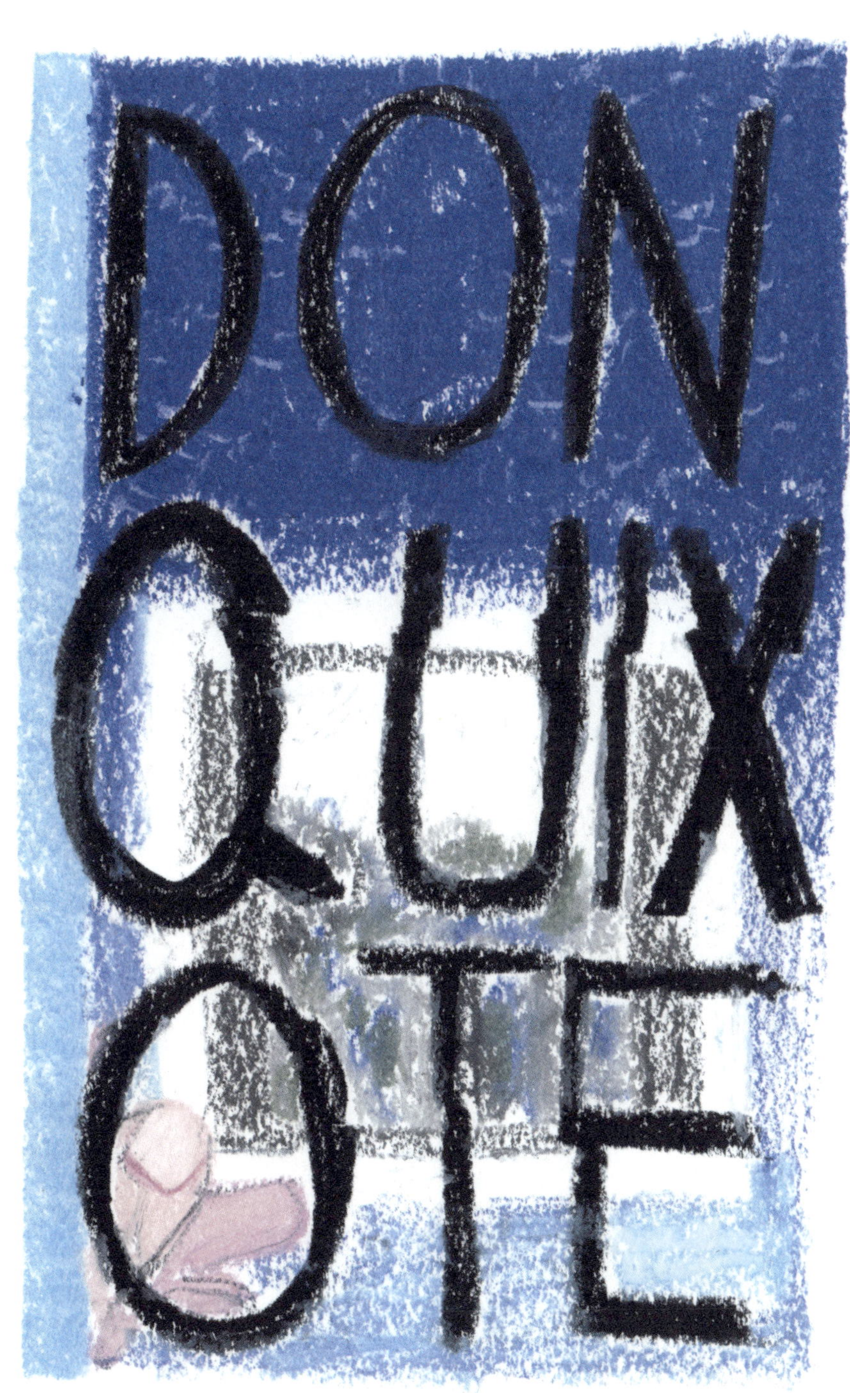
DON
QUIX
OTE

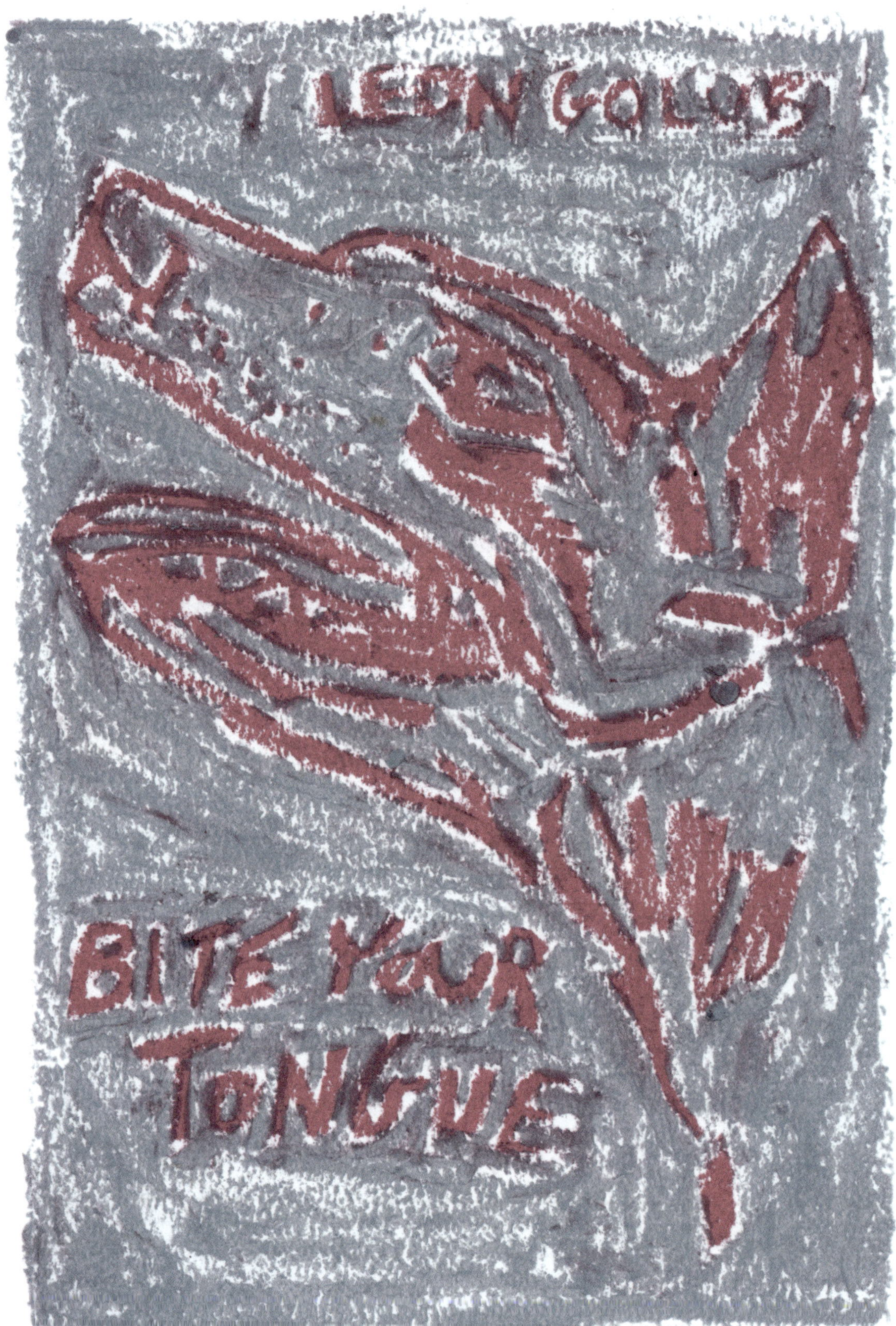
LEON GOLUB
BITE YOUR
TONGUE

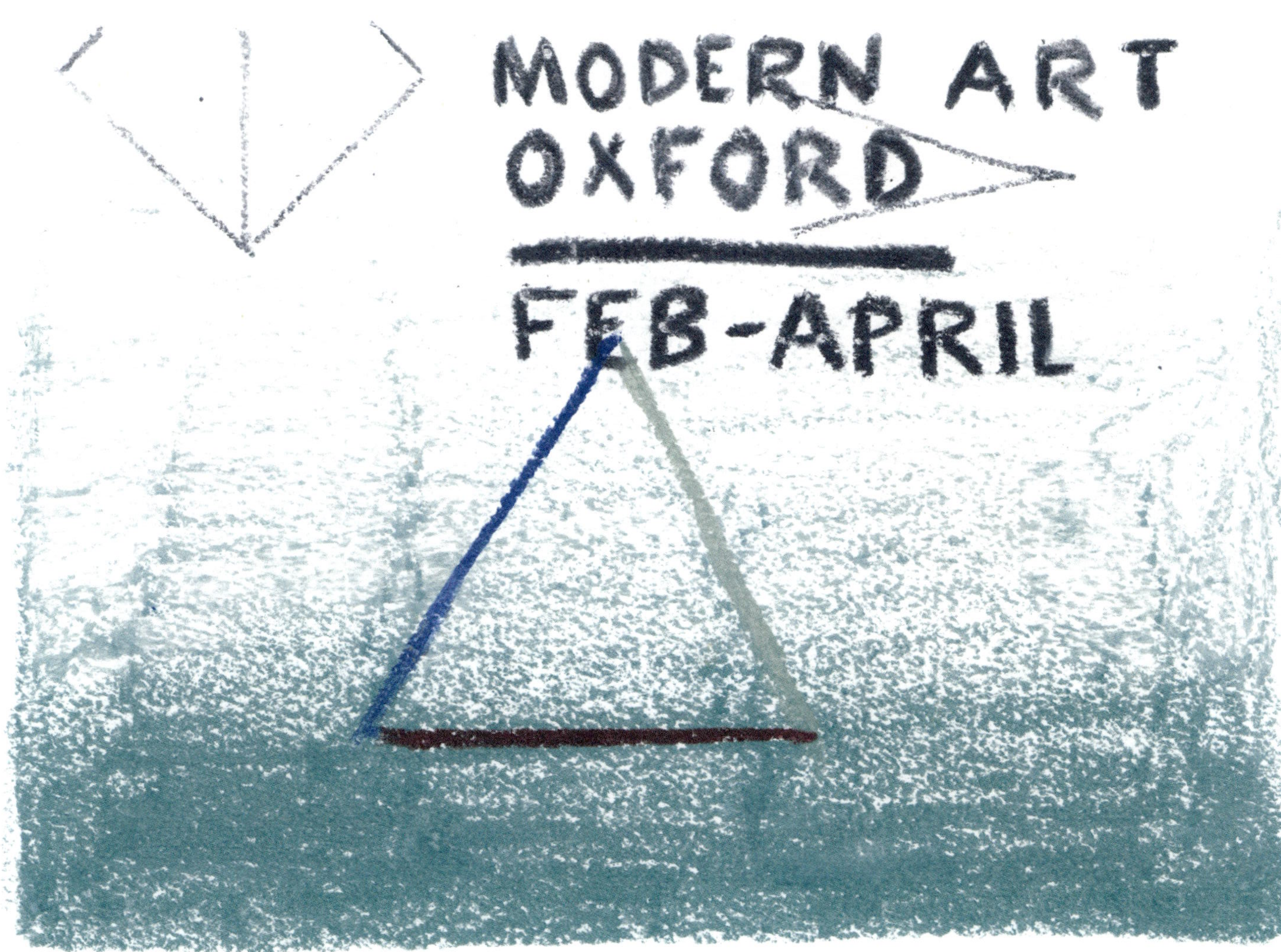
MODERN ART
OXFORD
FEB-APRIL

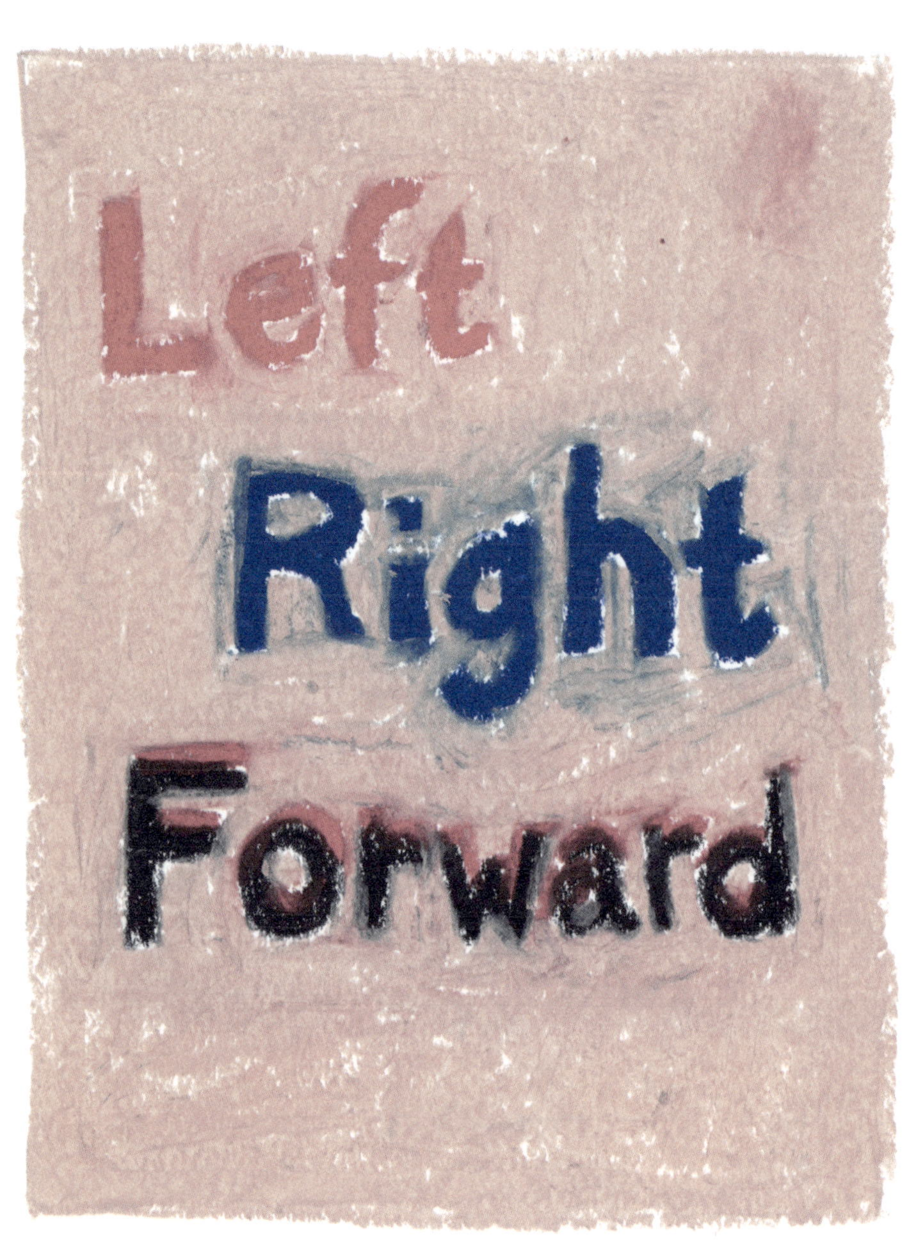
Left
Right
Forward

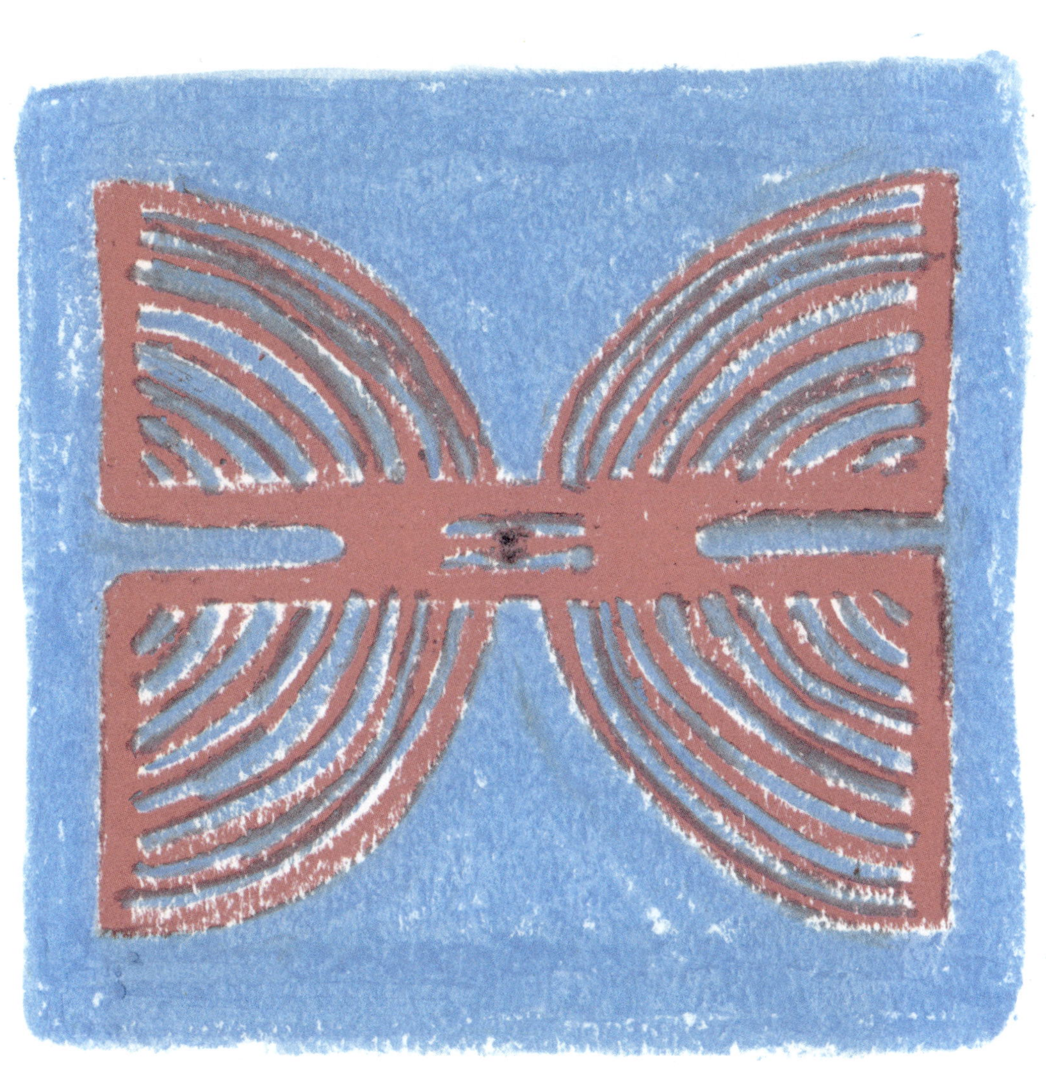

Paul Anthony Harford

Other Voices, Other Rooms

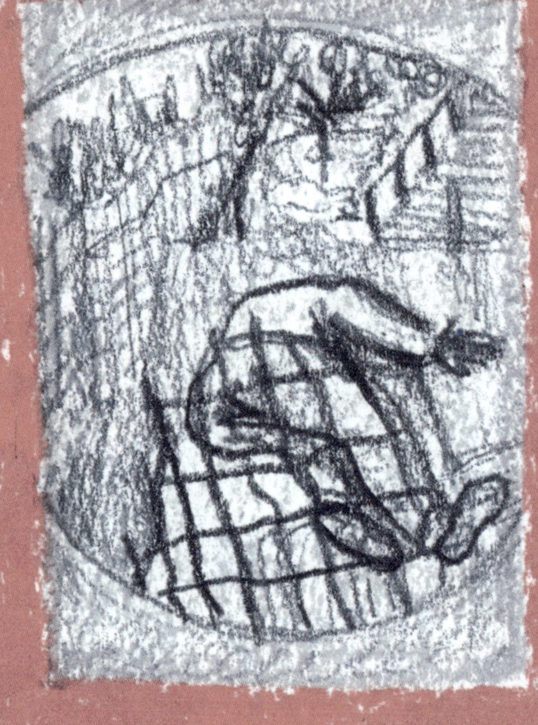

Metronomy

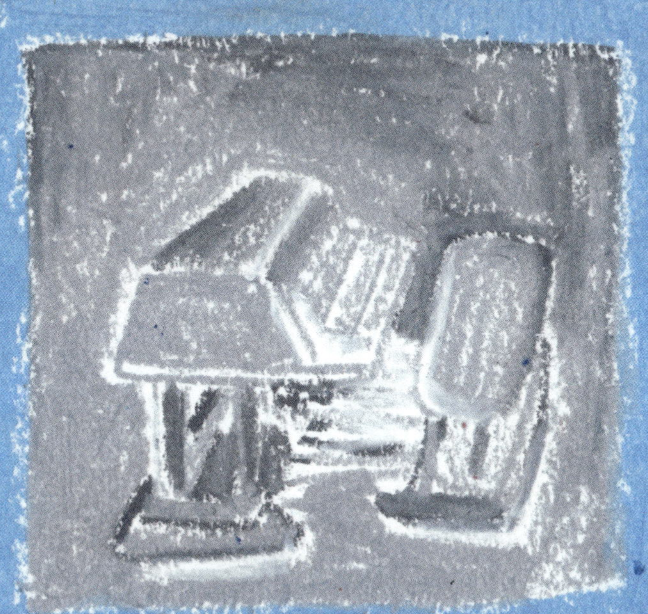

Zenith, Paris
3 Mars 2012

Rest in Peace

English Magic

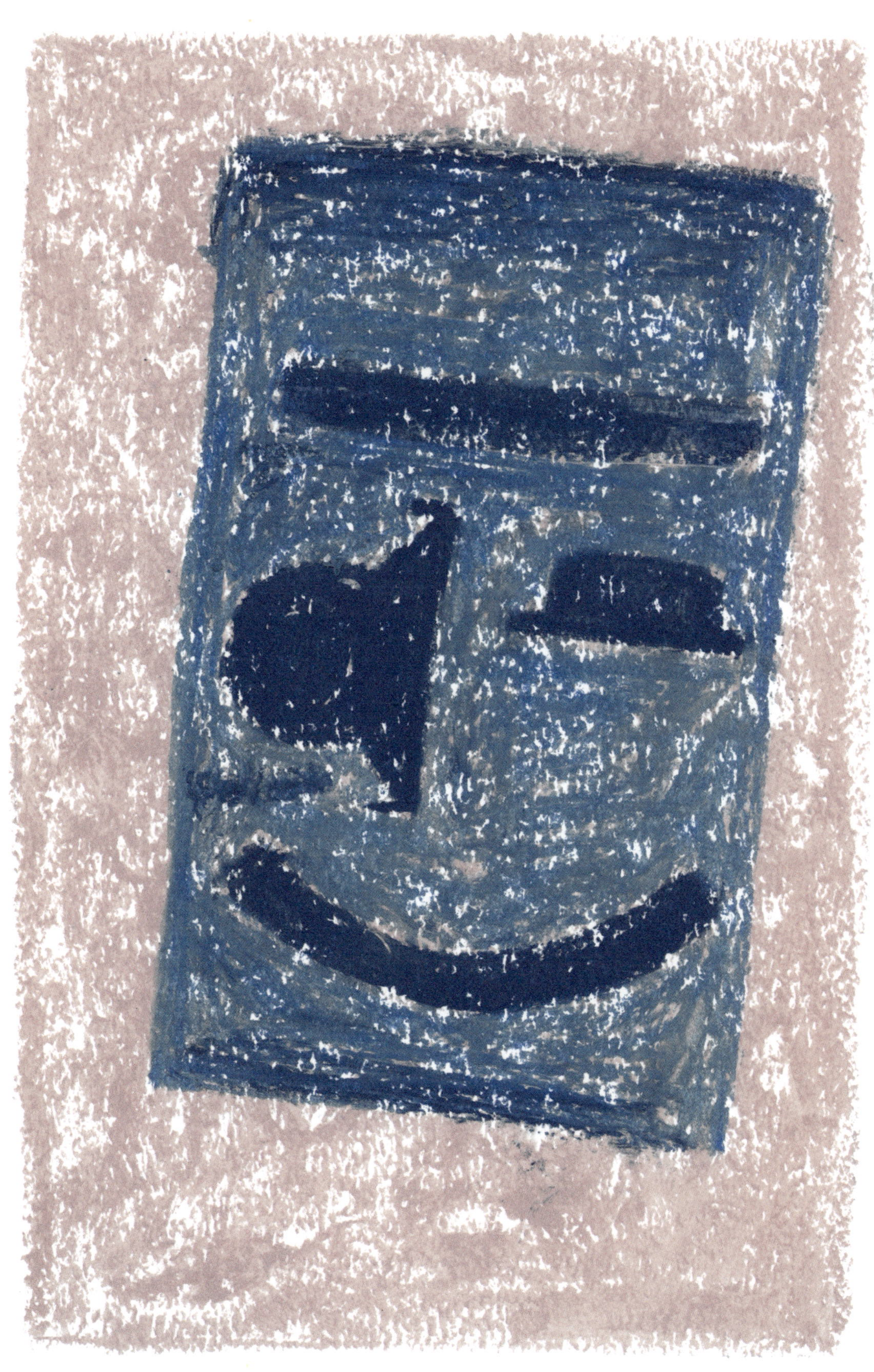

The Ballantyne Collection of
20th Century Studio Ceramics

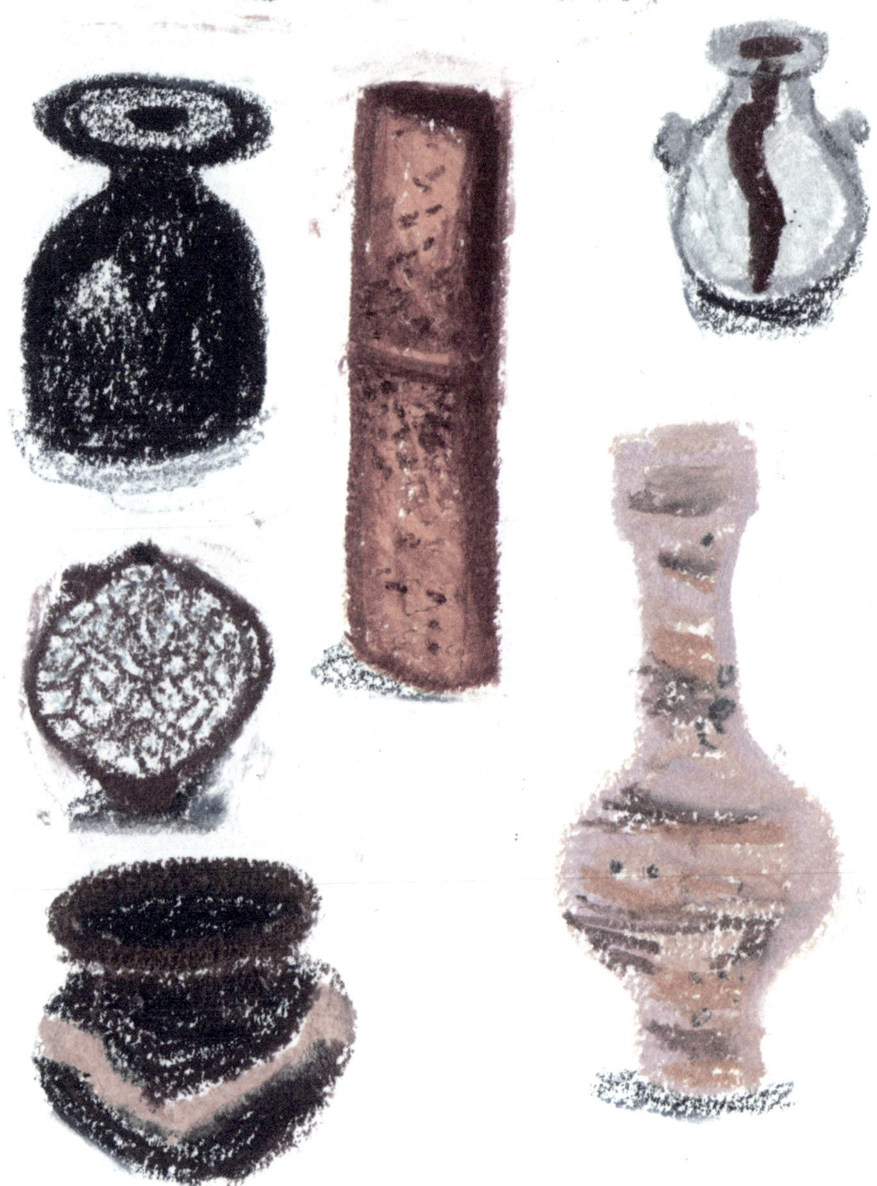